THE GOLDEN AGE MUSICALS OF
DARRYL F. ZANUCK

The
GOLDEN AGE
MUSICALS of
DARRYL F. ZANUCK

The Gentleman Preferred Blondes

BERNARD F. DICK

University Press of Mississippi / Jackson

The University Press of Mississippi is the scholarly publishing agency of the Mississippi Institutions of Higher Learning: Alcorn State University, Delta State University, Jackson State University, Mississippi State University, Mississippi University for Women, Mississippi Valley State University, University of Mississippi, and University of Southern Mississippi.

www.upress.state.ms.us

The University Press of Mississippi is a member of the Association of University Presses.

Manufactured in the United States of America
First printing 2022
∞

Library of Congress Control Number: 2021048516

Hardback: 978-1-4968-3861-2
E-pub Single: 978-1-4968-3862-9
E-pub Institutional: 978-1-4968-3863-6
PDF Single: 978-1-4968-3864-3
PDF Institutional: 978-1-4968-3865-0

British Library Cataloging-in-Publication Data available

CONTENTS

ACKNOWLEDGMENTS

My gratitude to Ned Comstock, Cinematic Arts Library, University of Southern California, for providing me with newspaper reviews of Twentieth Century-Fox musicals; Andrea Faling, archivist, Nebraska State Historical Society, for making copies for me of Zanuck's letters in the *Oakdale Sentinel* and various news stories about him in the local press; Tony Greco, for locating tapes of some rare musicals; Kristine Krueger, Margaret Herrick Library, for alerting me to the *Carousel* material housed there, thus enabling me to put together a case study of the musical; my wife, Katherine Restaino, for her constant encouragement; Sharon Rich, president, Mac/Eddy Club, for sending me a DVD of the rarely shown *Viennese Nights* (1930); MaryAnn Sena, former head of periodicals at the Frank Giovatto Library, Fairleigh Dickinson University (Teaneck campus), for tracking down some of Zanuck's short stories. I had a magnificent support staff.

In a special category is the third peer reviewer, who read my manuscript with great thoroughness and offered suggestions for revision which were enormously helpful; and the late Rudy Behlmer, whose *Memo from Darryl F. Zanuck* was the inspiration for this book, which I could never have written without it.

TEANECK, NEW JERSEY
MARCH 2021

THE GOLDEN AGE MUSICALS OF
DARRYL F. ZANUCK

INTRODUCTION

Darryl F. Zanuck (1902–1979) was unique among Hollywood's Golden Age producers. Over the years he headed production at three studios: Warner Bros., Twentieth Century, which he cofounded, and Twentieth Century-Fox after the merger of Twentieth Century and the Fox Film Corporation in 1935. He was also a published author who never intended to be a filmmaker. His goal was to be a fiction writer like his idol, O. Henry. He tried to imitate O. Henry's lean narratives with their surprise endings but only succeeded in writing some of the most florid prose in the history of the pulps. Zanuck had his first publication at the age of eleven. He sent his grandfather, Henry Torpin, a letter describing in detail a train trip he took from Los Angeles to Oakdale, Nebraska. Torpin thought it was so well-written that he sent it to the *Oakdale Sentinel*, which published it. It was the longest letter in the July 17, 1913, edition. That was Zanuck: if anything can be more, never make it less. He joined the Nebraska Sixth Infantry a day shy of his fifteenth birthday, lying about his age. He continued to send his grandfather letters during basic training and even after he shipped off to France as a member of the ambulance corps during World War I. His grandfather sent the letters to the *Oakdale Sentinel*, which gladly published his firsthand accounts.

When Zanuck was discharged in 1919, he set out in earnest to be a writer; four years later, he published a collection of four stories (really novellas) under the title *Habit* (1923). The *New York Times* reviewer criticized the style but could not deny that the "stories afford much entertainment." Zanuck had mastered the corkscrew plot, but he embellished it with garish prose. He could be evocative at times ("The fog had thinned to a transparent veil of pearl gray"), but mostly he overwrote ("tiny beads of perspiration glistening beneath the coiled wad of oily black hair that was his queue").

3

When he realized he would never be the next O. Henry, Zanuck tried to recast some of his stories as silent scenarios for the movies. To support himself, he turned to writing ads and then gags for such silent comics as Charlie Chaplin and Mack Sennett. He was gradually weaning himself away from overripe prose and adopting a more streamlined kind of writing required for ads and gags. Writing scenarios for two-reel series taught him economy, the art of compressing a story into fifteen minutes with a cliffhanger ending so the audience would return for the next episode. He understood plot in the classical sense of the ordered arrangement of the incidents, culminating in a tidy dénouement, as he showed in the scripts that Jack Warner (1892–1978), vice president of Warner Bros., hired him to create for the German Shepherd Rin-Tin-Tin. Warner was so taken with Zanuck's narrative skills and his ability to leave the studio on a Friday and return the following Monday with a completed script that, in 1926, he made him "supervisor," the term then used for a production head. Even a cursory survey of Zanuck's early screen stories and scenarios (chapter 2) reveals his mastery of linear narrative, pruned of the superfluous and redundant, and tidily resolved at the end. He was especially fond of parallel plots with complementary storylines. Zanuck's most ambitious attempt at parallel storytelling is *Noah's Ark* (1928), in which five characters from the first story set during World War I (1914–18) become biblical figures in the second, a retelling of the Great Flood and its aftermath.

Zanuck made a major contribution to the first feature-length musical, *The Jazz Singer* (Warner Bros., 1927), by adding dialogue to what had originally been planned as a silent movie with sound sequences of songs sung by the star, Al Jolson. By having the film end not with Jolson's singing "Kol Nidre" at his father's funeral but performing "Mammy" in blackface on stage at New York's Winter Garden, Zanuck turned what would have been a drama with some songs into a musical. *The Jazz Singer* was a show-business musical with a grand finale, which became Zanuck's specialty at the three studios where he headed production. Zanuck realized the importance of featuring well-known entertainers in musicals, drawing liberally from stage performers (Jolson, Fanny Brice, Vivienne Segal, Ethel Merman, Carmen Miranda, June Havoc, William Gaxton); vocalists (Russ Columbo, Helen Forrest, Dick Haymes, Perry Como, the Modernaires); and the Big Bands (Harry James, Glenn Miller, Benny Goodman, Tommy Dorsey, Woody Herman, Sammy Kaye, Charlie Spivak, and their orchestras). More than those of any other studio, Zanuck's musicals depicted the myriad forms and venues of American popular entertainment: saloons, music halls, concert halls, vaudeville, burlesque, variety shows, minstrel shows, the circus, the theater, motion pictures, radio, and television. His Twentieth Century-Fox musicals were known for their blondes: Alice Faye; Betty Grable, who ranked among the ten most popular stars of the 1940s, reaching first place in 1943; June Haver; Vivian Blaine, the "cherry blonde"; and the blonde who has been the subject of more books, articles, and speculation than any other Hollywood figure, Marilyn Monroe. Two other blondes, Sheree North and Jayne Mansfield, did not prove to be the successors to Marilyn that Zanuck was seeking. The blonde exception was the multitalented brunette, Mitzi Gaynor, who could act, sing, and, as a trained ballerina, dance on pointe.

The pulp writer in Zanuck never disappeared, even after he converted to rigidly linear narration in his scenarios. Zanuck, the pulp writer, who reveled in the lush and the florid, and Zanuck, the producer who insisted on judiciously pruned screenplays and scrupulously edited films, come together in his musicals, which are carefully plotted and lavishly staged, sometimes to excess (women costumed as desserts, including Jell-O, in *Billy Rose's Diamond Horseshoe* [1945] and as cosmetics in *The Dolly Sisters* [1945]). In 1940 only Zanuck would have hired Carmen Miranda, "the Brazilian Bombshell," overdressed, over-accessorized, and over-bejeweled in some of the clunkiest bracelets and necklaces ever to be worn in movie musicals. MGM would never have allowed Busby Berkeley's imagination to run riot as it did in "The Lady in the Tutti Fruiti Hat" sequence in *The Gang's All Here* (1943) with bananas turning into xylophone bars, culminating in the image of Miranda looking as if a gigantic bunch of bananas was spouting from her head. Yet the screenplay is the familiar boy-girl-rival formula with Alice Faye and Sheila Ryan vying for James Ellison's affections. The pairing off is typical of Zanuck's love of symmetrical plotting. Alice gets Ellison, and Sheila gets a Broadway show, which is a much better deal than wedding a war hero. If he were producing *Singin' in the Rain* (MGM, 1952), which starred Gene Kelly, Debbie Reynolds, and Donald O'Connor, he would probably have insisted on a rewrite. Gene gets Debbie, but Donald ends up with no one. He would have wanted another character who would be paired off with Donald at the end. In *Sweet Rosie O'Grady* (1943), Betty Grable ends up with Robert Young, but what about her social secretary (Virginia Grey)? Betty's former fiancé (Reginald Gardiner) is ready and willing, so the plot can be resolved with the union of two couples. No hanging threads, no ragged edges. If ripeness is all, symmetry is everything.

Zanuck distinguished between popular entertainment and prestige films. Musicals were the former. Thus production files for Twentieth Century-Fox's musicals do not contain the wealth of information found in those about films such as *The Grapes of Wrath* (1940) and *A Letter to Three Wives* (1949), which Zanuck believed would enhance the studio's reputation. The exception is the wealth of material on the making of *Carousel* (1956) in the Darryl F. Zanuck Papers at the Margaret Herrick Library, Fairbanks Center for Motion Picture Study in Beverly Hills, California. I have used this collection to present a case study of *Carousel*, a film in which Zanuck strongly believed, perhaps because he identified with the main character, Billy Bigelow. The memos and correspondence are extensive. The paper trail does not terminate in a dead end, which is so often the case with other production files. The *Carousel* material reveals a Zanuck so obsessed with symmetry that he altered the book of the original Rodgers and Hammerstein stage musical so that the movie version would open with Billy in a celestial purgatory and conclude with a terrestrial coda, with the bulk of the plot sandwiched in between as a flashback. Zanuck, who could be quite astute when it came to casting, was completely off target with *Carousel*, envisioning Frank Sinatra as Billy and, at one point, Judy Garland as Julie Jordan. Fortunately, the parts went to Gordon MacRae and Shirley Jones, but not without a heated exchange of memos.

Zanuck's musicals were unusual; unlike the traditional three-act screenplay, his musicals, for the most part, followed the two-act Broadway musical format with reprises or a medley at the end in the form of a curtain call, making them seem like Broadway shows. His musicals have never received serious treatment before, yet they were among the most popular of the 1940s and '50s. *The Golden Age Musicals of Darryl F. Zanuck: The Gentleman Preferred Blondes* is my effort to give Zanuck's musicals the attention they deserve.

Figures (production costs, grosses) cited in the text derive from Aubrey Solomon's invaluable *Twentieth Century-Fox: A Corporate and Financial History*, Filmmakers Series 20 (Lanham, MD: Scarecrow Press, 2002).

To distinguish between the films of the Fox Film Corporation and those of Twentieth Century-Fox, I cite the former as "Fox" and the latter as "TCF."

Although Twentieth Century-Fox ceased being hyphenated in 1984, it was still hyphenated during the period covered in the text.

Chapter 1

THE WRITER FROM WAHOO

Darryl Francis Zanuck (1902–1979) was born on September 5, 1902, in Wahoo, Nebraska, thirty miles north of Lincoln, the state capital. His father was a heavy drinker, and his mother became tubercular when he was six. Young Darryl never enjoyed the kind of idyllic family life depicted in MGM's Andy Hardy series. Twentieth Century-Fox, the studio with which he will always be associated, was not known for warm family movies, but rather for those about "families in stress" like the Joads in *The Grapes of Wrath* (TCF, 1940), who were forced off their land and took to the road in search of work; the women in *How Green Was My Valley* (TCF, 1941), who threw on their shawls and rushed to the mine for news of their men when they heard the shriek of the colliery whistle; the struggling Soubirous family in *The Song of Bernadette* (TCF, 1943), whose daughter was persecuted for claiming to have seen the Virgin Mary in a grotto; the Nolans in *A Tree Grows in Brooklyn* (TCF, 1944), in which a young girl with the soul of a writer maintained her optimism despite living in a tenement with her overworked mother and loveable but alcoholic father.

THE LETTER WRITER

Darryl Francis Zanuck understood stress. His mother had dreadful luck with men. Even after she divorced her first husband and remarried, it was to another abusive drinker. But a tension-ridden home life did not leave him scarred. Before America's entry into World War I in April 1917 made it possible for him to leave home, he found pleasure and perhaps even solace in writing, which was not so much a distraction as a compulsion. When he was eleven, Darryl sent his maternal grandfather, Henry Torpin, an account of the train trip he took from Los Angeles, where his mother and stepfather were living, to Oakdale, Nebraska, the Torpins' home, about ninety miles from Wahoo. Darryl and his grandfather were extremely close. Henry Torpin realized that, even at eleven, his grandson had a flair for writing, which alleviated the boredom of the classroom.

Henry Torpin was responsible for Darryl's first publication. He sent Darryl's letter to the *Oakdale Sentinel*, which published it on July 17, 1914. It was the longest letter in the paper, taking up two and a half columns. The editor even gave it a title: "Los Angeles to Oakdale: Observations of Darryl Zanuck, age 11, on his trip from Los Angeles, Calif., to Oakdale, Nebr., to spend his summer vacation with his grandparents, Mr. and Mrs. Henry Torpin." Written in the present tense, the letter reads like a scenario for a documentary, each detail a shot, and none too insignificant for inclusion: the street car ride to the station, the departure time, the train's speed, the temperature, a sandstorm that compelled "the writer" to leave the observation car; a stopover in Salt Lake City and a guided tour of the Mormon Temple; the various sights (cattle, sagebrush, "green hills and high mountains," a deer that "rolls down the hill, shot in the head"); and finally home. "At 1:15 a.m. we enter Oakdale and our trip is over," he wrote. Interestingly, Darryl referred to himself as "the writer," which implies much more than the one composing the letter. It was a title that spanned the arc of his career: pulp writer, gag writer, screenwriter, memo writer, and film producer who oversaw and monitored the writing of some of the greatest scripts to reach the screen such as *The Grapes of Wrath* (TCF, 1940), *How Green Was My Valley* (TCF, 1941), *Gentlemen's Agreement* (TCF, 1947), *The Snake Pit* (TCF, 1948), *A Letter to Three Wives* (TCF, 1949), *Twelve O'Clock High* (TCF, 1949), and *All About Eve* (TCF, 1950).

Determined to get away from his mother and wife-beating stepfather, Darryl joined the Sixth Nebraska Infantry (Nebraska National Guard) a day before his fifteenth birthday on September 4, 1917, claiming to be eighteen, which is exactly the age recorded in the Nebraska National Guard muster rolls. The deception worked, and in two weeks, Zanuck was at Camp Cody in Deming, New Mexico, as he wrote to his grandfather, who again sent his letter to the *Oakdale Sentinel*, which published it on September 21, 1917. At fifteen, he was writing simple but clear prose, unsentimental and economical, mostly in the present tense and stating just the facts, nothing more: the tent he slept in, the mess hall, and the drills.

When he was sent overseas in November 1918, he wrote his grandfather from Le Mans on November 28. As usual, Henry Torpin sent the letter on to the *Oakdale Sentinel*, which published it on December 27. As a member of the 136th Ambulance Corps, he

> helped carry twenty-six wounded men from the front lines to the rear in mud a foot deep. . . . My hand was struck by flying shrapnel but only scratched. My canteen was shattered. . . . We were on hand at 11 a.m. on the 11th of Nov. when the firing ceased as the armistice was signed. On the 20th we were sent back to Le Mans where we are now awaiting orders. We may go to the States or back to the 3rd Army of Occupation. Hope we go to the Statue of Liberty. . . . Well, here's love to all. I'll close hoping to be home by the 1st of January.
> —Darryl Zanuck

It was actually early April when Zanuck returned, as the April 4, 1919, *Oakdale Sentinel* reported: "Darryl Zanuck will arrive tomorrow after an absence of eighteen months with the army." However, he was not formally discharged until August 19, after which he supposedly spent six months in New York hoping to become a writer like his idol, O. Henry.

Zanuck had what the Roman satirist Juvenal called "*cacoëthes scribendi*" (*Satire* 7, 52), an insatiable desire (literally, "itch") to write. While he could construct a taut narrative, tying up all the plot threads, he could not create enduring literature, and his knowledge of human nature was limited to types familiar to the pulp peddlers (drug addicts, alcoholics, deceivers, adulterers, eccentrics, frauds, bullies, prodigal sons with college degrees, virtuous women, and those with a past, checkered or otherwise). Realizing that he was not suited to America's literary capital, he felt he stood a better chance in Los Angeles, which he knew well from visits to his mother and stepfather.

THE SHORT STORY WRITER

Los Angeles served a dual purpose: he could continue writing his stories and, at the same time, pitch some to the movies. Zanuck also learned how to deal with rejected material: Give it a makeover. In 1923, he converted three of his rejects, a short story and two scripts, into a four-story collection called

Habit, which comprised the title story, "The Scarlet Ladder," "Say It with Dreams," and the longest (and strangest), "The Forgotten City," in which prosperity returns to a New Mexico ghost town after a mentally unstable chemist discovers that a tonic made from the yucca plant can cure everything from dandruff to eczema and falling hair. After his discharge, one of Zanuck's many odd jobs included writing ads for Yuccatone, a hair restorer made from yucca, whose restorative properties were discovered by Native Americans—a point Zanuck emphasized with the slogan, "You've never seen a bald-headed Indian." He convinced Yuccatone's inventor, A. F. Foster, to subsidize the publication of *Habit*, promising to add a story promoting Yuccatone Hair Restorer. Foster agreed, and the dedication read: "Dedicated to my eminent friend, A. F. Foster, whose untiring efforts in desert research were finally successful in the remarkable discovery of the amazing ingredients contained in the desert yucca plant, and through whose hospitality to the author while devoted to the study of desert topics and characters, inspired the final narrative in this volume. Darryl Francis Zanuck." After *Habit* came out, receiving a generally a favorable review with reservations about the style from the *New York Times*, Foster's business went under when the alcohol in the bottles fermented and exploded in twenty-five drugstores. But by that time, Zanuck had gone Hollywood.

Zanuck grew up reading the pulps and dime store novels, which shaped his concept of storytelling. He seems to have preferred the pulps to serious literature, although one can sense the influence of Richard Henry Dana's *Two Years before the Mast* (1840) and Jack London's *The Sea Wolf* (1904) in the second story, "The Scarlet Ladder," set on board a freighter whose seemingly maniacal captain is conducting an unorthodox experiment on a shanghaied alcoholic, hoping to cure him of his addiction. The title, a riff on Nathaniel Hawthorne's *The Scarlet Letter*, refers not to Hester Prynne's "A" but to the ladder of advancement that one must climb "step by step to the top and success." The hero is such a climber, going from alcoholic and opium addict to Congressional Medal of Honor winner. That the ladder is scarlet has nothing to do with symbolism, but with Zanuck's choice of a title that would evoke an American classic—something "The Scarlet Ladder" is not.

All four stories have surprise endings in the O. Henry tradition. "Habit," the title story, reads as if it had been written in purple ink. Two of the characters are murdered, each in a different way in San Francisco's Chinatown with its casinos "crowded to the lily potted portals with throngs of heterogeneous denizens" and "gutter fires [that] blackened coal oil tins and cast grotesque shadows to mingle with the purplish halo of gaunt lamp posts." Ling Foo Gow, a hearing- and speech-impaired seller of lychee nuts, befriends Mell Wing of the "cherry-tinted smile," the abused wife of Bull Lung, "a mammoth hulk of muscle." When Bull Lung dies supposedly of a heart attack, only Ling Foo Gow knows the real cause of death. Always helping himself to the lychee nuts in Ling Foo Gow's bamboo basket, Bull Lung scooped up a handful nearest the top, which had been deliberately poisoned.

In "The Scarlet Ladder," the denouement is possible (most things are) but forced because of Zanuck's intention of transforming a wastrel into a hero. Ralph Weston, who had been drinking his way through the fleshpots of the South Pacific, is brought on board the *Blue Gull* against his will by a captain who seems to be another Wolf Larsen from *The Sea Wolf*. In his log, the captain refers to Weston as "the specimen," recording how he finally refused to eat food soaked in gin, thus proving the captain's theory: present an alcoholic with alcohol-drenched food and sooner or later he will recoil from the sight and taste of it. Since the captain has a daughter, who befriends Weston, the pairing off at the end is inevitable, but the revelation—that the captain, who has shown every sign of being a madman, is really a humanitarian with his own way of rehabilitating alcoholics—is rather like saying that a torturer is teaching his victim the art of endurance. Even more absurd is the ending, in which Weston is awarded the Congressional Medal of Honor for saving a group of Americans, including his father, who were stranded in Smyrna in 1921 during the Greco-Turkish War.

In the third story, "Say It with Dreams," the least likely murder suspect is a mime, not the vaudeville performer who pretended to be ten to travel half fare to San Francisco. She is now free to join her lover, a former mayor railroaded out of town for promoting a salve guaranteed to keep beards from growing but had the opposite effect. Zanuck brought the story full circle by having the ousted mayor return to the town to run for reelection. The final story, "The Forgotten City," is a perfect example of a narrative whose ending was planned in advance, with everything leading up to it adhering to the laws of verisimilitude. A railroad tycoon, exasperated by the antics of his wayward son, decides to teach him a lesson in responsibility by sending him off to Truceville, a nearly deserted town in New Mexico, with a dollar bill and a deed to a rundown hotel and some adjacent property. Truceville is inhabited chiefly by its founder, Granville Truce, and his daughter, Pauline. Truce is a wonderfully drawn character, dwelling in his own world somewhere on the far side of lunacy. He is also a chemist who has concocted a tonic and shampoo made from yucca that rids the scalp of dandruff, cures eczema, and restores hair. With the help of the once prodigal, and now regenerate, son, Truceville becomes a prosperous community and, of course, boy gets girl. Granville Truce is Zanuck's only fully realized character, whose orotund speech and aphorisms ("The most beautiful flowers blossom from the finest of seeds") make him sound like an elocutionist. Zanuck's grandfather, Henry Torpin, a former Pennsylvanian like Truce, was clearly the model. Young Zanuck loved to hear his grandfather reminisce about the time he survived an Indian massacre with arrow marks on his back to prove it. The humanity that shines through in Zanuck's portrait of Granville Truce is a tribute to Henry Torpin, a remarkable eccentric who established his own empire in Oakdale just as Truce did in the town to which he gave his name.

The January 1925 issue of *Physical Culture* contained remedies for bow legs, hair loss, and deafness; tips for homebuilders; and ads for correspondence courses in music and art. It also contained a short story, "Mad Desire" by Darryl Francis Zanuck, then a published author and budding scenarist. According to Zanuck's biographer, Mel Gussow, Zanuck wrote "Mad Desire" in 1920, "but publication was not until 1923." Gussow was off by two years, but "Mad Desire" was clearly written around the time of the first two stories in *Habit*. "Mad Desire" begins promisingly: an artist who "had killed two innocent people whom he believed to be his wife and her lover" went off to New Guinea, where he planned to commit suicide in atonement. "*Believed*?" After a steamy interlude in which the artist and his mistress overindulge in alcohol and opium, they forsake their vices and go in for clean living. Hint: the story was published in *Physical Culture*. Determined to outdo O. Henry with a climactic revelation, Zanuck identifies the couple that the artist thought he killed as a gangster and his wife, who decided to commit suicide rather than be liquidated by rivals. They chose poison, but when the wife could not bear the agony of a slow death, the husband shot her and then himself. When the artist arrived on the scene totally inebriated, he presumed the couple were his wife and her lover and shot them. But since they were already dead, it was only murder by intent. The ragged edges of the story have been clipped off, the loose ends tied up, and Zanuck received $500 for a stratospherically tall tale. Zanuck aimed "Mad

Desire" at *Physical Culture*, founded by fitness guru Bernarr Macfadden in 1899. The theme—overcoming vices through a healthy regimen and a stable relationship—was in keeping with the "Editor's Viewpoint": "Excesses constitute a monstrous evil." Zanuck understood the art of the pitch: tailor the story to the target audience. As a movie producer, he did exactly that.

Zanuck never shed the pulp writer side of himself. At Twentieth Century-Fox, his love of the lurid was reflected in thrillers like *I Wake Up Screaming* (TCF, 1941), in which the murderer of a young woman sets up a shrine to her memory, complete with candles; *The Lodger* (TCF, 1944), a variation on the Jack the Ripper story with a serial killer preying upon young woman, especially music hall performers; *Hangover Square* (TCF, 1945), in which a demented composer pounds away at the piano, oblivious to the flames that engulf the concert hall; *Kiss of Death* (TCF, 1947), in which a psychopath pushes an elderly woman in a wheelchair down a flight of stairs to her death; and *Panic in the Streets* (TCF, 1950), which takes place over a forty-eight-hour period as a doctor tries to avert a plague that threatens New Orleans.

Zanuck's pulp side is even more discernible in his musicals, splashier than any other studio's. Although the characters in his musicals often end up on Broadway, they get their start in seedy saloons, burlesque, vaudeville, and music halls—all lower-class venues. And for cinematic excess, no performer could compete with the overdressed, over-accessorized, oversized, and overwhelming Carmen Miranda in her platform shoes, floral and fruity head wraps, and costumes that looked as if they had been tailored by Technicolor. There was always purple ink in Zanuck's pen.

Chapter 2

THE WRITER IN HOLLYWOOD

Although Zanuck understood the difference between a scenario and a short story, and for a while worked in both forms simultaneously, he knew he could never make a living writing for the pulps. But he could toss off scenarios, which were just stories minus descriptive embellishments. Zanuck was never as much of a theatergoer as Louis B. Mayer (1885–1957) or Hal B. Wallis (1898–1986), but when he was in New York in 1919, he claims to have seen Langdon McCormick's *The Storm*, which opened on October 2, 1919, for a run of 282 performances. *New York Times* drama critic Alexander Woollcott dismissed the play as "an old fashioned melodrama" and "an almost forgotten form of rude entertainment" (October 3, 1919), although he was impressed by the climactic forest fire which he called "extraordinary." *The Storm* featured a snowstorm in the first act, a forest fire in the last, and a love triangle involving two men and a woman holed up in a cabin in the Canadian wilderness. The lead was Edward Arnold, who went on to become a much-admired character actor in Hollywood, as a lonely woodsman who offers to share his cabin with a British traveler. Complications result when a French-Canadian woman seeks refuge in the cabin, setting off currents of sexual tension as the elements respond to the storm brewing within. Zanuck felt that *The Storm* had great potential as a film. If McCormick had written it as a novella, it would have read like the ones that captivated the young Zanuck. It also had one of his favorite story templates: the triangular plot, which served him well in "Habit" (lychee nut seller, terrified wife, sadistic husband), "The Scarlet Ladder" (shanghaied American, captain, captain's daughter), "Say It with Dreams" (the vaudevillian, the salve salesman, the lecher), and "The Forgotten City" (the tycoon's son, the chemist, and his daughter).

THE SCENARIO WRITER

Zanuck claimed that, after optioning *The Storm* in 1919, he wrote an adaptation in the form of a "rough scenario," which he sent to Universal's story editor, Lucien Hubbard. Since the playwright's agent wanted $10,000, Zanuck raised the asking price to $15,000. Universal was looking for a suitable property for one of its stars, House Peters, who was cast as the woodsman in the 1922 film, with Matt Moore as the Brit and Virginia Valli as the woman, all of whom were upstaged by the hand-tinted forest-fire sequence. Another version has a friend handing Zanuck a copy of *The Storm*, which Zanuck adapted and sold to Universal for $525. Zanuck may have received $525 for his "rough scenario," but Universal probably paid $15,000 for the rights. That amount seems correct; at the time, the rights to a successful play—and *The Storm* ran an entire season—averaged $20,000.

Zanuck was writing so much during the 1920–24 period that he could not even keep track of his burgeoning *oeuvre*. Although he claimed he was responsible for all twenty-four episodes of *The Leather Pushers* (1922), the series only consisted of eighteen. H. C. Witwer's *The Leather Pushers* was the collective title of twelve stories, or "rounds," published in *Collier's Weekly* in 1920, about a former college football player, Kane Halliday, who, under the tutelage of a shrewd manager, evolved into the prizefighter Kid Roberts. In his heyday, the Kid entered the ring wearing "a blue silk bathrobe ornamented with pale peacocks and purple flowers." G. P. Putnam's Sons published the stories in book form the following year. Again, "rounds" replaced "chapters," with the milieu remaining the same: the boxing world described in colorful slang and wild comparisons, with an occasional anachronism like "gentle reader."

The Leather Pushers (1922), in altered form, became a popular series (sometimes referred to as a "serial") produced by Universal Pictures, starring Reginald Denny, one of Universal's most popular and versatile actors, as Kane Halliday/Kid Roberts. Zanuck indeed wrote the scripts for the second, *Round Two*, and the tenth, *When Kane Met Abel*. Zanuck's scripts seem to be more like continuities, sequential arrangements of the incidents—the ideal format for episodes in a silent series. This type of plot construction would also explain how he could turn out so many scenarios in so short a time. He began doing this kind of writing since he was eleven and wrote his grandfather a letter detailing, incident by incident, the train trip he took from Los Angeles to Oakdale, Nebraska.

Since "Round Two," the second of *The Leather Pushers*, has been preserved, one can see exactly how much plot Zanuck was able to pack into an episode and how smoothly the narrative progresses. There is even a flashback which occurs so unobtrusively that it is only later that you realize you have watched something that occurred in the past. Zanuck's titles matched Witwer's "tough guy" prose—colorful (a "pork-and-beans" fight manager), slangy ("youse guys"), and nasal ("Noo Yawk"). The first scene is set "Somewhere in New York's Roarin' Forties," specifically a rooming house where Kid Roberts, "a famous college athlete whose dad went broke," lives with Joe Murphy, a fight manager, who bought the Kid for $100 from the cigar-chomping "Dummy" Carney. In case the exposition is too much, a title comes on stating that "for the benefit of them which came in late, I want to explain," followed by a brief summary. Carney decides he wants the Kid back, threating blacklisting if Murphy refuses. Instead, Murphy bets Carney that the Kid will knock out his opponent in the second round. Just before the fight begins, there is a scene in which the Kid tells his bankrupt father that somehow he will make enough money to pay off his debts. The scene at first seems out of place, particularly since both father and son are in evening clothes until you realize that it is a flashback to an earlier incident—an excellent touch on Zanuck's part, since it restates the reason the son became a boxer. There is no round two knockout, and the Kid's socialite fiancée returns her engagement ring, which Murphy promptly takes to a pawn shop. Looking straight into the camera, Murphy teases the audience: "I got great stuff for the Kid, so don't miss Round Three." Zanuck understood the way a series works: Write every episode as if it were a cliffhanger.

THE ZANUCK FORMULA

Zanuck never used the term, "linear narration," but he clearly understood beginning-middle-end plot structure, which he termed "A-B-C." Nor did he think a well-crafted script was inferior to a intricately plotted one with multiple points of view like *A Letter to Three Wives* (TCF, 1949) or *All About Eve* (TCF, 1950). He accepted and, in fact, embraced what he called the "formula film." In his memo to Milton Sperling, producer of *Crash Dive*

(TCF, 1943), a World War II drama, Zanuck acknowledged that while it may be a formula film, "if the background and atmosphere are interesting, if the theme is patriotic, if the action is exciting, . . . the fact that it is A-B-C doesn't make the slightest difference." What mattered to Zanuck was that the characters, "while formula, were honest."

Thus at Twentieth Century-Fox, musicals were far more formulaic than they were at MGM, where the best aspired to some level of art (*Meet Me in St. Louis, An American in Paris, Singin' in the Rain, The Band Wagon, Gigi*). Twentieth Century- Fox's best musicals centered around triangular relationships, frequently within the world of show business: the heroine caught between two males (*Moon Over Miami, Sweet Rosie O'Grady, Coney Island*, and its remake, *Wabash Avenue*); the heroine and her competition for the hero (*Week-End in Havana, The Gang's All Here, Hello, Frisco, Hello, Nob Hill, My Blue Heaven*); the heroine torn between marriage and career (*The Dolly Sisters*); the heroine torn between mink coat and medical student (*Billy Rose's Diamond Horseshoe*); the heroine torn between marrying the chauvinistic hero and supporting women's suffrage (*The Shocking Miss Pilgrim*); the heroine's husband becomes a star and hits the bottle, after which wife starts divorce proceedings and is courted by a millionaire, but returns to her seemingly reformed spouse (*When My Baby Smiles at Me*); the heroine's ancestor helps her save her kingdom from the conquering hero (*That Lady in Ermine*).

If there are two sisters in the plot, there must be a double pairing off of the siblings with their beaus (*The Dolly Sisters*); if three (*Three Little Girls in Blue*), a triple. If there are three children in a family of entertainers (*There's No Business Like Show Business*), two sons (Donald O'Connor, Johnnie Ray) and a daughter (Mitzi Gaynor), there must also be a triple pairing off: O'Connor gets Marilyn Monroe; Gaynor, Hugh O'Brien; and Ray, the deity (he becomes a priest). When there are two sets of couples, one should be older than the other: Ethel Merman and George Sanders/ Vera-Ellen and Donald O'Connor in *Call Me Madam*, Beatrice Kay and William Gaxton/Betty Grable and Dick Haymes in *Billy Rose's Diamond Horseshoe*; and June Havoc and Jack Oakie/Betty Grable and Dan Dailey in *When My Baby Smiles at Me*.

The formula need not result in a formulaic film. Zanuck compared the musicals, *Carnival in Costa Rica* (TCF, 1947) and *State Fair* (TCF, 1945), noting how the former, even in its first drafts, would only be a pedestrian

A-B-C musical (boy from Kansas and girl from Costa Rica resolve their differences), while the latter not only had a score by Richard Rodgers and Oscar Hammerstein and believable characters in equally believable situations, but most important, had "charm," which was lacking in the plot-heavy story of an arranged marriage between the wrong people that ends with the would-be groom marrying the right woman, and the would-be bride, the right man. *State Fair* works from the two children-from-the-same-family template and their romantic involvements: the daughter (Jeanne Crain) with a reporter (Dana Andrews); the son (Dick Haymes) with a singer (Vivian Blaine). Daughter gets reporter, but son does not get singer, who is married. Instead, he returns to his girlfriend. There is the traditional pairing off within a linear structure (a state fair with competitions and contests, rocky romance, and an unexpected but plausible resolution) characterized by simplicity and "charm."

It was common knowledge that Zanuck had been a writer and continued to write even after becoming "supervisor," the term then used for production head, at Warner Bros. On April 26, 1936, screenwriter, playwright, and Screen Writers Guild (SWG) president Ernest Pascal tried to enlist Zanuck's support of the guild as the screenwriters' sole bargaining agent, citing—but not documenting—the "abuses" the writers incurred at the hands of producers (Zanuck being the exception). Perhaps out of flattery, Pascal added that if Zanuck had "confined his extraordinary talents to screenwriting," *he* would have been SWG president. Zanuck probably would have agreed, but he was not about to endorse unionism, which he compared to curing a patient (the movie industry) that is "strong, healthy, and normal." Instead, Zanuck reminded Pascal of what it was like when he began in the business, walking from Hollywood to Culver City and Universal City, because he lacked carfare, and living "in the back room of a bungalow with two other 'almost writers.'" Yet within four years (1922–26), as Zanuck told Pascal, he "wrote twenty-one produced feature scenarios, sixty-five produced two-reel scenarios, and made thirty-one produced adaptations." There is no way of verifying Zanuck's claim, but he may very well have been correct, given the lack of so much verifiable information from this period. The Wikipedia entry on Zanuck, derived from the Internet Movie Database (imdb.com) and the *American Film Institute Catalog*, includes a "select filmography" that attributes thirty scenarios written between 1922 and 1925 to Zanuck, seventeen of which were shorts.

DARRYL F. ZANUCK AS "GREGORY ROGERS," "MELVILLE CROSSMAN," AND "MARK CANFIELD"

Most of Zanuck's credits for features made between 1924 and 1928 only carry story credit. During that period, fourteen were written under the pseudonyms "Gregory Rogers," "Melville Crossman," and "Mark Canfield." When Zanuck wrote both story and screenplay, he used a pseudonym for the story and his own name for the screenplay; "Gregory Rogers" was credited with the story and Darryl Zanuck for the screenplay of *Hogan's Alley* and *Two Weeks in Paris* (both 1925). Zanuck continued to use pseudonyms until 1944. At first he used them "because he imagined that was what *real* writers did," like his role model, William Sydney Porter, who wrote under the name of O. Henry. When Zanuck came to Warner Bros. in 1924, he may have chosen to reserve his own name for what he considered "important" films or to give exhibitors the impression that the studio had more writers than it actually did. He retired "Gregory Rogers" after *The Midnight Taxi* (1928), but retained "Mark Canfield" and "Melville Crossman" when he needed a name for a story that he had written for one of his productions, not wishing to attribute it to himself either because the subject matter might be too controversial or the plot too formulaic. Thus, "Mark Canfield" is credited for the story of *Baby Face* (1933), a rather daring pre-Code movie in which Barbara Stanwyck played a woman whose idea of upward mobility is sleeping with her bosses; and Melville Crossman for *China Girl* (1942), a World War II drama about an interracial romance that ends tragically.

George F. Custen has provided the best assessment of Zanuck as a writer when he acknowledged that creating a plot was Zanuck's "greatest gift," adding that "Hollywood paid far more attention (and a good deal more money) for what Zanuck could *not* create: the conventional, prestigious forms of the written culture—the novel, the play, and the short story." Yet, as a production head, Zanuck knew how to get the right people to turn these "prestigious forms" into prestigious films. Jack Warner was amazed at Zanuck's ability to turn out screen stories, scenarios, and an occasional screenplay, including *Eve's Lover* (1925) and *A Broadway Butterfly* (1925), both as "Gregory Rogers": "[Zanuck] could write ten times faster than any ordinary man." Warner was right; he could even write for a German Shepherd.

THE RIN-TIN-TIN QUARTET

Mal St. Clair, who had directed many of the two-reelers written by Zanuck, had been asked to direct a series of films for Warner Bros.' newest star, Rin-Tin-Tin. At a meeting with Jack Warner and his brother Harry, Zanuck pitched his idea for a Rin-Tin-movie, even playing the dog. Warner knew he had a writer in Zanuck and the star of a series in Rin-Tin-Tin after *Find Your Man* (1924), written by "Gregory Rogers." It was an unusual detective story with Rinty (called Buddy) as witness to a murder of which his master is falsely accused. Buddy helps his master escape from prison and saves him and his girlfriend from drowning before tracking down the murderer. What Zanuck brought to the screenplay was a true situation-complication-resolution story arc, the kind at which he excelled: Buddy witnesses a murder in a timber camp, which explains his ability to identify the murderer (situation); his master is accused of the crime, imprisoned, and escapes with help from Buddy, who later saves him and his sweetheart from drowning (complication); Buddy, after being tied up and muzzled by the murderer's henchman, breaks free and exposes the perpetrator, the timber camp foreman (resolution)—all in seventy minutes.

One of the better films in the Rin-Tin-Tin series is *The Lighthouse by the Sea* (1924) from another "Gregory Rogers" script, adapted from a play by Owen Davis. Rinty shared billing with Louise Fazenda, better known at the time than Rinty due to her appearances in Mack Sennett's Keystone comedies. This time, however, Fazenda was cast in a melodrama as the daughter of a blind lighthouse keeper, who performs his chores so no one will be aware of his condition. Rinty is worked into the plot when a shipwreck survivor arrives at the lighthouse with his dog. Naturally, the survivor and the daughter fall in love, but there can be no happy ending until the survivor and Rinty rescue her from liquor smugglers.

In *Jaws of Steel* (1927), again with a story by "Gregory Rogers," Rinty had to prove he is not a threat to the community by saving a child from danger. *Tracked by the Police* (1927), the last "Gregory Rogers" story for the series, is an improvement over *Jaws of Steel*, showcasing the star at his ingenious best. Rinty—now known as Satan, "loyal and true with the heart of a lion and the soul of a child"—has enjoyed a close relationship with his master, Dan Owen (Jason Robards Sr.), ever since he was a Red Cross dog during World War I. Dan, who is overseeing the construction of an Arizona dam, clashes with the foreman, who, with his disgruntled crew, retaliates by opening the locks and causing a flood. But the villains have not counted on Rinty's ability to close the locks by biting down on the lever and turning it off. He indeed has "jaws of steel." Rinty does the same with the lock on a door to release his master. At this point, Zanuck drops the dam plot and introduces a parallel subplot: Dan and his beloved, Marcella Bradley (Virginia Brown Faire), whose dog, Princess, becomes Rinty's soul mate. The affection that the dogs show for each other is genuinely moving, so much so that one ceases to think of them in canine terms, but as lover and beloved, especially when the villains throw Princess into the river, bringing the plot to the brink of tragedy. Rinty assumes she has drowned, and Zanuck leads the viewer to suspect as much. But this is a film of many surprise twists. Just when you think the dam plot has been resolved or shelved, it recurs when the villains turn saboteurs and open the locks again. Rinty turns off the levers and rescues Marcella, who was almost raped by the foreman. In the final shot, Rinty and Princess (who apparently can swim) and Dan and Marcella seem to have formed a four-member household. Zanuck's concentric plot (Dan/Marcella, Rinty/Princess) and subplot (foreman and his gang) keeps the narrative from faltering, since the viewer literally does not know what will happen next.

Perhaps because he did not think the Rinty movies were worthy of him, Zanuck chose not to use his own name. However, they were perfectly respectable entries in the series, representing the kind of storytelling that shows that the author clearly knew how many complications he could introduce before the plot went into overload. Zanuck's range of plot templates confirms Jack Warner's claim that Zanuck could write anything. The stories seemed to spring from his imagination like saplings. In 1924, in addition to his two Rin-Tin-Tin films, there was *The Millionaire Cowboy*, which would have been familiar to anyone who read his four-story collection, *Habit*. Zanuck simply converted the fourth story, "The Forgotten City," into a screen story, in which father sends spoiled son to a ghost town, whose sole inhabitants, except for some Mexican bandits, are the flamboyantly eccentric father and his daughter; the son, spiritually renewed, capitalizes on the father's discovery, drives out the bandits, brings the town back to life, and marries the daughter. Since Zanuck no longer had to extol the merits of Yuccatone, he kept the idea of the restorative power of yucca extracts but changed the product from a hair restorer to a rust remover.

DARRYL F. ZANUCK, SUPERVISOR

At some point in 1927, Zanuck was elevated from "writer" to "supervisor," or, as *Moving Picture World* (October 22, 1927) dubbed him, "first lieutenant to Jack Warner, studio chieftain." "Supervisor" was the original name for production head or executive producer, although when Carl Laemmle asked his son, Carl Jr., to replace Roy Walsh as Universal's "general manager," Carl Jr. agreed, provided his title be "general manager in charge of production," which, in effect, meant production head. Beginning as a writer, and then as a writer who revised the scenarios of others, Zanuck discovered the magic of editing, which was not all that different from doctoring scripts. The function of an editor, both in print and visual media, is to improve a work by pruning it of excrescences that have grown over it until the final product has a linear leanness. Zanuck fancied himself a "pretty good cutter," as he reminded Michael Curtiz in his memo (April 29, 1954) about Twentieth Century-Fox's CinemaScope production of *The Egyptian* (1954), which Curtiz was directing. Although Zanuck assembled a rough cut of the film, the final editing was done by Barbara McLean, on whom Zanuck relied heavily. In an oral history interview, McLean described how Zanuck would sit next to her in the projection room, "and when he didn't like something, he'd just touch you on the arm." Her ability to interpret Zanuck's way of signaling dissatisfaction made it easier for her to either eliminate what displeased him or, if it was only a matter of excising a few seconds of screen time, cut the scene in such a way that audiences would not be aware it had been trimmed.

McLean was an extraordinary editor, nominated seven times for the Best Editing Oscar and winning for *Wilson* (TCF, 1944). Twentieth Century-Fox tied with MGM for the number of editing nominations between 1936 and 1951: eleven, with one win each (TCF for *Wilson*, MGM for *National Velvet* [1945]). Zanuck was also a creative editor in a different way. He knew instinctively how to excise or revise dialogue that was redundant or overly literary and to improve a performance by deleting or trimming shots that showed an actor at a disadvantage (exaggerated reactions, unconvincing line readings). What really made Zanuck a great producer was his understanding of dramatic structure, which required, besides a well-crafted script, the elimination of the superfluous. He found Philip Dunne's first draft screenplay of *The Robe* (TCF, 1953) too novelistic, asking for the removal of "any line or speech that may even be halfway superfluous" to give the film "tempo, pace, and drive," which it eventually received, resulting not only in the studio's first CinemaScope production but also in a blockbuster; budgeted at a little over $4 million, *The Robe* grossed $32 million worldwide.

Tempo, a film's speed or pace, is a recurring phrase in Zanuck's memos. He urged John Ford to "pick up the tempo" in *Young Mr. Lincoln* (TCF, 1939), even after deleting a scene in which the shabbily dressed Lincoln, riding on a mule through Springfield, Illinois, where the Booths were performing in *Hamlet*, caught the attention of one of the Booth children who stared up at him as if he were a curiosity piece. The scene would have added a touch of irony to the film, but Zanuck found it "superfluous," another favorite word. In a 1941 memo to directors and producers of the studio's A-films, or those given high budgets, he expressed himself more clearly that he ever did before: no matter how well-crafted the screenplay, if the action is not paced properly, the audience will be left in a state of ennui.

"Tempo is the cure for a script that may be well written but crawls along at a snail's pace and will fold up and die while the audience is waiting for the next thing to happen." What mattered was gradation of tempo, which did not have to be trip hammer style like *His Girl Friday* (Columbia, 1940), which was appropriate for a movie set in the newspaper world. But to Zanuck, uniformity of pace produced monotony. His musicals, particularly those with a show-business setting, are a good illustration of what he meant by tempo. Important plot elements are established early in *Wabash Avenue* (TCF, 1950), in which Victor Mature returns to a Chicago saloon now owned by Phil Harris, who won it from him in a poker game. It is evident that Mature is planning to win it back. Harris is enamored of his star, Betty Grable, but before she does her first number in the film, "Sister Kate," another character is introduced, an amiable drunk, who will play a significant role in the plot. In another Betty Grable movie, *The Shocking Miss Pilgrim* (TCF, 1947), there is even more plot before anyone sings. The title character is a "typewriter," an early term used for a typist, in this case one who becomes involved in the women's suffrage movement, much to the displeasure of her chauvinist boss (Dick Haymes). As he becomes more interested in her than her secretarial skills, it is time for a song, which does not advance the plot, but exists only because (a) the songs were by

George and Ira Gershwin; (b) Dick Haymes was a popular vocalist and recording artist; and (c) audiences expected singing, if not dancing, in a Betty Grable movie.

DARRYL F. ZANUCK, ARISTOTELIAN

Plotting mattered to Zanuck. If verisimilitude was impossible, and plausibility was doubtful, then probability was the last recourse. Zanuck thought of screenwriting in terms of building: the writer must provide a foundation that can support the narrative as it mounts steadily to a climax. It is only when a writer locates the story's base line that it can develop into a full-grown narrative. In a firmly worded memo (June 25, 1946) to John Ford, Zanuck admitted liking the script of *My Darling Clementine* (TCF, 1946), except for the "construction of the continuity" and the "inconsistencies." Zanuck felt that, despite the title, too much attention was focused on Clementine Carter (Cathy Downs), which detracted from the relationship between Wyatt Earp (Henry Fonda) and the tubercular "Doc" Holliday (Victor Mature) and obscured the contrast between the virtuous Clementine, who seems destined for the heroic Earp, and the earthy Chihuahua (Linda Darnell), Holliday's Latina lover. Zanuck clearly favored Chihuahua, who becomes a tragic figure. He deleted the brawl between the two women, rightly realizing that it would be completely out of character for the prim and proper Clementine. He also cut several of Clementine's scenes, including one in which she dissolved in tears at James Earp's grave, which made little sense, since she had never met him; and another in which she berated Doc Holliday, calling him "a coward" and accusing him of "running away from life." Zanuck "recommended" that he edit the film personally, as he did Ford's *The Grapes of Wrath* and *How Green Was My Valley*, by which he meant creating a narrative continuity, a technique he had mastered much earlier when he was writing *The Leather Pushers*, so that the sequences would follow each other in order once the incongruities, inconsistencies, and redundancies had been removed. The rest—rhythm, alternation of shots, exit-entrance matches, cutaways, transitions (fades, dissolves), inserts, etc.—would be left to the editor, which, in the case of *My Darling Clementine*, was Dorothy Spencer.

Since Zanuck never read Aristotle's *Poetics*, he would not have known that back in the fourth century BCE, Aristotle insisted (*Poetics* XV, 307) that characterization must be true to life (*homoion*) and consistent (*homalon*). These were Zanuck's criteria as well. After reading the first ninety-six pages of "My Heart Tells Me" (retitled *The Miracle on 34th St.* [TCF, 1947]), Zanuck felt that Doris Walker, Maureen O'Hara's character, was not "true to life." That she became believable—a single parent who raised her daughter not to believe in Santa Claus before later realizing that children need their myths—is due to writer-director George Seaton's heeding Zanuck's criticism, resulting in a television Christmastime perennial.

If someone had told Zanuck what Aristotle had written about characterization, he probably would have shrugged and said: "What else can it be other than true to life and consistent?" Everything derived from plot, which, to Aristotle, was the "soul" and "first principle" of the play. If the plot was structured in accordance with the laws of verisimilitude (literally, "life likeness"), the characters would be as plausible as the story they inhabit. Zanuck was an Aristotelian at heart.

Chapter 3

THE SOUND (LITERALLY) OF MUSIC

"When I took over at Warner Brothers . . . Jack *practically* gave me a free hand," Zanuck boasted to Mel Gussow, his biographer. "*Practically*" is the right word. *Moving Picture World* (March 26, 1927) referred to Zanuck as "associate executive," the second in command to Jack Warner, who was "in personal charge of production." In Hollywood, Zanuck's elevation in rank was less noteworthy than the August 6, 1926, premiere of Warner Bros.' first Vitaphone production," *Don Juan*, at its flagship theater, the Warners', on Broadway and Forty-Seventh Street; and that of *The Jazz Singer* on October 6, 1927, at the same theater.

In 1925, Sam Warner (1887–1927) convinced his brothers Albert (1894–1967), Jack (1898–1986), and Harry (1881–1958) that the Vitaphone sound-on-disk system developed by Bell Telephone Laboratories and Western Electric, in which sound recorded on 16-inch, 33 1/3 rpm shellac disks is synchronized with the picture, would soon do away with the need for live musical accompaniment at showings of films. With financial assistance from Goldman Sachs, Warner Bros. leased the Vitaphone system from Western Electric for $800,000, intending to lease it to other studios if it proved successful, which it did. Sam Warner was not thinking in terms of talking pictures, but rather of silent films with musical accompaniment, with the goal of bringing the sound of great orchestras and vocalists to moviegoers. There was no spoken dialogue *in Don Juan*, just intertitles. But there was sound: swords clashing, bells tolling, and a theatrically made up John Barrymore kissing, drinking, dueling, and leaping off balconies. *Don Juan* was preceded by an introduction by Will Hays, president of the Motion Picture Producers and Distributors of America (MPPDA), who waxed rhetorical with arms extended, intoning that "the influence of motion pictures is as far flung as all the tomorrows." A mini-concert followed, illustrating Vitaphone's ability to reproduce sound on film. The New York Philharmonic played the overture to Wagner's *Tannhaüser*, followed by eight musical shorts including Giovanni Martinelli performing "Vesti la giubba" from *Pagliacci*; Marion Talley, "Caro nome" from *Rigoletto*; and violinist Mischa Elman playing Dvorak's "Humoresque." Of historical interest was American soprano Anna Case in "La Fiesta," which featured the Cansinos, the "Spanish Wonder Dancers," one of whom was Eduardo Cansino, whose daughter and occasional dancing partner was Marguerita Cansino, later known as Rita Hayworth. After intermission, *Don Juan* came on the screen. *New York Times* critic Mordaunt Hall (August 7, 1926) was thrilled by the concert and commended Warner Bros. for being "sufficiently astute" to make *Don Juan* the post-intermission attraction when the audience was in the mood for a story with enough romance, swordplay, and intrigue to hold its attention for 112 minutes.

THE JAZZ SINGER (1927)

Zanuck played no role in the production of *Don Juan* nor did he attend the New York City premiere. To him, it was a lavish swashbuckler notable for its soundtrack, beautifully gowned women, and John Barrymore performing his own stunts. *The Jazz Singer* was something else. If auteurism was in vogue in 1927 and producers were identified by name, the opening title would have read "*The Jazz Singer*, a Darryl F. Zanuck Production, an Alan Crosland film." The Academy of Motion Picture Arts and Sciences awarded Warner Bros. a Special Oscar for *The Jazz Singer*, which Zanuck accepted on behalf of the studio. It was, after all, *his* production. The Academy considered the film ineligible for consideration as Best Picture because a "talkie" would put the other nominees (*The Last Command*, *The Racket*, *Seventh Heaven*, *The Way of All Flesh*, and *Wings*), all silent films, at a disadvantage. Zanuck's acceptance speech was unusually brief: "This award is dedicated to the late Sam Warner, the man responsible for the successful usage of the medium." Sam had died the day before the October 6 premiere, at the age of forty from pneumonia caused by sinusitis and a brain abscess. Because of the funeral, none of the brothers attended the opening of *The Jazz Singer*, which, as the Academy acknowledged, "has revolutionized the industry."

The January 1922 issue of *Everyone's Magazine* included a short story by Sampson (later Samson) Raphaelson, "The Day of Atonement," about a cantor's son, Jackie Rabinowitz, who refuses to follow in his father's footsteps and reinvents himself as Jack Robin, vaudeville headliner. Three years later, Raphaelson turned the story into a play eventually called *The Jazz Singer*, which opened on Broadway on September 14, 1925, with George Jessel in the leading role. Warner Bros. purchased the screen rights for $50,000. Jessel was expected to star, but for various reasons, none of which can be verified (salary, script, the unproven Vitaphone process), he was replaced by a celebrated performer, whose own transformation from Asa Yoelson to Al Jolson paralleled his character's metamorphosis from Jackie Rabinowitz to Jack Robin. Warner Bros. probably preferred Jolson to Jessel, even offering him $75,000, part of which would be reinvested in the film for a share of the profits. More than *Don Juan*, *The Jazz Singer* was a natural for Vitaphone. Unlike Raphaelson's three-act drama, the movie version consists of eight sequences with synchronized sound and musical numbers that included Jolson singing a chorus of "My Gal Sal" and the opening of "Waiting for the Robert E. Lee," "Dirty Hands, Dirty Face," "Toot, Toot, Tootsie," "Blue Skies," "Mother of Mine, I Still Have You," "Kol Nidre" at his father's funeral, and the climactic "My Mammy." The hybrid soundtrack was comprised of four to ninety-two bars from over eighty musical selections.

There was also spoken dialogue for which Zanuck claimed credit: "I was on the set when they were rehearsing the part where Jolson sings to his mother. . . . Suddenly it dawned on me, why don't they have a conversation. The mike was on! I said, 'Why doesn't Jolson turn to his mother and say, 'Mama, I wanna sing a song for you.' Then the guy turned the sound machine on early. When they played it back, there was Jolson's voice clear as a bell. That was when the talking thing started."

The microphone was actually open earlier during the filming of the "Dirty Hands, Dirty Face" number, which was received so enthusiastically that Jolson raised his hand to stop the applause and shouted, "Wait a minute! Wait a minute! You ain't heard nothin'. You wanna hear 'Toot, Toot, Tootsie!?' All right, hold on, hold on. Lou, listen, play 'Toot, Toot, Tootsie.' Three choruses you understand. In the third chorus I whistle. Now give it to 'em hot and heavy. Go right ahead." In the scene that Zanuck recalled, Jolson didn't say, "Mama, I wanna sing a song for you." First, Jack tells his mother (Eugenie Besserer) all he will do for her when he becomes a star. Then he pounds away at the piano, singing a jazzed-up version of Irving Berlin's "Blue Skies," in the middle of which his father, the cantor, enters looking horrified. "Stop!" he shouts. And everything did. The entire scene between Jack and his mother was improvised, with Jolson doing all the talking and Besserer reacting in character, coy and motherly, as if she realized she couldn't get a word in if she tried. While Jolson was his flamboyant self, Besserer seemed subdued. The placement of the microphone favored Jolson, leaving Besserer sounding natural but indistinct. When Jake's father arrives as his son is belting out "Blue Skies," the film reverts to silent mode with the dialogue on title cards ("Papa, have you no word for your son?") and the actors becoming voiceless. Clearly, the dialogue portion of *The Jazz Singer* was not a fluke. The director, Alan Crosland, and Zanuck probably encouraged Jolson and Besserer to improvise the scene to see how well it played with spoken dialogue. If it did not play well, the dialogue could always be written on title cards. Crosland and Zanuck must have been sufficiently pleased with the improvisation to keep it in the film, despite the faintness of Besserer's voice. But the real start of the "talking thing" was not the result of an open mic that was originally intended for "Toot, Toot, Tootsie" but picked up Jolson's introduction as well. It was a Vitaphone short in which Jolson both sang and spoke.

A PLANTATION ACT (1926)

Zanuck seems to have forgotten that when *The Better 'Ole* (Cockney for "hole"), the scenario for which he coauthored, played at New York's Colony Theatre in October 1926, it was preceded by five Vitaphone shorts, the last of which was Al Jolson in *A Plantation Act*. Appearing in blackface and looking as if he had just come from picking cotton, Jolson launches into "When the Red, Red Robin Comes Bob, Bob Bobbin' Along" after which, as if anticipating applause, he says, "Wait a minute, wait a minute. You ain't heard nothin' yet." He then introduces "April Showers," after which he says the same. He refers to his final number, "Rock-a-Bye Your Baby with a Dixie Melody," as a "Mammy Song," comparing it to "Mother Machree," a favorite of Irish tenor John McCormack, which hardly qualifies as a "Mammy Song." Jolson then takes several curtain calls and blows kisses.

If *A Plantation Act* has the immediacy of a live performance, it is because it was filmed at the Manhattan Opera House on West Thirty-Fourth Street on September 7, 1926, while Jolson was in rehearsal for a tour of his hit show, *Big Boy*, and shown a month later at the premiere of *The Better 'Ole*. But it was *A Plantation Act* that awed critics and audiences alike, who marveled at Jolson's delivery and the sound of his voice. Thus *A Plantation Act*, not *The Jazz Singer*, which arrived the following year, can be considered the first talkie (though it wasn't the first feature talkie). It is therefore difficult to believe that *The Jazz Singer* was planned as a silent with a soundtrack like *Don Juan*, or that the exchange between Jack and his mother would not have been heard if the mic had not been on. If audiences had heard Jolson speak the year before in a short, why should they be denied hearing him in a feature? Old myths die hard. However, as George F. Custen, who studied Zanuck's shorthand notes for *The Jazz Singer*, has shown, Zanuck made changes in the title cards, eliminating those that were "superfluous"; made edits that improved the rhythm; and revised the ending so that the film concludes with Jolson wowing the audience with "Mammy" instead of the cantor's death (as the play did). *The Jazz Singer* was truly a Darryl F. Zanuck production.

Vitaphone proved an expensive proposition for exhibitors, who were initially reluctant to convert to a system that might prove to have as many problems as the Kinetophone, the Edison Corporation's sound-on-disk format, which was plagued by faulty synchronization. But the brothers were undaunted. The success of *Don Juan* ($1.258 million) and *The Jazz Singer* ($2.625 million) convinced Warner Bros. that the process was only the beginning and that the "all-talking" movie was imminent. Zanuck was involved in a number of Vitaphone productions, all of which were released as silents in theaters that were not wired for sound.

HIS INFINITE VARIETY

In 1926, Zanuck wrote or coauthored the stories, scenarios, or adaptations of a number of films, some under his own name (*Across the Pacific*, *The Better 'Ole*, with director Charles Reisner, starring Charlie Chaplin's younger half-brother, Sydney "Syd" Chaplin, who was also a master of pantomime and physical comedy); *The Cave Man*, an adaptation of Gelett Burgess's comedy of the same name; *The Little Irish Girl*, which Zanuck adapted from a short story, "The Grifters," by Edith Joan Lyttleton; *Oh, What a Nurse!*, another adaptation, this time of a story by playwright Bertram Bloch (*Dark Victory*), and playwright and Oscar-winning screenwriter Robert E. Sherwood (*The Road to Rome*, *The Petrified Forest*, *There Shall Be No Night*, *The Best Years of Our Lives*), with Sydney Chaplin in drag; and *The Social Highwayman*, for which Zanuck shared writing credit with Philip Klein and Edward T. Loew Jr.

In 1927, the year he officially became production head, he was responsible for the following productions: *The Missing Link*, another Charles Reisner-Darryl Zanuck collaboration, with Reisner directing Zanuck's screenplay from a story by "Gregory Rogers"—another case of Zanuck reserving his name for the screenplay and attributing the story to his nom de plume; *Irish Hearts*, from a story by "Melville Crossman;" *Simple Sue*, another "Melville Crossman"-Darryl F. (he was now using the middle initial) Zanuck film with "Crossman" credited with the story and Zanuck and Albert Kenyon with the screenplay; *Black Diamond Express*, with a screenplay by Harvey Gates derived from an original story by "Mark Canfield"; *Old San Francisco*, a Vitaphone eight-reeler, produced by Zanuck himself with a screenplay by Anthony Coldeway from an original story by Zanuck, who felt the film, whose climax was the 1906 earthquake, merited his name.

The First Auto (June 1927) is notable for the amount of music in it. It was released ten months after *Don Juan* and four months before *The Jazz Singer* and supervised by Zanuck, who also wrote the original story. Zanuck was well aware that the Vitaphone system could enhance melodramas like *Old San Francisco* with its earthquake climax and *The First Auto*, "a Romance of the Last Horse and the First Horseless Carriage," with its racing scenes and car crash. Warner Bros. was apparently testing the audience's reaction to Vitaphone with a familiar soundtrack and at least one audible spoken word. The soundtrack consists of music from such familiar songs as "In My Merry Oldsmobile," "In the Good Old Summer Time," and "For He's a Jolly Good Fellow." It also supposedly contains three spoken words, one of which is clearly heard: "Go!" at the start of a race between a horse and a horseless carriage, culminating in a victory for the horse. The other two may have been muffled by the jeering that erupted from the crowd watching the driver lose control of the vehicle, which keeps backfiring as it barrels through fences and finally over a cliff and into a lake.

Other 1927 films include *The Desired Woman* (also known as *The Desert Woman*), another "Mark Canfield" (story)-Anthony Coldeway (screenplay) collaboration about love, lust, and murder in the desert; *Slightly Used*, a Vitaphone production, with story credit going to "Melville Crossman"; *Jaws of Steel*, Zanuck's third and last Rinty movie as "Gregory Rogers"; *Good Time Charley*, with Zanuck receiving story credit under his own name.

During 1927, Warner Bros. released eleven films that bore the Zanuck brand; in 1928, six; and in 1929, three. As Hollywood entered the sound era, the assembly line method of moviemaking would continue, but the screenplay would literally become a play intended for the screen (albeit with the same kind of construction that playwrights have traditionally used). It was the same onward thrust of the narrative, the same building to a climax, and the same tapering off in a resolution. The difference was the dialogue, which would be written, whenever possible by professionals: novelists, nonfiction writers, playwrights. Zanuck knew he was a storyteller, but not a playwright or a great screenwriter. At the same time, he had one gift that other production heads lacked: he knew how to fine-tune a screenplay and make it better. He also knew that for motion pictures to take on the mantle of respectability, Warner Bros. needed writers who could go beyond what he did: elevate the screenplay to a kind of literature. He would never have phrased it that way, but he was clearly thinking in those terms.

Meanwhile Zanuck would write stories for films that were largely silent with a synchronized score and sound effects such as *Tenderloin* (1928), which contained four sequences of spoken dialogue that amounted to fifteen minutes of screen time. When the film premiered at the Warners' Theatre in New York on March 14, 1928, it was preceded by some musical shorts, including the overture to Offenbach's *Orpheus in the Underworld* and Beniamino Gigli and Giuseppe de Luca in the duet for tenor and baritone from Bizet's *The Pearl Fishers*, which were well received. However, when the film came on, *New York Times* critic Mordaunt Hall noted (March 15, 1928) that "the spectators were moved to loud mirth during the spoken episodes of this lurid film." Consequently, the four dialogue sequences were reduced to two. Zanuck at least did not have to bear the brunt of the derision. He only wrote the story under the name of "Melville Crossman"; the adapters, Edward T. Lowe Jr. and Joseph Jackson, were responsible for the dialogue, and Michael Curtiz for the direction. What the actors needed was a dialogue coach, a position that at the time did not exist.

"Gregory Rogers" received story credit for *Pay As You Enter* and *The Midnight Taxi* (both 1928), "Melville Crossman" was credited for the *State Street Sadie* (1928) story. However, Zanuck had no problem using his name for the story of *Noah's Ark* (1928), which, as author George F. Custen has shown, he supervised so thoroughly that he should have been given associate producer credit, which he would have received if such a title existed. At least he is named in the opening credits: "Story by Darryl Francis Zanuck." Anthony Coldeway did the adaptation, and De Leon Anthony was responsible for the titles, many of which were excerpts from the Book of Genesis. Anthony, who was also in charge of the Warner Bros. film library, composed the titles for a number of Warner Bros. films (fifteen in 1929, including *Honky Tonk, The Time, The Place, and the Girl, Skin Deep, The Gamblers, Gold Diggers of Broadway,* and *Disraeli*). The *Noah's Ark* titles, while not literary, avoid the artificial quaintness that have made those in many silent films seem like verbal embroidery.

NOAH'S ARK (1928)

Warner Bros. originally conceived *Noah's Ark* as a silent, but after the success of *Don Juan* and *The Jazz Singer*, the studio decided to add some spoken dialogue to the second half of the film as a way of heralding the arrival of the sound era at least in its incipient form. Zanuck used modified bookend framing, beginning with a shot of the ark and a title from Genesis 6 about the Lord's decision to destroy the earth because of the wickedness of humankind, followed by a series of other titles about an event that occurred after the Great Flood: the building of the Tower of Babel (Genesis 11) that was to reach heaven, an act that angers the Lord who creates linguistic confusion, which may have been an etiological explanation of the diversity of tongues. That the Flood and the Tower are not connected temporally or even causally did not seem to matter to Zanuck, who was looking for examples of humankind's arrogating to itself what belonged to the Lord.

Next there is another unrelated incident: the worship of the Golden Calf (Exodus 32), to which the Israelites resorted when Moses went up to Mount Sinai to receive the stone tablets—a perfect opportunity for an orgy, into which are interpolated shots of stock market ticker tapes, suggesting that the bullish and bearish markets resulted from the attempt to build the infamous tower to heaven: "Towers of Babel multiply throughout the world and brother wars with brother." The opening sequence, really a prologue, is a biblical and historical montage, with examples of man's wickedness (idolatry, avarice) and the Lord's punishment in the form of a world war, which precedes the flood narrative. World War I, Zanuck's first encounter with death and devastation when he was a mere teenager, had ended with an armistice a decade before *Noah's Ark* went into production. It was still fresh in Zanuck's memory when he conceived the idea for the film, but knew it could not be exclusively about the Great Flood but rather about a similar disaster caused by humankind's reversion to ways that would anger the deity: rivalry among nations trying to outdo each other in the acquisition of colonies, military strength, nationalistic fervor, and alliances that would provide them with allies should war erupt, which it did.

Noah's Ark, then, is double plotted: a title introduces the World War I plot: "1914 The Orient Express from Paris to Constantinople." On the train, two Americans, Travis (George O'Brien) and Al (Guinn "Big Boy" Williams), Nickoloff (Noah Berry), a Russian spy, and a clergyman (Paul McAllister) are discussing religion when a storm arises that is so intense that it brings down a bridge and causes the train to crash. By now, train wrecks and storms had become convenient plot devices, but the idea of a deluge as a metaphor for war, the minister's comparison, is strikingly new and justifies the Flood sequence. One of the passengers is a German woman, Mary (Dolores Costello), whom Travis later marries. When America enters the war in April 1917, Travis enlists and eventually meets up with Mary, whom he saves from execution after Nickoloff falsely accuses her of being a German spy. The deluge comparison is the cue for the flood story, with actors from the World War I plot playing their biblical counterparts: O'Brien and Williams as Noah's sons, Japheth and Ham; Dolores Costello as Miriam, Japheth's intended; McAllister as Noah; and Noah Beery as the fictitious King Nephilim.

Realizing that the biblical section of *Noah's Ark* needed a good vs. evil plot line, Zanuck noticed that in Genesis 6, prior to the story of Noah, mention is made of the Nephilim, a race that has been variously interpreted as mythological beings, warriors, or even fallen angels. Zanuck seems to have preferred the "fallen angels" theory, which appealed to his taste for melodrama. Assuming that the Nephilim must have had a ruler, Zanuck gave them one, an idolater who appeases the gods with human sacrifices, although there is no evidence that the Nephilim committed such atrocities. There are, however, references to human sacrifice in the Bible, with which Zanuck may have been familiar, such as 2 Kings 21:6, in which Manasseh, king of Judah, sacrificed children to the Canaanite god, Moloch. (In the Bible, human sacrifice is considered especially abhorrent to the Lord.) Zanuck made Nephilim into another Manasseh. He wanted an arch fiend for the plot; not finding one in Genesis 6, he created his own, King Nephilim, who orders the sacrifice of a virgin (Miriam) and the blinding of Japheth, which is also fictitious. Zanuck simply transferred Samson's blinding (Judges 16:21) to Japheth. Unable to tolerate any more debauchery, the Lord instructs Noah to build his ark before he sends the flood and, miracle of miracles, Japheth's sight is restored, so he can rescue Miriam. A rainbow arches over the horizon, and the war is over. "War is now an outlaw," the clergyman announces in the epilogue. Famous last words.

The biblical segment of *Noah's Ark* is an eye-filling spectacle designed to outdo Cecil B. DeMille, who had set the standard in *The Ten Commandments* (1923); and the flood was so authentically torrential that three extras were alleged to have lost their lives, although that was probably not the case. Structurally, *Noah's Ark* is the reverse of *The Ten Commandments*, in which the Moses story occupies the first third of the film, with the rest devoted to the divergent career paths taken by two brothers, one of whom becomes a carpenter like Jesus, and the other an unscrupulous contractor and later a murderer. *Noah's Ark* begins with a prologue drawn from incidents in the Hebrew Bible depicting impiety, lawlessness, and greed before moving into the main action set in the 1914–18 period. Midway in the film, Zanuck returned to the Hebrew Bible for the Great Flood sequence to which he added another example of depravity in the character of King Nephilim. Zanuck showed early in his career with his short story, "Say It with Dreams," the third story in *Habit*, that he could run two narratives together and achieve a joint resolution. At the end of *Noah's Ark*, the Flood and World War I plot lines converge as two horrific events seem like mirror images of each other.

MY MAN (1928)

Zanuck's last 1928 film, *My Man*, was a movie with music, rather than a musical. He took story credit as "Mark Canfield" for what is basically a silent film with some sound sequences, notably musical numbers. *My Man* marked the film debut of Fanny (earlier Fannie) Brice, then thirty-seven, playing a character called Fannie Brand, who goes from costume company employee to Broadway star. *My Man* is significant for several reasons, chief of which is Brice, who sang the song for which she is most famous, "My Man," in addition to "Second Hand Rose," which became one of Barbra Streisand's specialties; "I'm an Indian"; "If You Want the Rainbow (You Must Have the Rain)"; and "I Was a Floradora Baby." It was also another show-business musical, the kind that Zanuck favored and at which Twentieth Century-Fox would excel. *My Man* had a flimsy plot with a silly complication: the coquettish sister's attempt to sabotage Fannie's wedding by trying to ensnare the groom. But all is forgiven when Fannie becomes a star, and the wedding goes on as planned.

Zanuck would retell the Fanny Brice story in greater detail in *Rose of Washington Square* (TCF, 1939), with Alice Faye as the title character singing "My Man" in her own languid way but not with Brice's suppressed heartbreak. As a disguised biopic, *Rose of Washington Square* proved too close for comfort, and Brice sued the studio for $750,000, resulting in an out-of-court settlement.

As Warner Bros. moved from part-talkies to all-talkies, and the screenplay replaced the scenario, Zanuck's responsibilities increased, requiring him to improve the work of others, which left him little time to write on his own. Zanuck wrote the stories for three 1929 releases, two under pseudonyms and one under his own name. "Mark Canfield" received story credit for *Madonna of Avenue A*; and "Melville Crossman," for *Hardboiled Rose*, a part-talkie with Myrna Loy. Zanuck regarded *Say It with Songs* (1929) as sufficiently important to warrant lending it his name, which looms large after the title: the titles read *Say It with Songs* "by Darryl Francis Zanuck." This was Al Jolson's third movie and a complete talkie, as opposed to *The Jazz Singer* and *The Singing Fool* (1928), which were partial. It was also another melodrama that gained traction from cliché overload. The characters are subjected to a series of misfortunes that would even have appalled Dickens, who flirted with bathos but never descended into it. Al Stone (Jolson), an entertainer with a short fuse, accidently kills a man who came on to his wife and is sent to jail. After his release, an accident leaves his son paralyzed and aphasic. A surgeon who was once in love with Stone's wife agrees to operate on the boy provided his mother has sole custody of him.

The operation is a success, but the boy still cannot speak until his mother plays Stone's recording of "Little Pal," which restores his voice in addition to reuniting Stone with his family.

Warner Bros. hoped that "Little Pal" would be as popular as *The Singing Fool*'s "Sonny Boy"; it never was, although Paul Robeson's version is an art song compared to Jolson's lachrymose delivery. At least Zanuck was not responsible for the treacly lyrics ("Little Pal, if Daddy goes away / Promise you'll be good from day to day") that Jolson milks for all their weepy sentiment. *Say It with Songs* embodied the melodrama and pathos of *The Jazz Singer* and especially *The Singing Fool*, in which Jolson had to go on stage after visiting his dying son in the hospital and sing "Sonny Boy" for the third time. Although Zanuck was not involved in the writing of *The Singing Fool*, he knew audiences expected something similar in *Say It with Songs*: a climax that would open up the tear ducts. Although the critics were dry-eyed, the public was not. *Say it with Songs*, budgeted at $388,000, grossed $5.9 million worldwide.

Since the other studios had joined the movie musical bandwagon, Zanuck knew he had to distinguish the Warner Bros. product from the others. Thus, a big component of the "all-talking, all-singing" film version of Sigmund Romberg's *The Desert Song* (1929) was that it was in two-strip Technicolor. Why stop with a few color sequences? *On with the Show* was all-talking, all-singing, and all-color, grossing $2.415 million. *Gold Diggers of Broadway* (1929) did even better: around $4 million.

GOLD DIGGERS OF BROADWAY (1929)

Gold Diggers of Broadway turned out to be one of the top-grossing pictures of 1929, and according to *Film Daily*, one of the ten best of that year. It was based on Avery Hopwood's three-act comedy *The Gold Diggers*, which enjoyed a healthy run of 717 performances on Broadway from September 30, 1919, to June 18, 1921. Zanuck may well have seen it when he spent six months in New York after being discharged from the army. The play starred the doyenne of sophisticated comedy, Ina Claire, as Jerry Lamarr, a showgirl tired of moving majestically across the stage as Lady Liberty in a tired revue. When a wealthy man asks Jerry to convince his nephew to end his dalliance with a chorus girl because he believes such women are interested only in snaring rich husbands, she attempts to disabuse him of that notion and in the process falls in love with him. The reviews ranged from "screamingly funny at times" (*New York Times*) to "vulgar and immoral" (*The Drama*). This was exactly the kind of show that would appeal to Zanuck: broad, a bit bawdy, sometimes raucous, intermittently witty, and peopled by colorful characters. Since the play centered around performers in a show, Hopwood's plot, which remained pretty much intact, needed a score to make it into what was becoming Warner Bros.' specialty: the show-business—in this case, backstage—musical with a dénouement that anticipates *42nd Street* (1933): the star sustains an eye injury, and Jerry goes on in her place, singing and dancing as if she had always been slated for the lead. Although *Gold Diggers of Broadway* is presumably a lost film, the soundtrack is intact, and the few sequences available on YouTube suggest a musical with a breathtaking finale.

Unlike the numbers in MGM's *The Broadway Melody* (1929), a showbiz musical with a soundstage look, those in *Gold Diggers of Broadway* are unmistakably theatrical. The audience is always aware that they are watching a Broadway show and even see the cast milling around onstage before the curtain goes up. By filming the numbers in long and medium shot, director Roy Del Ruth preserved the wholeness of a stage experience. The effect is like seeing the action from an orchestra seat in a theater. It may not be the most imaginative use of the camera, but it suits a film with a cast that seems to have been born in a trunk. The three principals and the choreographer were all trained on the stage: Winnie Lightner (Mabel) came from the theater via vaudeville, and Nancy Welford (Jerry) had performed in London's West End and New York before arriving in Hollywood for an extremely short-lived movie career. The stepfather of American-born and British-raised Conway Tearle (Stephen Lee, the rich uncle) was a Shakespearean actor-manager, in whose company Conway performed before branching out on his own. Larry Ceballos choreographed a number of Broadway musicals between 1921 and 1929, including Bert Kalmar and Harry Ruby's *No Other Girl* (1924) and Cole Porter's *Fifty Million Frenchmen* (1929), after which he settled in Hollywood working as choreographer and dance director (including *Murder at the Vanities* [1935], *Copacabana* [1947], and *Valentino* [1951]).

The finale, "The Song of the Gold Diggers," most of which has been preserved, is pure theater. You know it is taking place on a stage since there is even a suggestion of footlights. After the ladies of the chorus (no chorus girls, these) parade on stage looking like models in a fashion show, Jerry bounces on, urging young women to dig like forty-niners. But she sings the number so playfully that she made gold digging seem like another form of dating. Men in tuxes line up beating time with their canes, and the chorus descends Ziegfeld-style stairs. Dancers do high kicks and perform on pointe. Acrobats do somersaults, with two of them forming a human wheel barreling across the stage. The entire number is sheer kinesis, dizzying in its frenetic pace. The curtain was supposed to come down after Mabel as Lady Liberty (Jerry's role in the original) delivers her one line, "I am the spirit of the ages and the progress of civilization," which has been giving her trouble. She gets the first part right, but then mutters, "Dammit, I forgot that second line." Curtain. The End.

While *Sally*, *The Show of Shows*, and *Gold Diggers of Broadway* (all 1929) were in color, *Paris*, with Irene Bordoni, and *Footlights and Fools*, with Colleen Moore (both 1929), were only partly in color; others, completely in monochrome like *Honky Tonk*, Sophie Tucker's "all-talking, all-singing" film debut. Some—*The Time, the Place, and the Girl*, *The Painted Angel*, and *Is Everybody Happy?* (all 1929)—are considered lost films. By 1930, Zanuck wondered if the moviegoing public was becoming indifferent to musicals. He was right.

Chapter 4

THE MUSICAL RECESSION

Encouraged by the success of *The Jazz Singer*, Jack Warner and Zanuck believed they could cash in on what seemed to be a musical craze by making musicals the studio's specialty, at least until such time as the public ruled otherwise. The genre had become a novelty, like sound. Just as Warner Bros. tried to add a few spoken words to some of its 1927 movies, then spoken dialogue in films that could also be shown as silents, it did the same with music. Some films were musicals in name only; they could have easily been done without any musical enhancement. Others were full-fledged musicals, adapted from operettas (*The Desert Song*) or Broadway shows (*No, No, Nanette*) that had been musicals to begin with. In 1930, of the studio's seventy-four releases, twenty-one were musicals, most lacking distinction. Paramount released fourteen musicals in 1930, five of which are significant in terms of film history: *Glorifying the American Girl*, supervised by the great Florenz Ziegfeld himself; *Roadhouse Nights*, Jimmy Durante's debut film; *Paramount on Parade*, which showcased the studio's contract players including non-singing actors such as Jean Arthur, Ruth Chatterton, and Fredric March; *Let's Go Native*, one of Leo McCarey's early sound films with some odd casting: Jack Oakie, Jeanette MacDonald, Kay Francis, and Skeets Gallagher; *Animal Crackers*, the Marx Brothers' second sound film, worth viewing just to watch Groucho use Margaret Dumont as a stooge and hear him sing "Hooray for Captain Spaulding"; and the best of all, Ernst Lubitsch's *Monte Carlo*, with Jeanette MacDonald singing "Beyond the Blue Horizon" in a train compartment wearing only a slip. The same was true of MGM: twelve 1930 musicals, two of which are notable for their casting: *The Rogue Song*, with Metropolitan Opera baritone Lawrence Tibbett; and *A Lady's Morals*, with Met Opera soprano Grace Moore as Jenny Lind, "the Swedish nightingale," singing "Casta Diva" from Bellini's *Norma*; the third,

Montana Moon, revealed Joan Crawford as an accomplished dancer (she does an exotic number with Ricardo Cortez) and singer, talents she rarely displayed in her later pictures.

The 1930 musical of historical significance did not come from one of the top studios, but from Universal: *King of Jazz*, conceived and directed by John Murray Anderson, best known for his Broadway revues with their mix of musical numbers and sketches, often satirical and topical. *King of Jazz* was that kind of entertainment. There was no plot, just a tribute to Paul Whiteman and His Orchestra and an attempt to authenticate the African origins of jazz in Walter Lantz's witty animated sequence, "Paul Whiteman in Africa," in which a lion pursues Whiteman to Ferde Grofé's orchestration of George Gershwin's "Rhapsody in Blue," which Whiteman introduced in 1924. Universal even spoofed the film that would win the studio its first Best Picture Oscar: *All Quiet on the Western Front* (1930), in a skit called "All Noisy on the Eastern Front."

The special effects (the orchestra comes into view from a keyboard played by multiple pianists) and the attempt to trace jazz back to its African roots led to the unwanted intrusions of drum beats in the *Rhapsody in Blue* sequence. Universal may have also thought that it was producing something arty by concluding with "Finis" instead of "The End." Still, *King of Jazz* was more cinematic than any musical that year. But the public was indifferent, and the box-office receipts indicated as much. Bing Crosby aficionados will remember it as the singer's film debut, although he had little to do in what was essentially Universal's homage to the "King of Jazz" himself, Paul Whiteman.

THE FORGOTTEN AND THE FORGETTABLE

As the 1930s began, Zanuck assumed that audiences were so taken with musicals that quality did not matter. He did not seem to be aware that an excess of mediocrity could result in a backlash. Warner Bros.' 1930s musicals were a mix of Broadway musicals (mostly minor ones) and straight plays (minor and obscure), a few original scripts (without much distinction), and two operettas written especially for the screen (one of which is worth making an effort to see). Some came out under the First National banner. Since Warner Bros. owned all of First National in 1930, there was no competition between them. First National was "merely a trade name under which a certain portion of Warner Bros. product would be . . . distributed." In general, the more prestigious films were Warner Bros.; the less prestigious, First National. An exception was *Sally* (1929), the movie version of Jerome Kern's 1920 musical that was a triumph for Marilyn Miller, which was a First National release. Miller fans were disappointed, since only three of the original twelve songs remained in the final release print.

TOO MANY, TOO SOON: 1930

The Warner Bros. musicals of 1930 suggest that Zanuck was so anxious to corner the market that he sacrificed quality for quantity. *Song of the West* derived from the stage musical, *Rainbow*, with a score by Vincent Youmans and Oscar Hammerstein II; it was filmed in Technicolor and starred John Boles and Vivienne Segal. Although the studio had little faith in the film and "shortened it by two reels" after "miserable previews," it grossed over $900,000, largely on the strength of John Boles's popularity with filmgoers after *The Desert Song*. *Song of the West* is considered a lost film, but has the distinction of being the first musical to be filmed entirely on location in Lone Pine, California, which had become a favorite setting for westerns and especially for the climax of Raoul Walsh's *High Sierra* (Warner Bros., 1941) atop the nearby Mt. Whitney.

No, No, Nanette (First National) was another adaptation of a Vincent Youmans stage musical and another lost film. At least 1930 audiences had a chance to hear two of the show's best numbers, "Tea for Two" and "I Want to Be Happy," which were all that remained of the original score. *She Couldn't Say No*—adapted from a minor stage play of the same by Benjamin M. Kaye that had a three-month run on Broadway in 1926—is another lost film that had Winnie Lightner singing five songs by Joseph A. Burke (music) and Al Dubin (lyrics). *Spring Is Here* (First National) derived from Rodgers and Hart's 1929 Broadway musical of the same name with only three of the original songs intact: the title song, "Yours Sincerely," and the ever-popular "With a Song in My Heart." *Showgirl in Hollywood* (First National) was written for the screen. One of the numbers sums up the plot: "There's a Tear for Every Smile in Hollywood," although for cockeyed optimists, there is the summary song, "Hang on to Your Rainbow." *Hold Everything* was originally a 1928 Broadway show with music by Ray Henderson, and lyrics by Buddy DeSylva and Lew Brown. The film version is lost, but the soundtrack survives in the Vitaphone Soundtrack Collection, so one can at least hear "You're the Cream in My Coffee" sung by Georges Charpentier. *Song of the Flame* (First National) was a Technicolor adaptation of the 1925 operetta with a book by Oscar Hammerstein and Otto A. Harbach and music by Herbert Strothart and George Gershwin. Three songs from the original survived but constituted minor Gershwin.

Oh! Sailor, Behave! (Warner Bros.) is unimpressive, although its lineage is not: Elmer Rice's *See Naples and Die*, in which Claudette Colbert had starred on Broadway. It is not so much a musical as a comedy with a few numbers, sung by Charles King, who appeared to better advantage a year earlier in MGM's first musical, *The Broadway Melody* (1929). The misbehaving sailors implied in the title are not from Rice's play but were added to introduce the team of (Ole) Olsen and (Chic) Johnson, billed in the ads as "America's funniest clowns," so they could make their film debut doing the kind of slapstick comedy for which they were famous.

Mammy, with Al Jolson as an end man in a minstrel show, is unusual in the sense that it originated as a story by Irving Berlin entitled "Mr. Bones," who also provided Jolson with five new songs, not exactly vintage Berlin ("Swanee River," "When You and I Were Young, Maggie," and "Yes, We Have No Bananas," were by other songwriters). Hoping to provide Jolson with a song that would prove as popular as "Mammy," which he introduced in *The Jazz Singer*, Berlin wrote "To My Mammy," which Jolson sings to his mother in the film. It's just as treacly as "Mammy," except that it is a son's confession that no matter how the world treats him, there is always his "mammy." Jolson is not in blackface when he's at the piano, pouring his heart out about his "mammy," a term for a Black woman who serves as a nanny for a white family. The "mammy" is played by Louise Dresser, who has all she can do to hold back tears when Jolson indulges in his patented form of slick sincerity, proclaims that no matter what happens, he can always cling to his Mammy.

Sweet Kitty Bellairs (Warner Bros.) is an interesting example of a movie that started life as a novel adapted for the stage with great success by David Belasco, filmed as a silent in 1916 with Mae Murray as the flirtatious Kitty, and turned into a Technicolor musical fourteen years later with Claudia Dell. The revelation is the singing voice of Walter Pidgeon, whose rendition of "My Love, I'll Be Waiting for You" makes one wonder why it took him so long to do a Broadway musical, which he finally did in 1959 when he costarred with Jackie Gleason and Robert Morse in *Take Me Along. Bride of the Regiment* (First National) is another film that went through several iterations before arriving as a 1930 Technicolor musical. It began as an operetta, *Die Frau im Hermelin* (*The Lady in Ermine*), which became a stage musical in 1922, a silent film in 1927, retitled *Bride of the Regiment* in 1930, and remade as a Twentieth Century-Fox musical with Betty Grable as *That Lady in Ermine* in 1948. The plot is the same in each version: a countess saves her husband's life and herself from shame with the help of a painting of her great grandmother in an ermine cloak that comes to life. The film was considered quite racy in its time, with Myrna Loy doing an exotic dance and Walter Pidgeon's character not knowing whether or not he had sex with Vivienne Segal (but assumes he must have from her behavior). Pidgeon and Segal blend their voices harmoniously in "Dream Away." While Segal was a Broadway luminary, one wonders how Pidgeon would have fared if he pursued a career in musical theater.

Golden Dawn originated as Oscar Hammerstein and Otto A. Harbach's operetta of the same name that ran for 184 performances during the 1927–28 season. *Golden Dawn* is typical of the way Africa, "the dark continent," was portrayed on stage and screen. Racial sensitivity was virtually nonexistent. In the stage version, there was even a character called "Dago," who was eliminated from the film. Hollywood would not offend Italians, but Blacks were different. The *New York Times* (July 26, 1930) review did not address the racial stereotypy but was largely critical of the photography. Set in East Africa during World War I, *Golden Dawn* catered to the popular conception audiences had about Africans (unenlightened) and the occupying Germans (Huns). Dawn of the title (Vivienne Segal) believes that the native woman who raised her is her mother; the Germans believe that Dawn is of mixed race. Racists need not worry: both of Dawn's parents turn out to be white—a fact that saves her from being sacrificed. The revelation about Dawn's background explains the title; if it had been "Dusky Dawn," it would have been alliterative, but would have required a totally different plot and a predominately Black cast, which would have made for a far more exciting moviegoing experience

Top Speed (First National) is another adaptation, this time of the 1929 Broadway musical of the same name by the songwriting team of Harry

Ruby (music) and Bert Kalmar (lyrics). Before the film was released in late August 1930, Zanuck, sensing that the public had had a surfeit of musicals, cut all of the Ruby and Kalmar numbers and for some reason added three by Joseph A. Burke and Al Dubin for the version released domestically, although international audiences heard six of the original twelve songs. It is worth seeing for Joe E. Brown, the wide-mouthed, rubber-faced comic whom most moviegoers only remember from *Some Like It Hot* (United Artists, 1959), in which he delivers the classic fade-out line, "Nobody's perfect." *Dancing Sweeties* did not derive from the theater but from "Three Flights Up," a story by Harry Fried, who is better known as the story editor of the television series, *The Untouchables* (1959–61) and *The F.B.I.* (1965–66).

Bright Lights (First National), from an original screenplay by Humphrey Pearson, was filmed in 1929 in two-strip Technicolor, and could only have been made before the enforcement of the Motion Picture Production Code, which would never have approved the ending, in which some of the characters lie to shield the reputation of a stage star (Dorothy Mackaill), whose tawdry past would otherwise have been made public. Fearing a box-office disaster, Zanuck cut some of the numbers before the film was released, leaving out, among others, "Man about Town" with Mackaill in a tux prefiguring the signature attire of Fred Astaire.

BIG BOY (1930)

Big Boy, also released in early September 1930, proved that even an Al Jolson vehicle was not immune to the studio's policy of converting movies that were once musicals into movies with some musical numbers. Zanuck may also have had second thoughts after *Mammy* failed at the box office. *Big Boy* (the title is the name of a racehorse) was another Jolson-in-blackface movie, this time starring the performer as a Black stable groom who becomes a jockey and exposes corruption at the race track. Jolson had played the same role in the 1925 stage musical. Warner Bros. had such great hopes for the film that it booked New York's Winter Garden for the opening. Jolson's shows were regularly performed there, with a runway added on that allowed him to go out into the audience, and on one knee, with arms extended, step out of character and sing to his admirers who responded with an ovation. It was rock-star showmanship, narcissistic perhaps, but unashamedly theatrical. Movie audiences saw *Big Boy* without the original score, which was replaced by one with six songs by different teams. In addition, Jolson also sang the spiritual "Let My People Go" ("Go Down Moses"), with a chorus of farm workers in a flashback in which he played his character's father. What is extraordinary about his delivery is that Jolson succeeds in sounding genuinely African American, the sound wrenched from his heart without the folksy warbling and faux sincerity to which he often resorted. At the end of the film, Jolson steps out of character, appearing as himself along with the cast as if he were on stage for a curtain call, expressing his hope that the audience enjoyed the film and adding that "no Jolson show would be complete without a Jolson song." No, he will not sing "Sonny," but instead launches into "Tomorrow Is Another Day. And what would a Jolson musical be without a reference to his "little Mammy" waiting for him in their old Kentucky home with a Southern ham in the window? The rendition is hammy enough, but one cannot deny, as Momma Rose proclaimed in *Gypsy*, that "some people got it and make it pay." Jolson had "it," and he parlayed "it" into a style, a signature, and a career.

One doubts that Zanuck conceived *The Life of the Party* (Warner Bros., 1930) as a musical when he wrote it under the name of "Melville Crossman." The plot was a throwback to Zanuck's *The Telephone Girl* series (1924), about two young women and their adventures. In *The Life of the Party*, two ex-song pluggers—Flo (Winnie Lightner) and Dot (Irene Delroy)—lose their jobs selling sheet music and turn to gold digging in Havana, where they find husbands, though not the kind they originally envisioned. At some point, Zanuck thought that *The Life of the Party* might profit from some songs, but when the public began showing its indifference to musicals, he eliminated all but one, "Poison Ivy," which is not a musical number but a song Flo is plugging about a husband who expected his wife to be subservient but "got poison ivy instead of a clinging vine." The film is decidedly pre-Code, not only in its moral tone but also in its language. While Flo and Dot are complaining about their jobs, Flo spots the store owner and says, "Pansy," slang for an effeminate or gay male. With the enforcement of the Production Code in 1934, films that contained words like "pansy," "nance," and "fairy" would not be approved by the Production Code Administration.

As was the case with all of Warner's Broadway refits, Jerome Kern's *Sunny* (First National) was stripped of much of the original score, although the plot, based on the book by Otto Harbach and Oscar Hammerstein, remained pretty much the same. Marilyn Miller, who starred in the original, repeated her role as the title character, "Sunny" Peters, an American circus performer appearing in Britain who falls in love with a fellow American. The plot was silly, and the score was not Kern's best, although it included the still sung "Who?" Because of Miller's reputation, *Sunny* proved a financial hit for Warner's, but not enough of one to convince the studio to produce the same number of musicals in 1931.

LESS IS LESS: 1931

By now, Warner Bros. had learned its lesson. The studio released five musicals in 1931: *The Hot Heiress*, *Her Majesty, Love*, *Viennese Nights*, *Children of Dreams*, and a revised *Kiss Me Again*. *The Hot Heiress* (First National) was the reverse of *Sally*: rich girl (Ona Munson, best known as Belle Watling in *Gone with the Wind*)/poor boy (Ben Lyon)/rich girl's meddling friends. It was a screwball comedy with three Rodgers and Hart songs, none of which was memorable, although the slangy "You're the Cats" had a kind of sweet innocence: "You're the cats, you're the berries." *Her Majesty Love* (First National), a remake of the German film, *Ihre Majestät die Liebe*, was the reverse of *The Hot Heiress*: rich boy (Ben Lyon, now a wealthy playboy)/poor girl (Marilyn Miller, in her final film as the daughter of an ex-circus performer played by W. C. Fields, in his first talkie/boy's opposing family. There were only four songs by Walter Jurmann and Al Dubin, plus the Bridal Chorus from *Lohengrin* and the Wedding March from Mendelssohn's *A Midsummer Night's Dream*. The film is worth viewing just to see three great comics, Leon Errol, Ford Sterling, and Chester Conklin, in a single film in addition to the inimitable Fields, who shocks a table of snobs at a restaurant by juggling plates and apples. From her few films, one would never know that Marilyn Miller was such a Broadway icon that she has been memorialized atop the landmarked I. Miller Building at 1552 Broadway in Times Square. Alongside the arched windows are golden nooks with statues of four divas sculpted by Alexander Calder, each epitomizing a different art form: Mary Pickford (movies), Rosa Ponselle (opera), Ethel Barrymore (theater), and Marilyn Miller (the Broadway musical).

VIENNESE NIGHTS (1931)

In early 1930, Warner Bros., inspired by the success of *The Desert Song* (1929), commissioned Sigmund Romberg and Oscar Hammerstein to create four original operettas for the screen, the first of which was *Viennese Nights* (1931). The originality of *Viennese Nights* is questionable. It was a typical operetta lower-class/upper-class romance, this time with tragic overtones. Elsa Hofner (Vivienne Segal), a cobbler's daughter, is torn between two army officers: Franz von Renner (Walter Pidgeon), who can offer her wealth and status; and Otto Stirner (Alexander Gray), who can offer her a life filled with music, as he demonstrates in the film's most lyrical moment, "I Give You a Love Song," which becomes a glorious duet with Gray's robust baritone blending with Segal's silvery soprano and soaring to a rapturous climax. Money wins out, and Elsa marries Franz. Neither she nor Otto has a happy marriage. Otto marries a woman without an ear for music, causing him to abandon his dream of becoming a composer and playing instead in an opera orchestra. For a resolution, Hammerstein went back to an earlier Romberg operetta, *Maytime* (1917) and a rich girl (Otille)/poor boy (Richard) plot, in which each marries someone else, much to their regret. However, their grandchildren have better luck, with Otille's granddaughter marrying Richard's grandson.

To get Elsa's granddaughter to marry Otto's grandson, Hammerstein had to advance the action from 1890, when the story begins, to 1930, where it ends. Otto is now dead, and Elsa is preparing for her granddaughter's wedding to a man she does not love (but who has money). Irony of ironies, the granddaughter is in love with Otto's grandson, who has become the composer his father aspired to be. Recalling how she chose money over love, Elsa encourages her granddaughter to marry the grandson. The ending is almost a double wedding, one physical, the other spiritual. Elsa, now approaching death, is in a park where she sees Otto—or rather, his spirit. She joins him as her spirit leaves her body, and what they were denied on earth is realized in the hereafter. Strangely, *Viennese Nights*, one of Warner's few impressive early musicals, can currently only be viewed at UCLA's Cinema and Television Archives. (I was fortunate to see it on a DVD kindly provided to me by Ms. Sharon Rich, president of the Mac/Eddy Club.) Unless there are estate restrictions, it should be released on the Warner Archive home-video label, if, for no other reason than to see and hear the great Vivienne Segal, who was so ill-served in *Golden Dawn* and who brought such elegance and style to *Viennese Nights*.

Children of Dreams was the second and last original Romberg and Hammerstein operetta. Although it was originally filmed in Technicolor, most audiences saw it in black-and-white after the studio realized that even in the few places where it was shown in color, the public was left unimpressed, hoping for a repeat of the team's *Viennese Nights* but getting instead the story of a fruit picker's daughter who becomes an opera singer and later returns to her father's orchard where she is reunited with the boy she left behind. When Jack Warner saw how abysmally musicals were doing, he bought out Romberg and Hammerstein's contract, which called for two more original operettas.

In 1925, First National released *Mademoiselle Modiste*, a silent version of Victor Herbert's operetta *Mlle. Modiste*, produced by and starring Corinne Griffith as Fifi, who graduates from saleswoman to international star. When Warner's decided to film the operetta with an added subplot as *Toast of the Legion* (Fifi's lover is a legionnaire), the studio had still not reckoned with the public's increasing apathy toward movie musicals because of their recycled plots and stale sameness. After its tepid reception in late 1930, the film was withdrawn from circulation and rereleased in early 1931, with most of the score cut, as *Kiss Me Again*. Originally shot in two-strip Technicolor, only a black-and-white version survives, but it is worth viewing just to hear Bernice Claire, who sounds uncannily like the lustrous Jeanette MacDonald, sing the title song to Walter Pidgeon, who briefly joins her.

Warner Bros. suffered a net loss of $7,918.604 in 1931, which accounts for its one musical in 1932: *Crooner* (First National), a cynical variation on the obscurity-to-fame-to-obscurity trajectory, in which a saxophonist (David Manners) achieves fame with a different kind of instrument: his voice amplified by a megaphone, which makes him into a Rudy Vallee-like crooner. Drunk (literally) with success, he becomes affected and overbearing, eventually hitting the skids, leaving only his long-suffering girlfriend (the magnificent Ann Dvorak) to comfort and perhaps rehabilitate him. There was also another reason for the paucity of musicals in 1932: after the success of *Little Caesar* (1930) and *The Public Enemy* (1931), Zanuck realized that Warner's had created a type of movie that other studios could only imitate: the crime film, along with its subspecies, tabloid melodrama. Warner's already had two great actors, Edward G. Robinson and James Cagney, who could work both sides of a two-way street, on either the right or the wrong side of the law. If Warner's was to embark upon another musical cycle, the musicals should have the toughness of the crime film—not schmaltzy operettas or rocky road romances, but movies about show business as a blue collar profession devoid of glamour and glitz that would not deny the existence of a Depression but would not highlight it, either. The theater was not a temple of high art but a job. Women were dames, not ladies. Dancers were hoofers working their legs off, not artistes. Boy would get girl, but both had to work. There was no time for career vs. marriage angst. The story would be realistic enough so that audiences would not ask themselves, "Why are we watching musicals at a time when one-third of the nation is unemployed?" The solution was simple: Razzle dazzle, Depression-style.

In *42nd St.*, Zanuck found the formula to woo moviegoers back to musicals.

Chapter 5

"NAUGHTY, BAWDY, GAWDY, SPORTY FORTY-SECOND STREET"

42ND ST. (1932), THE NOVEL

When Zanuck read Bradford Ropes's novel, *42nd St.*, it must have reminded him of the kind of fiction he would have produced if he had devoted himself exclusively to writing. Ropes (1905–1966) had been a dancer, actor, and author, whose novels *42nd St.* (1932) and *Stage Mother* (1933) were filmed by Warner Bros. and MGM, respectively. Ropes's experience in the theater resulted in the novel for which he is chiefly known, *42nd St.*, the backstage story behind the production of a Broadway musical, *Pretty Lady*, whose title conjures up images of women in frilly dresses and picture hats and men in cashmere sweaters and white pants. The show is the exact opposite; it seems to have been a revue which, by its very nature, was plotless: a mix of comic routines, dance, particularly tap, a torchy number or two, and some specialty bits. The reader never learns much about *Pretty Lady*, but a good deal about those associated with it. The British-born director, Julian Marsh, whose "clothes were impeccable" and whose "taste in cravats vivid but unerring," is gay; his lover, Billy Lawler, is the male ingénue. Ropes, who can be quite open in his book about the sexual escapades of his characters, is uncommonly discreet about Marsh's and Lawler's homosexuality, probably because it added nothing to the plot, which is a series of vignettes about everyone involved in the production from the producers and the creative team to the female lead and the supporting cast, whose aspirations, love lives, and fears constitute the bulk of the novel, until the out-of-town opening and the Broadway premiere, when the action picks up and barrels along toward a resolution.

The language in the novel is tangy and also blatantly homophobic ("fag," "faggot," "nance," "queer"). The leading lady refers to Billy as "Miss Lawler." Occasionally Ropes would hear the muse, and the language would turn literary, as if Gotham had become O. Henry's Baghdad on the Hudson, with glitter to spare: "To Marsh it seemed as though the yellow street lamps sent their rays reaching jealously toward those aloof stars, seeking to draw from them a millionth part of their unearthly splendor." But every time Ropes tried to deflect the narrative from pulp to art, he realized there were multiple relationships that had to be interwoven. The wife of dance director Andy Lee, who threatens to expose her husband's affair with a minor, has no qualms about sleeping with Pat Denning, the gigolo of the star, Dorothy Brock, who is forced to play up to (and perhaps sleep with) an influential backer. Denning is a truly egalitarian ladies' man, setting his signs on newcomer Peggy Sawyer, who is torn between him and Terry Neill, a fellow cast member who encourages her and even teaches her the time step. These characters are palpably human in their needs.

The specter of the Great Depression, although unmentioned, hangs over the action (it broods over the film) with performers desperate for a job, even if it's just a bit in the second act. One can even be sympathetic to the alcoholic Dorothy Brock, who knows that she can light up a stage with her presence, but not with her voice. Even the minor characters are sharply drawn. The exceptions are Marsh and Lawler, who remain faceless. Although Marsh drives the action, he remains in the wings, a shadowy presence whose directorial genius has to be taken on faith. And Billy Lawler's main role is that of a plot resolver: when Brock, in a drunken stupor, falls down a flight of stairs and sustains a concussion, it is Billy who persuades Marsh to put on Peggy in her place. Peggy is not the dewy-eyed novice that she is in the film. When a Columbia undergrad becomes familiar, she turns on him, calling him a "cheap, half-baked kid." She has clearly been around the block more than once. The novel ends with her triumph and her request that in their duet, the tenor refrain from starting the second verse so soon. "Who the hell does he think he is?" Peggy is a diva in the making, the next Dorothy Brock.

42ND STREET (1933), THE FILM

For the movie version of *42nd St.*, in which "Street" is spelled out, the plot went through Hollywood's rinse cycle, with sex reduced to strictly het-erosexual innuendo. There is nothing glamorous about the theater, as the pavement-pounders know who toil away in obscurity, glad to have a job to pay the rent. *42nd Street* never becomes a musical until the end. Most of the film is a series of intersecting storylines: the determination of Julian Marsh (Warner Baxter), no longer gay but also not particularly interested in women, to make *Pretty Lady* into a hit even if it means behaving tyranni-cally to the company; the romantic entanglements of Pat Denning (George Brent) with Dorothy Brock (Bebe Daniels) and, later, with Peggy Sawyer (Ruby Keeler); Brock's cozying up to the main backer, now a sugar daddy (a cuddly Guy Kibbee); Peggy, pursued by both Denning and a straight Billy Lawler (Dick Powell); Brock's indisposition (now a broken ankle). The storylines stop crisscrossing until opening night, when we finally get a look at *Pretty Lady*, whose title suggests pristine entertainment like Jerome Kern's *Cousin Lucy* or *Sweet Adeline*, but is nothing of the sort.

Zanuck wanted a racy, pungent script, which Whitney Bolton's thirty-eight-page treatment gave no indication of becoming, as film scholar Rocco Fumento has shown in his detailed analysis of the film's genesis. The final screenplay is credited to Rian James and James Seymour, the latter a Harvard-educated writer, producer, and dialogue director, with theatrical roots on his father's side. Both were suited to the task, James more so than Seymour. James had been an arts and entertainment col-umnist for the *Brooklyn Eagle*, a stunt man, and a vaudevillian. He knew the milieu, as he showed in his novel, *Love Is a Racket*, with its assortment of unprincipled characters, which Warner Bros. turned into a 1932 film directed by William A. Wellman.

In their screenplay, James and Seymour captured the feverish anticipa-tion that gripped Depression-era Broadway when news that "Jones and Barry are doing a show" begins circulating, attracting hopefuls desperate for a chance to work, even if it means the humiliation of the "cattle call," where they exchange wisecracks and size each other up, some going out of their way to mislead the naïve, and others being as considerate as competitors can be. Never has auditioning been subject to such a glaringly unflattering light. Civility is almost nonexistent. When Peggy Sawyer, straight out of

Sioux City (Maine in the novel), asks to find "the gentleman in charge," she is told, "second door on your right, dearie," which happens to be the men's room. Slightly flustered, she goes to the room on the left and discovers Billy Lawler in his underwear. It's a great meet-cute: a virginal novice and a juvenile lead without his pants.

Sexually, the movie is rather tame. The dialogue is more suggestive than risqué. Ann Lowell (Ginger Rogers) is known as "Anytime Annie" ("She only said 'no' once and then she didn't hear the question"). Lorraine (Una Merkel) admonishes one of the chorus boys, "You've got the busiest hands." A chorine is described as making $45 a week and sending her mother $100. Innocuous dialogue, even for 1933—but not for 1936, when Joseph Breen headed the Production Code Administration. In his letter to Jack Warner (August 26, 1936), he wrote that he would not approve the film for rerelease because of its "general flavor of suggestiveness." "You've got the busiest hands" had to go, along with the pun on "make": Man #1: "Just trying to make her . . ." Man #2 interrupts "'Make her' is right." Breen also wanted the elimination of the scene in which Bebe Daniels is lifted up from the floor after breaking her ankle because of the "undone exposure of her breasts," as if she had suffered a wardrobe malfunction, which was not the case. Her cleavage was what caught Breen's all-discerning eye. On September 25, 1936, A. J. McCord of the Editing Department informed Breen that "all the eliminations you have asked for and prints that will be sent out on re-issue have been made." How different it was on December 27, 1932, when James Wingate, representing the Hays Office, informed Warner Bros. that the script was "satisfactory under the Code."

Breen raised no objection to the final sequence, which is all that one sees of *Pretty Lady*. It requires a leap of faith to accept the fact that plucky Peggy Sawyer could replace glamorous Dorothy Brock, who knew how to add sexual shading to her big number, "You're Getting to Be a Habit with Me." Sawyer is a hoofer, whose idea of tap is to attack the floor as if were something intractable that had to be stomped into submission. There is no indication that Brock could hoof, or that Sawyer could handle innuendo. But the *42nd Street* finale, staged by Busby Berkeley, is so breathtakingly cinematic, so totally un-Broadway (no stage could accommodate whizzing cars and policemen on horseback) that you realize this could not possibly be *Pretty Lady* but instead Berkeley's attempt to bridge the gulf between Broadway and Hollywood by uniting them on a particular kind of stage: a soundstage. What matters is that Peggy Sawyer heeds Julian Marsh's command, which has echoed throughout the decades: "Sawyer, you're going out a youngster, but you've got to come back a star." This is a pure movie line, which obviously was never in the novel.

The finale is a three-part sequence ("Shuffle Off to Buffalo," "I'm Young and Healthy," and the title song), each of which stands independent of the other, so that it is impossible to make any narrative sense out of it. The effect is like watching three sketches in a musical revue, one following the other, which is generally the case in that kind of non-narrative entertainment. *Pretty Lady*, then, must have been conceived as a revue, not a book musical. In "Shuffle Off to Buffalo," two newlyweds (Keeler and Clarence Nordstrom) board the Niagara Limited, he with a "Just Married" sign on his back. The cooing couple project such an air of innocence as they sing "Shuffle Off to Buffalo" that references to starting a family ("Someday the stork may pay a visit") seem like unwelcome intrusions of carnality. Berkeley then has the train separate in two, revealing the interior and prompting applause from the audience. Anyone expecting consummation on this Honeymoon Express will get it by metaphor: the bride's limp hand dangling from the lower berth's curtain. The newlyweds are not the only couple in the sleeper, which becomes evident when the curtains are pulled back, revealing the ladies of the chorus.

"I'm Young and Healthy" is a masterpiece of Busby Berkeley's choreography and Sol Polito's cinematography, a triumph of black-and-white filmmaking. Dick Powell in a white tuxedo jacket, white bow tie, and black pants enumerates his qualifications to Toby Wing—her hair blindingly platinum, her white gown trimmed in ermine with matching muff—as they are framed against a black background, so that the composition is a study in monochrome so rich that it seems to be a spectrum unto itself. Berkeley plays with geometry, as Powell and Wing revolve on a turntable, surrounded by men dressed like Powell and women in less ostentatious ermine outfits. When the women form a human wheel, Berkeley cuts to a high shot that makes their conjoined bodies look like a magnified snowflake, delicate and lacey. But the *pièce de résistance* is the final tracking shot between the inverted V formed by the women's legs, at the end of which are the beaming faces of Powell and Wing. Whether Berkeley was objectifying the female form, eroticizing it, creating geometric compositions, or catering to male fantasies is unclear; one could argue that he was doing all four.

In the climactic number, "42nd St.," Ruby Keeler appears in a two-piece black-and-white ensemble: jaunty white derby, a black top with a white collar and puffed sleeves with polka dots, and a black detachable skirt with a side opening, inviting us to the intersection of high-and low-life, "where the underworld can meet the elite." When she exits on the running board of a cab (another example of celluloid Broadway), you realize she was dancing on top of it. The scene then changes to another section of Forty-Second Street, not the fabled theater-studded stretch between Broadway and Eighth Avenue, but closer to Hell's Kitchen, around Ninth and Tenth Avenue. Actually, this is not the real Forty-Second Street, but a simulation: Hollywood's idea of what the Crosswords of the World might mean to the average moviegoer who knew of its fabled reputation second hand. Native New Yorkers would have known the difference, but they would have also understood that they were in fantasy land. The locals descend on the street, creating an urban vibe and flooding the block with diversity: a policeman, an apple seller, a barber and his customer, banana vendors, African American boys tapping away. Then, the camera suddenly tracks up to a hotel window, where a woman screams as a man breaks into the room, causing her to jump out of the window and into the arms of a stranger. They engage in a mad dance that becomes a dance of death, ending with her assailant stabbing her in the back. But this is only one aspect of "the big parade," and an unsavory one at that, which has no place in the grand finale with the chorus deployed in rows with their back to the audience. When they turn around, they hold pieces of the set that, in combination, form a skyscraper, atop of which are Keeler and Powell. He whispers something to her, perhaps that it's time for the number to end. She nods, and they pull down an asbestos curtain. End of show.

In the final scene, Marsh is waiting in the alley outside the theatre as the first-nighters exit, extolling Sawyer's performance. One even dismisses Marsh's contribution, attributing the show's success to the star. Warner Baxter's look of resignation masks the dejection he feels but does not express. It's the equivalent of shrugging and saying, "That's show business." It is from the final close-up of Marsh lighting a cigarette and looking joylessly pensive that we realize *42nd Street* is not really about the making of a hit musical and the elevation of a member of the chorus to stardom, but about the tragedy of Julian Marsh, who is suffering from more than clinical depression. There have been intimations that he is in poor health, and, in fact, may be dying. Marsh senses that his days are numbered, which is why he tells the producers early on: "It's my last show. It's got to be my best." And it was.

Zanuck told Mel Gussow that after failing to convince Jack Warner that the musical was due for a revival, he had *42nd Street* shot clandestinely. When Warner saw the finished product, he agreed. "It was a huge hit," Zanuck boasted, "and it began a whole new musical cycle." The logical follow up to *42nd Street* was *Gold Diggers of 1933* (1933), with some of the same cast members (Ruby Keeler, Dick Powell, Ginger Rogers, Guy Kibbee) and Busby Berkeley as choreographer. Zanuck was not involved with *Gold Diggers of 1933*, which was supervised by Robert Lord, who was the equivalent of a line producer—a kind of overseer and, in some cases, a troubleshooter especially when a picture appeared to be going over budget. The film was released in late May, more than a month after Zanuck left Warner Bros. on April 15, 1933, after which Hal B. Wallis took over Zanuck's job and title, listing *Gold Diggers of 1933* as one of his productions in his autobiography, *Starmaker*.

When Zanuck told Mel Gussow, "When I took over at Warner Brothers . . . Jack Warner *practically* gave me a free hand," he was telling the truth. Jack Warner ran the studio; Zanuck ran production They functioned well as a team, but it was a different situation with Jack's brother, Harry, the studio's president. Unlike his womanizing brother, Harry was staunchly moral, which might have contributed to his animus toward Zanuck, who was not. There will always be speculation about the circumstances under which Zanuck left Warner Bros. Zanuck claimed the reason was the across-the-board salary cuts that were instituted in 1933 because of the studio's net loss of $14 million in 1932. Zanuck was charged with implementing the cuts. At first he agreed, even taking a cut himself. When the Motion Picture Academy of Arts and Sciences and the accounting firm of Price Waterhouse decided that the cuts could be restored, Harry refused. Zanuck, rather than appear powerless, resigned "as a matter of principle."

THE GRAND EXIT

Zanuck was not the type to take the high ground, nor was principle ever a motivating factor. He wanted Jack Warner's job and title: vice president in charge of production, in short, studio boss. Knowing he could not have it at

Warner Bros., he was ready to move elsewhere. Wallis implied in his auto-biography that perhaps Zanuck did not leave voluntarily. He recounted the time the two of them were having dinner at the Brown Derby, in which Jack Warner had a third interest. Harry Warner dropped in and asked Zanuck to step outside. When Zanuck returned to the table, he was "flushed and irritable." When Wallis asked what happened, he replied, "The inevitable. I'm leaving Warners and I'm not coming back. Joe Schenck offered me a job and I'm going to take it."

Wallis implies that Harry fired Zanuck, which is not widely believed. Their dislike, if not outright hatred, of each other was well known, but Harry also knew that Zanuck was too valuable to the studio to let go. What Wallis does imply, however, is that Zanuck had the offer from Schenck before April 15, 1933, the official date of his resignation, although another account has him meeting with Schenck three days after that date. We will never know what Harry and Zanuck argued about outside the Brown Derby that evening. Perhaps Harry knew that Zanuck was negotiating with Schenck and accused him of being an ingrate and defecting for a better-paying job in the worst year of the Great Depression. (Harry, "the self-appointed conscience of the Warner family," was adept at playing the guilt card.) The more likely scenario is that Zanuck used Harry's refusal to reinstate the cuts as an excuse for leaving so that he and Joseph Schenck could form Twentieth Century Pictures, an independent company releasing through United Artists.

Chapter 6

ON THE TWENTIETH CENTURY

Joseph Schenck (1876–1961)—the older brother of Nicholas Schenck (1880–1960), president of Loew's, Inc., the corporate parent of MGM—was one of the original Jews who invented Hollywood, to use Neal Gabler's description of the creators of the studio system. The brothers Schenck were Russian immigrants who began as pharmacy owners before discovering that there was more money to be made in the amusement park business, first operating a concessions stand in Fort George in upper Manhattan, which attracted the attention of Marcus Loew, with whom they built Palisades Amusement Park in Bergen Country, New Jersey. Loew owned a large number of theatres, with which the Schencks became involved: Joseph booking films, and Nicholas assisting Loew in running his ever-growing theatre chain. Three years after the formation of MGM in 1924, Marcus Loew died, and Nicholas became president of Loew's, Inc. Joseph, meanwhile, had become a producer. With his wife, actress Norma Talmadge, they formed the Norma Talmadge Film Corporation in 1917. When the financially strapped D. W. Griffith, one of the original founders of United Artists, left the company for a more lucrative arrangement with Paramount, Joseph Schenck came on as board chairman of United Artists in 1924 and returned the studio to financial stability. Schenck, then, was the ideal partner for Zanuck. He had connections and, as head of United Artists, was in a position to distribute the product of Twentieth Century Pictures.

On July 13, 1933, three months after Zanuck left Warner Bros., Twentieth Century Pictures came into existence with Schenck as president. Zanuck was first vice president in charge of production, and Louis B. Mayer's son-in-law, William Goetz, was second vice president. Financing came from three sources: Mayer—who was so anxious that the husband of his younger daughter, Edith, find a place in the business, knowing that he would never be the equal of his other son-in-law, producer David O. Selznick, the husband of his older daughter, Irene—that he put up $100,000; Consolidated Film Industries, a film processing laboratory, an undisclosed amount; and Bank of America, which supplied the lion's share, $3 million. Emil Kosa Jr., a painter and later a matte artist, created the logo: a two-tiered monolith with "20th" at the top and "Century" under it, illuminated by crisscrossing searchlights. Composer Alfred Newman provided the accompanying fanfare. When Twentieth Century merged with the Fox Film Corporation, "Fox" was placed beneath "Century."

BROADWAY THRU A KEYHOLE (1933)

The ad for *Broadway Thru a Keyhole* (1933), Twentieth Century's second release, read like a mini organizational chart: "Joseph Schenck presents Walter Winchell's *Broadway Thru a Keyhole*. A Darryl F. Zanuck Production." Zanuck had what he always wanted: his own production unit. The film was one of five musicals that Twentieth Century made during its brief existence (1933–35). *Broadway Thru a Keyhole* derived from an original story by gossip columnist Walter Winchell, who also functioned as off screen narrator, even broadcasting the denouement on his radio show. Ray Binger supplied the visual effects, one of which was irising-in and -out of scenes in the form of a keyhole, as if the film were a peep show; and the audience, peeping Toms. The keyhole iris was really a gimmick; there is nothing particularly sensational or original about "the underworld meets show business" plot. But what is intriguing about *Broadway Thru a Keyhole* is its resemblance to, and its echoes of, earlier films that Zanuck produced at Warner Bros., which leads one to suspect the hand of Zanuck, who never met a script he didn't annotate and may well have shaped the final screenplay attributed to C. Graham Baker and Gene Towne. It is the kind of musical that Zanuck would have produced if he were still at Warner Bros.

The setting is still "naughty, bawdy, gaudy, sporty, Forty-Second Street," with a detour to Miami. When an old-timer gives a pep talk to a newcomer (Constance Cummings), telling her the show must go on, one can't help but recall Warner Baxter's reminding Ruby Keeler that she's going out a youngster but must come back a star. However, this is not the street where the "underworld can meet the elite." There is no elite, but there is an underworld, a rather benign one—the kind in which racketeer Frank Rocci (Paul Kelly) does an old friend a favor by getting her daughter, Joan Whelan (Cummings), a job at a club owned by Tex Kaley, played by the speakeasy queen herself Texas ("Hello, Suckers") Guinan. Rocci is attracted to Joan, who is drawn to a singer she met in Miami, Clark Brian (Russ Columbo). A rival mobster has Joan kidnapped on her wedding day, and Rocci is seriously wounded by a police officer while trying to rescue her. Just as *42nd Street* ended with Julian Marsh all alone feeling the emptiness of a hollow victory with the success of *Pretty Lady* attributed to Peggy Sawyer, *Broadway Thru a Keyhole* ends with Rocci in a hospital bed, looking as rueful as Marsh. He has been told his prognosis is favorable but he is not sure. He asks to be remembered at that Times Square institution, Lindy's. As "Give My Regards to Broadway" is heard plaintively on the soundtrack, Rocci gazes out of the hospital window at the Great White Way, bringing the film full circle from its glittering opening to its thoughtful end.

Broadway Thru a Keyhole is blatantly pre-Code, with gay slurs ("Peter Pansies"), double entendre ("You know how I am on an empty stomach"), and racy dialogue ("You seem to be having hand trouble"). Jack Haskell's Busby Berkeley-inspired choreography positioned the dancers in circular and intersecting arrangements, at one point with their faces inside musical notes. A high shot showed them linked together like a human wheel. In "When You Were the Girl on a Scooter and I a Boy on a Bike," the chorus girls ride scooters, pedaling right into the lens. Zanuck was using an old formula: a mix of melodrama, song and dance, and recognizable performers from the stage and vaudeville.

MOULIN ROUGE (1934)

Moulin Rouge (1934) could easily have been a romantic comedy, inspired as it was by Ferenc Molnár's *The Guardsman*, in which an actor, suspecting his actress-wife of infidelity, disguises himself as an amorous guardsman and succeeds in seducing her. The clever wife, however, tells him that she knew his identity all along. *Moulin Rouge* is the reverse. The wife, Helen Hall (Constance Bennett), is still an actress, whose playwright husband (Franchot Tone) is opposed to her continuing in the theater. Eager to appear in his new play, which will star Racquel from the Moulin Rouge (and who also happens to be her twin sister), Helen proposes that she and her sister change places so she can star in the show and at the same time test her husband's fidelity. Since *Moulin Rouge* is pre-Code, the moral implications of such an exchange are left to the imagination. *Moulin Rouge* is comparatively innocuous and played with enough sophistication to steer the plot away from "Did they or didn't they?" territory. The highlight is Constance Bennett in a black gown with sparkling accessories singing the Harry Warren and Al Dubin standard, "Boulevard of Broken Dreams," in a French accent, sounding like a jaded observer of life's passing parade. Russell Markert, founder and choreographer of the Rockettes of Radio City Music Hall, staged the musical numbers with the same kind of wholesomeness he brought to the shows at the Music Hall—a bit of Berkeley for the masses, but mostly Markert. These were not chorus girls; they were fast-stepping, high-kicking chorus ladies.

Lottery Lover (1934), from a screenplay coauthored by Billy Wilder, is another so-called musical (four songs) about a sailor (Lew Ayres) who wins a lottery organized by his peers to woo a performer from the Folies Bergère and in the process falls in love with a chorus girl from Canada. Wilder's biographer dismisses *Lottery Lover* as "tired and formulaic," noting that the same plot would be recycled to better effect twenty-five years later in Blake Edwards's *The Perfect Furlough* (1959), starring Tony Curtis and Janet Leigh.

FOLIES BERGÈRE (1935)

Folies Bergère (1935), sometimes known as *Folies Bergère de Paris*, originated as a play, *The Red Cat* (1934), by Rudolph Lothar and Hans Adler that had a short run (thirteen performances) on Broadway in September 1934. Zanuck either saw it, as the late Robert Osborne claimed when he introduced a screening of the film on Turner Classic Movies, or, more likely, backed it after he realized it could be a great vehicle for Maurice Chevalier, whom he was eager to woo away from MGM once he learned that Chevalier and production head, Irving Thalberg, were at an impasse regarding salary. Zanuck also know that Chevalier had played a dual role in *Love Me Tonight* (Paramount, 1932) similar to the one in *Folies Bergère*, in which he would be playing both a song-and-dance man and a baron. Chevalier had become a favorite with American audiences from such Paramount films as *The Love*

Parade (1929), *The Big Pond* (1930), and especially *One Hour with You* (1932), with Jeanette MacDonald. The essence of debonair, Chevalier could invest a lyric with a throatiness that seemed like a subtler form of heavy breathing. No matter what songs he sang, they always seemed to be about sex or to imply it. Chevalier did not sing songs as much as seduce them.

In *Folies Bergère*, a music hall entertainer's uncanny resemblance to a wealthy baron comes in handy when the baron must fly to London to negotiate a bank loan because of a failed African mine. The entertainer is hired to impersonate the baron at an important reception with the understanding that the baron's wife (Merle Oberon) remains unaware of the deception. The baron's advisors feel differently and inform her, allowing the writers (of which Zanuck was one) to leave audiences wondering if the wife will knowingly yield to her husband's lookalike or tease him into a harmless dalliance. Complications arise when the entertainer leaves the reception to return to the music hall at the same time as the baron unexpectedly returns home. Informed of the impersonation, the baron decides to see whom his wife prefers as a lover: the entertainer or himself. Since the Production Code was now being rigorously enforced, and the National Legion of Decency had become the self-appointed custodian of public morality, *Folies Bergère* became an all-innuendo/no-action movie. Nothing happens except a flirtation that leads to the wife's realization that she can be attracted to two men who have nothing in common except their appearance. The entertainer and the baron realize that each has something that attracted the baroness. The entertainer can also offer something the baron cannot: an accomplished dancing partner and singer who knows what mood music is meant for. Although *Folies Bergère* was successful, it marked Chevalier's last appearance in an American film until he played Audrey Hepburn's father in Billy Wilder's *Love in the Afternoon* (1957), in which he proved that, behind the boater hat, spiffy suit, and cane, there was an actor who just needed the right role to reveal it.

THANKS A MILLION (1935)

Thanks a Million (1935) made it official: "A Darryl F. Zanuck Twentieth Century Production Presented by Joseph Schenck." Since Nunnally Johnson based his screenplay on an original story by "Melville Crossman," the film was nominally Zanuck's. By the time it came out in late October 1935, Twentieth Century had merged with Fox to become Twentieth Century-Fox, which released *Thanks a Million*. No longer did Zanuck and Schenck need United Artists as distributor. *Thanks a Million* had the makings of a great political satire. The performers in Fred Allen's traveling company are stuck in a small town for two hours, forced to wait in the pouring rain for a bus bound for New York. A few of them take refuge at a political rally for the Commonwealth Party's candidate for governor, who is not only an alcoholic but also a windbag. When he becomes so inebriated that he cannot deliver his campaign speech, one of the troupe (a cherubic looking Dick Powell as Eric Land) is recruited to read it, which he does so effectively that the party bosses recruit him. Land, eager for a career in radio, agrees only if he can sing at each rally. When it becomes apparent that the Commonwealth candidate is a hopeless drunk, the bosses persuade Land to run instead, even though he insists he knows nothing about politics.

Land seems to be enjoying his new celebrity until he is asked to sign a document agreeing to reward those who financed the campaign by appointing them to key positions within the government. Land discovers his conscience and exposes the political machine publicly, urging his audience to vote for the opposition. Fleeing town to escape retaliation by the political machine, Land and his girlfriend (Ann Dvorak, a more than acceptable singer and dancer) are stopped by the police who, when they discover Land's identity, show him a newspaper headline, "Land Elected Governor."

Since Powell was cast in the lead, *Thanks a Million* had to be a quasi-musical. Powell croons the title song and "Sittin' on a Hilltop," but the most impressive number is a poorly motivated excuse to introduce the great Paul Whiteman and His Orchestra. When the opposition party discovers that the voting public is attracted to singers, they hire Whiteman to perform "New O'leans," with Ramona on piano providing the vocal, backed up by the King's Men. Ramona's rendition of "New O'leans" is the film's highlight; it is a bluesy number that Ramona sings languidly about a lady with a checkered past who is now no longer in demand. Nothing else in the film matches the artistry of "New O'leans."

All four Twentieth Century musicals have something in common: the main characters belong to the world of show business, which Zanuck has favored ever since *The Jazz Singer* back in 1927. Show business with its various forms and venues would be a staple of the Twentieth Century-Fox musical.

Chapter 7

THE HYPHENATED STUDIO
Twentieth Century-Fox

O f all the founders of the great studios, William Fox (1879–1952) emerges as both the most innovative and tragic. His story has been told several times—by Neal Gabler within the context of early Hollywood history in *An Empire of Their Own: How the Jews Invented Hollywood* (1987); by Upton Sinclair in *Upton Sinclair Presents William Fox* (1933), which seems to have been Fox's memoir as edited by Sinclair; Glendon Alvine in his impressionistic *The Greatest Fox of Them All* (1969); Aubrey Solomon in his wonderfully concise *Twentieth Century-Fox: A Corporate and Financial History*; and, perhaps definitively, by Vanda Krefft in *The Man Who Made the Movies: The Meteoric Rise and Tragic Fall of William Fox* (2017). Since there would be no Twentieth Century-Fox Film Corporation without the Fox Film Corporation, it is only fitting that "the greatest Fox of them all" receive his due.

Like Paramount's Adolph Zukor (1873–1976), William Fox was born in Hungary, the eldest of thirteen children, whose German Jewish parents emigrated to America when he was a year old and settled in a tenement on New York's Lower East Side. His father's aversion to work caused Fox to leave school at eleven. He took jobs wherever he could find them, first selling candy and pretzels and eventually finding work in the garment industry where he excelled as a coat liner and later became a partner in a cloth-shrinking company. Fox and a friend, Cliff Gordon, worked up a vaudeville act which proved unsuccessful. But this was the first decade of the twentieth century, when the "flickers" were gaining in popularity. Movies were often shown as part of a vaudeville program largely because theater owners, suspicious of the new medium, regarded them as "chasers," assuming they would trigger an exodus so the theater could be cleared for the next show. But then special theaters were built for movies alone: nickelodeons. Fox was unusually prescient. He saw the future of film in its nascent form and in 1904 purchased a combination penny arcade/movie theater in Brooklyn in which there were kinetoscope machines (coin-operated peep shows) downstairs; and a theater, upstairs. Between showings in the upstairs theatre, he introduced singalongs in which the audience would sing the lyrics from illustrated slides with piano accompaniment. Fox understood show business and would have agreed that "it's a Barnum and Bailey world, just as phony as it can be." But the audiences bought it. Fox, rather than depend on other film exchanges for product, formed his own, the Greater New York Rental Company.

Carl Laemmle (1867–1939), whose Independent Moving Picture Company (IMP) was the forerunner of Universal Pictures, is credited for hastening the dissolution of the Motion Picture Patents Company (MPPCo), a trust composed of ten companies that pooled their patents on cameras and projectors, essentially forming a monopoly with the purpose of squeezing out the independents. The Trust ruled that only licensed projectors could be used for which exhibitors were required to pay two dollars a week in order to show pictures made by companies that were part of the MPPCo, which distributed them through the General Film Company. Laemmle held out, except for a brief period when he joined MPPCo to have access to its licensed films, which were of higher quality than those of the independents. When he acquired a sufficient number, he surrendered his license.

Fox's Greater New York Film Exchange was the only licensed exchange that General Film did not own. Fox agreed to sell, but he and Jeremiah J. Kennedy, president of General Film, could not agree on a price. While offers were being made and rejected, Fox's Exchange remained in business. But once Fox refused Kennedy's offer of $75,00, demanding $750,000 instead, the Trust canceled his license. He sued the MPPCo in 1912, citing the Sherman Antitrust Act. The litigation dragged on for several years, and the case was eventually settled out of court. Fox didn't get his $750,000 but had to settle for $300,000. By 1915, the MPPCo had receded into history, and Fox and Laemmle could take some credit for its demise.

Fox was now ready to move into production. In 1913, he renamed the Greater New York Rental Company the Box Office Attraction Film Rental Company. At the time, the "Hollywood of the East" was Fort Lee in New

Jersey's Bergen Country. Filmmakers could board a ferry at 125th Street to take them across the Hudson to Edgewater, New Jersey, from which they could hop on a trolley to Fort Lee with its dusty roads and dense woods, ideal for westerns; and the Hudson Palisades, perfect for cliff-hangers. Rambo's Tavern located on a dirt road had an upstairs where the actors could change and a downstairs where they could eat. Fox set up his company, renamed Box Office Attractions, first at the Éclair Studio on Fort Lee's Linwood Avenue and later at the nearby Willat Studio, which would constitute his East Coast base of operations.

On February 1, 1915, a final name change occurred: Box Office Attractions was folded into the Fox Film Corporation, which was not long for Fort Lee. The West Coast was gradually eclipsing Fort Lee as the center of moviemaking because its climate was conducive to year-round production. No longer did the film pioneers have to bear the expense of heating their hangar-like studios in winter. Fox believed that his company's future lay in Southern California. After leasing studio space in the Edendale district of Los Angeles, now known as Echo Park, Fox was ready to go Hollywood and in 1916 "bought twelve and a half acres on both sides of Western Avenue at the Sunset Boulevard intersection," which became the first Los Angeles home of the Fox Film Corporation, with Sol M. Wurtzel (1890–1958) as Fox's executive assistant and Winfield A. Sheehan (1883–1945) as general manager, both of whom would play major roles in the development of the studio, including discovering talent and producing. Sheehan also established exchanges abroad and created a newsreel division that became Fox Movietone News.

Needing a corporate presence in New York and never satisfied with a mere office, Fox purchased property on Tenth Avenue and Fifty-Fifth Street which became the imposing Fox Film Corporation Building. It was important for Sheehan and Wurtzel to become bicoastal, on the lookout for stage performers like Will Rogers, Walter Pidgeon, Madge Bellamy (who became Sheehan's lover), and Lola Lane to add to the studio's talent pool. Fox preferred the East Coast where he had a mansion on Long Island adjoining the Woodmere Golf Club and an office in the Fox Building on Tenth Avenue with "colored-glass windows, thickly carpeted floors, and a desk behind which he sat in solitary grandeur." As soon as Fox Film Corporation came into existence in 1915, Fox began putting together a starry company that included Theda Bara, William Farnum, Betty Blythe, and Tom Mix. Fox was not publicity shy; he starred Evelyn Nesbit—the girl in the red velvet swing, whose jealous husband, Harry Thaw, killed her lover, architect Sanford White—in the provocatively titled *The Woman Who Gave* (1918).

Stars, however, have limited incandescence, as Winfield Sheehan realized. Fox began to rely heavily on Sheehan, whom he eventually made vice president and unofficial production head. Sheehan believed that film was basically a director's medium. Accordingly, he brought in a number of directors, believing they could raise the Fox Film Corporation from a fledgling operation to a major studio. Once Sheehan became production head, the quality of the Fox product improved considerably—for example, John Ford's *Three Bad Men* (1926), *Hangman's House* (1928), and *Four Sons* (1928); Howard Hawks's *The Road to Glory* (1926); Raoul Walsh's *What Price Glory* (1926), *The Loves of Carmen* (1927), and *Red Dance* (1928); and Frank Borzage's *7th Heaven* (1927) and *Street Angel* (1928). F. W. Murnau's *Sunrise* (1928), one of the greatest of the silents, is in a class by itself, honored by the Academy of Motion Picture Arts and Sciences for "artistic quality of production." The actress of the year was Janet Gaynor, voted Best Actress for not one but three pictures: *7th Heaven*, for which Frank Borzage received an Oscar as Best Director; *Street Angel*; and *Sunrise*, for which Charles Rosher and Karl Struss also won for their poetic cinematography.

Fox became interested in sound movies in 1925, envisioning a sound-on-film process that would produce a seamless synchronization between sound and image. The system became known as Movietone, which was largely the creation of Theodore W. Case, whose patents Fox purchased, along with the patents to Tri-Ergon, the sound-on-film creation of three German inventors, hoping to make Fox Movietone the only process for making talkies—in short, creating a monopoly, which was exactly what he fought against when he challenged the MPPCo in court. Fox had become an empire-builder. He built a new studio on forty acres in West Los Angeles, which opened in October 1928. Unlike the Western Avenue studios, Movietone City was used for films made with the Fox Movietone system. It was indeed a city, complete with a hospital, police and fire departments, and cottages for the actors. Once the imperial residence had been completed, Fox started a massive theater chain whose jewel in the crown was the world's largest movie palace, the 5,920-seat Roxy on Seventh Avenue and West Fiftieth Street in New York, dubbed "the cathedral of the motion picture."

Fox may not have realized it, but he was ready for a fall. The year 1929 began auspiciously. In February, the Academy Awards were announced, with the Fox Film Corporation scoring wins in four categories: Best Actress, Director, Writing, and Cinematography. Fox's elation was short-lived. The marriages of both daughters ended in divorce. On July 17, he was injured in an automobile accident in which his chauffeur was killed. He spent ten days in the hospital and was never the same. A concussion was ruled out, although a heart attack was not. He may have experienced some kind of brain trauma, since his behavior became unpredictable. Then came "Black Tuesday," October 29. The events that followed have been vividly told in page-turner fashion by Vanda Krefft in her authoritative biography of Fox, written with the careful pacing of a novelist who knows how to speed up the narrative as it builds toward a climax which, inevitably, is the dethrone-ment of the monarch. In his efforts to monopolize exhibition, Fox bought 660,900 shares of Loew's stock for $73 million, which he was desperate to sell. But there were no buyers. A $6.3 million loan from Eastman Kodak buoyed up his spirits for a while. But then Winfield Sheehan turned against him, deservedly taking credit for running the studio, implying that Fox was "a mere figurehead."

On April 7, 1930, Fox realized it was torch-passing time and sold his voting shares to Harley L. Clarke, who knew nothing about movies, and after nineteen months, was through. And by July 1935, so was the Fox Film Corporation. Only a merger would save it. There was one taker: Twentieth Century. Schenck and Zanuck realized that a merger with Fox Film would give them Movietone City. No longer would they be the poor relations of United Artists but they would have their own studio where they could make and distribute their films. The logical name for the new studio would have been Fox-Twentieth Century. Zanuck demurred: "I insisted on Twentieth Century-Fox." And on July 19, 1935, Twentieth Century-Fox officially came into being. Zanuck originally selected an office on the first floor of the Administration Building in the Spanish Colonial Revival style. But he soon realized that as vice president, production, he needed something in keeping with his title and moved to a four-room office suite with a bedroom and bath, to which eventually were added a screening room, barber shop with shoe shine stand, a stream room, and swimming pool. Unlike the other movie czars who preferred to reign from the top floors, Zanuck preferred the first. If he thought his choice made him seem more egalitarian, he was wrong. The employees referred to Building 88 as "The Temple," which would make Darryl F. Zanuck the high priest of Twentieth Century-Fox.

Chapter 8

THE LAST DAYS OF FOX FILM

The Fox films of the early sound era are significant chiefly for the seminal work of such directors as Raoul Wash, John Ford, Frank Borzage, and Henry King, who helped define the classical Hollywood style. Between 1929 and 1932, Walsh made nine films at Fox, the best of which were *In Old Arizona* (1929), for which Warner Baxter won a Best Actor Oscar; *The Big Trail* (1930), filmed in Grandeur, Fox's widescreen process, selected for preservation by the National Film Registry, and notable also for John Wayne's appearance in a starring role; *The Man Who Came Back* (1931), another pairing of the popular team of Janet Gaynor and Charles Farrell; *Me and My Gal* (1932), a romantic comedy-gangster movie hybrid with Spencer Tracy and Joan Bennett, which was a flop in its day but significant for demonstrating Walsh's ability to portray tough female characters (the gum-chewing Bennett) as men's equals, including those later portrayed by Ida Lupino in *High Sierra* (Warner Bros., 1941) and *The Man I Love* (Warner Bros., 1946), Ann Sheridan in *Silver River* (Warner Bros., 1948), and Virginia Mayo in *Colorado Territory* (Warner Bros., 1949). During the same period, Borzage won another Best Director Oscar for *Bad Girl* (1931) and also had the distinction of directing Will Rogers's first sound film, *They Had to See Paris* (Fox, 1929).

It is impossible to make a case for John Ford's Fox films of that period: *The Black Watch, Salute, Strong Boy* (all 1929), *Born Reckless, Men without Women, Up the River* (all 1930), *The Brat* and *The Sea Beneath* (1931) could hardly be said to prefigure *How Green Was My Valley, My Darling Clementine*, and *The Searchers*. *Up the River* is significant for the feature film debuts of Spencer Tracy and Humphrey Bogart (they had each made some movie shorts), starring as convicts in a state penitentiary. What the film does bring out is Ford's skillful handling of male bonding with one male being the reverse image of the other (e.g., Henry Fonda and Victor Mature in *My Darling Clementine* [1946], John Wayne and Henry Fonda in *Fort Apache* [1948], Dan Dailey and James Cagney in the *What Price Glory* remake [1952], John Wayne and Jeffrey Hunter in *The Searchers* [1956], and John Wayne and James Stewart in *The Man Who Shot Liberty Valence* [1962]).

Henry King made his first film for Fox, *Lightnin'*, in 1930 and a few years later was on his way to becoming Hollywood's leading exponent of Americana in Fox's *State Fair* (1933) and *Carolina* (1934). After the merger of Twentieth Century and Fox, King continued to idealize American life in *The Country Doctor* (1936), with the Dione Quintuplets; *Ramona* (1936); *Alexander's Ragtime Band* (1938); *Jesse James* (1939), a sympathetic portrait of the outlaw; *Wilson* (1944), Zanuck's personal tribute to the president; *Maryland* (1940); *Margie* (1946); and *Wait Till the Sun Shines, Nellie* (1952). Three of his greatest TCF films starred Gregory Peck experiencing the loss of grace under pressure (*Twelve O'Clock High, The Gunfighter, The Snows of Kilimanjaro*).

THE FOX MUSICALS, 1929–35

The musicals were a mingled yarn consisting of

- —films that could easily have been done straight but were musically embellished because some executive (Winfield Sheehan, perhaps) felt the script was not strong enough to stand on its own;
- —the musical revue with a hint of a plot;
- —the operetta, a form too rarefied to become a genre, since such movies do not play well outside of major cities where audiences are more accepting of artifice;
- —the movie conceived as a musical in which the numbers move the action along but rarely drive it;
- —the specialty film which requires song and/or dance to showcase a unique talent.

Raoul Walsh's *The Cock-Eyed World* (1929) was the sequel to *What Price Glory* (1926) with the same cast (Victor McLaglen as Quirt and Edmund Lowe as Flagg) and writers. It might have worked as a stage musical, but the further exploits of Quirt and Flagg seem like the forerunner of the *Road* movies with Bing Crosby, Bob Hope, and Dorothy Lamour, who over the years (1940–52) went all over the map. In *The Cock-Eyed World*, Quirt and Flagg go from Russia to Latin America with a stopover in Brooklyn. It's mildly bawdy (puns on "fanny" and "behind") with a few superfluous songs, the best known being "K-K-K Katy" and "You're the Cream in My Coffee." The songs seem to have been added to show off Fox's Movietone process, particularly since neither McLaglan nor Lowe could sing,

Unlike MGM's *The Hollywood Revue of 1929*, Paramount's *Paramount on Parade* (1930), Warner Bros.' *The Show of Shows* (1930), and Universal's *King of Jazz* (1930), which were plotless variety shows, *Fox Movietone Follies of 1929* had a discernible storyline that would take on a definitive form four years later in *42nd Street*: the understudy (Lola Lane) in a Broadway revue who goes on for the star and, of course, becomes one herself. Since the show in question is a revue, the songs in *Fox Movietone Follies of 1929* (the best known of which is "That's You, Baby" sung by Jackie Cooper and Sue Carol) were the sort that one would hear in this type of entertainment and were never intended to advance the plot. Similarly, the plot of *42nd Street* unfolds independently of *Pretty Lady*, the show that set it in motion. Unfortunately, *Fox Movietone Follies of 1929*, which premiered at the Roxy in Grandeur, Fox's 75 mm process, and shown elsewhere in 35 mm, is considered a lost film.

Fox's lone operetta was *Married in Hollywood* (1929), adapted from Oscar Straus's operetta *Hochzeit in Hollywood* (*Hollywood Wedding*, 1928), a variation of the prince-and-the-commoner plot, in which a Balkan prince, who becomes enamored of an American performer and is forced to flee his country with his lover; after getting caught up in a revolution, they end up in Hollywood, where she achieves stardom and he finds work as an extra. The final reel is all that has survived. In the finale, filmed in Multicolor, a short-lived color process that gave way to Cinecolor in 1932, the couple appear in the star's latest vehicle, which bears the same title as the film, leading one to suspect that the movie in which she is starring is a facsimile of the one we have been watching.

DELICIOUS (1931)

Delicious (1931) could not have been anything other than what it is: an original musical written for the screen with a score by George and Ira Gershwin, based on a story by Guy Bolton, who also coauthored the screenplay with Sonya Levien. *Delicious* was the Gershwins' first attempt at a Hollywood musical, although three of George's songs had been used in *Song of the Flame* (Warner Bros., 1930). *Delicious* begins promisingly—in steerage on a boat headed for Ellis Island, where immigrants of various nationalities create their own melting plot: the Irish dance jig; a Russian woman sings the doleful "Ochi Chornye"; and an Italian and a Russian (Mischa Auer of the popping eyes) argue about whose country's music is better. On board is Heather Gordon (Janet Gaynor), a young Scots woman, who is convinced that "Mr. Ellis of Ellis Island" will ask immigrants to recite the national anthem, which Heather tries teaching them. Then it is time for a plot twist, involving Heather and a polo player (Charles Farrell), whom she had met earlier when she crashed first class. Love has to conquer all, since Gaynor and Farrell had already made four films together and now were regarded as inseparable.

Since Fox cut most of the score, only a few numbers remain. The title song, performed by the Brazilian Raul Roulien improbably cast as a Russian, was inspired by Heather's pronouncing "delicious" as if it were quadrisyllabic ("del-is-i-us"). There is something so disarmingly sincere about the silly lyrics that you're suddenly amazed that such innocence exists. But then the immigrants are expecting, if not streets of gold, then papered with dollar bills. In a dream sequence, reporters interview Heather, and a chorus of Uncle Sams welcome her to the melting pot, as bank notes rain down on her from the Statue of Liberty. The sequence is mildly satirical without being cynical, prefiguring the Gershwins' Broadway musical that opened the same year as *Delicious*, *Of Thee I Sing*, in which nothing is sacred, including presidential campaigns, the Supreme Court, war, motherhood, and the Constitution.

The only other music of note in *Delicious* occurs in an expressionistic scene which includes six minutes of Gershwin's *New York Rhapsody* (aka, *Rhapsody in Rivets*), in which Heather envisions New York as a place of menace with skyscrapers towering over her, intensified by the dissonance. Gershwin revised the score, calling it his *Second Rhapsody* (the first was *Rhapsody in Blue*), which premiered in 1932. *Delicious* is a pleasant enough diversion but significant only for the remnants of Gershwin's score.

ADORABLE (1933)

Adorable (1933) was never a stage operetta like *Married in Hollywood* but could easily have been. It was an adaptation of the German film, *Ihre Hoheit befielt* ("Her Grace Commands," 1931) cowritten by Billy (then Billie) Wilder, which, as his biographer notes, revolves around a theme that the writer-director would use repeatedly in his American pictures: deception, in this case doubled. The princess of a mythical country (Janet Gaynor), eager to sample life as it is lived by the working class, attends a servants' ball disguised as Mitzi, a manicurist. A lieutenant in the royal regiment is immediately attracted to her and identifies himself as Karl (Henry [Henri] Gravat), a deli worker. Since the princess cannot marry a deli worker, the "king," who happens to be her kid brother, makes the lieutenant a prince.

The score by George Marion Jr. and Richard Whiting, a prolific composer who died much too young at forty-six, consists of three songs, one of which, the title song, is heard ad nauseam in the picture and sung so often that the rhymes ("adorable," "explorable," "deplorable") became cringingly predictable. Then there are the performances. Janet Gaynor was in her early thirties, looked in her mid-twenties, and sounded like a teenager. She was, literally, adorable, but without the requisite charm that the role required. Gravat enjoyed greater success in France, where his continental suavity and dark looks were more typical of a romantic lead. Lubitsch could have made the film work even with Gaynor, who needed a costar like John Boles or Walter Pidgeon to counterbalance her fluttering femininity with masculine grace.

MUSIC IN THE AIR (1934)

Music in the Air (1934) it is a generally faithful version of the Jerome Kern-Oscar Hammerstein Broadway hit of 1932, which ran for 342 performances. The movie, for which Billy (still Billie) Wilder coauthored the screenplay, was not as fortunate. It was one of the worst-performing films of 1934. The plot was too sophisticated for mass audiences who were alienated by the theatricality of John Boles and Gloria Swanson as songwriter and prima donna, respectively, who are so self-enraptured that they do not realize that they are bound together by their narcissism. A trio from a small town in Bavaria—a local composer (Al Shean, recreating his stage role), his daughter (June Lang), and the school teacher (Douglass Montgomery) in love with her—experience culture shock in Munich where they plan to get the composer's song, "I've Told Every Little Star," published. Instead, they find themselves enmeshed in the world of the theater when the prima donna (Gloria Swanson) makes a play for the teacher; and the songwriter (John Boles), for the daughter. To the prima donna, the teacher is a wholesome distraction from the artifice of the stage; to the songwriter, the daughter is the stock ingénue in the flesh, whom he tries to make into a star when the prima donna quits the show. But the daughter is hopelessly inadequate, and the prima donna returns to the only world she knows, while the trio return to their Bavarian village.

The score was reduced from thirteen songs to eight. The best known, "I've Told Every Little Star," is heard at the beginning and then reprised, but the equally memorable, "The Song is You," for some reason was dropped. The revelation is Swanson, who possessed a steely soprano that could take flight without becoming shrill but was never really able to soar. Sadly, Swanson told Barbara Walters in a 1981 interview, now available on YouTube, that she never wanted to be a movie star but an opera singer. She might not have succeeded in opera, but she certainly exhibited a flair for musical theater. Anyone who thought that Swanson's Norma Desmond in Billy Wilder's *Sunset Boulevard* (Paramount, 1950) was a revelation should study her Frieda Hatsfeld in *Music in the Air*, whose screenplay Wilder coauthored with Howard Young. The mannerisms are all there: the imperiousness, the narcissism, the tooth-bared smile, the eyes that could be elongated or stretched into slits, and above all, the bravura unapologetically displayed for all to marvel at. Unfortunately, Swanson was so disappointed with the negative reaction to the film that she swore she would retire from the movies, deigning to return seven years later for *Father Takes a Wife* (RKO, 1941), another failure after which Swanson seems to have retired from the screen until Wilder offered her *Sunset Boulevard*. When Wilder decided to tailor *Sunset Boulevard* to Swanson's persona, he must have her Frieda in mind. What is Norma Desmond other than Frieda Hatsfeld past her prime?

SONG O' MY HEART (1930)

When Fox offered John McCormack $500,000 to make his film debut in *Song O' My Heart* (1930), the vehicle not only had to be authentically Irish but plotted simply enough so that the great tenor would not have to do much acting. Since he was in his mid-forties and a bit portly, he could not pass for a romantic lead but simply became Sean, a middle-aged man in an Irish village bringing joy to everyone, especially children, who thrilled to his rapturous voice. While McCormack's body had thickened over the years, his voice had not lost its brilliance. He could still manage a falsetto, spinning it out carefully but never cracking in the process. Exactly why Sean is not sharing his gift with the world is unclear until midway in the film, when we learn that Mary (Alice Joyce), the love of his life, was forced by her aunt to marry a rich man who later deserted both her and her son and daughter, the latter played by a very young Maureen O'Sullivan. Apparently, Sean once had a lucrative career, even playing La Scala, until his lost love made him too despondent to perform professionally. He finally agrees to make his New York debut and go on tour. The debut is worth sitting through eighty-five minutes of thwarted love and Irish whimsy. Mary's death brings Sean back to the village, where he promptly arranges a wedding for her daughter and takes her son with him on tour.

Since Frank Borzage excelled at films about true love and its obstacles, he was able to poeticize the doomed romance between Sean and Mary, at one point framing her in the doorway as he sings "The Rose of Tralee" for his sister, but reserves the end of it for her. Shot in 75 mm in the Grandeur process (but shown in most theatres in 35 mm), *Song O' My Heart* is exquisitely photographed in the soft, low-key lighting that to Borzage was the perfect metaphor for romance. But it is McCormack's singing that can still produce a nationalistic rush even in one who is not Irish when he turns "Ireland, My Ireland" into a universal anthem. The musicals of the Fox Film Corporation were no better or worse than its comedies and dramas. *Song O' My Heart* was a hit, earning $1.2 million, but it is really a curiosity piece. But none of the Fox musicals ranked with Warner Bros' *42nd St*reet, RKO's *Flying Down to Rio*, Paramount's *One Hour with You* and *Monte Carlo*, MGM's *The Broadway Melody*, or Universal's *King of Jazz*, all of which are historically significant.

When Zanuck became production head of the newly formed Twentieth Century-Fox in the summer 1935, he realized he had to fill what looked like a rather shallow talent pool. There were the Fox regulars, such as Spencer Tracy, Joan Bennett, Janet Gaynor, and Will Rogers. Tracy would soon be leaving for MGM, where better roles awaited him; Gaynor was not Zanuck's idea of a star; Bennett would make a few films at Twentieth Century-Fox including Fritz Lang's *Man Hunt* (1941), one of her best, but was never associated with any one studio; and Rogers was too popular to drop. Zanuck was taken with Loretta Young's soft-edged beauty and also her chameleon-like ability to turn vixen or virgin, depending on the role. She would stay—for a while.

But what impressed him most was a performer Fox had signed in 1934, and for whom Zanuck had great plans at Twentieth Century-Fox: Alice Faye. "You can bet your last dollar that Faye will be a star."

Chapter 9

ZANUCK'S FIRST BLONDE

Alice Faye

Alice Faye (1912–98) began her career as a dancer and graduated to the chorus of *George White's Scandals of 1931*, which enjoyed a run of 202 performances. The revue featured, among other soon-to-be Broadway legends, Ray Bolger and Ethel Merman, who introduced the standard, "Life Is Just a Bowl of Cherries." Two members of the cast became famous in other media: Rudy Vallee as a band leader, crooner, and occasional movie and stage star; and Alice Faye as the onetime queen of the Twentieth Century-Fox musical. Although Alice was only a Broadway novice, Vallee was taken with her looks and her talent. Vallee was then a well-known recording artist, whose rendition of "Life Is Just a Bowl of Cherries" was one of 1931's best-selling records. He also had his own band and hosted *The Fleischmann's Yeast Hour* (later known as *The Rudy Vallee Show*) on radio, which helped promote the careers of Milton Berle, Beatrice Lillie, Frances Langford, and, not surprisingly, Alice Faye. Vallee liked the way she used her voice, softly spun and mellow when a ballad called for warmth, which she delivered in a languid style that was dreamy without being somnolent. As a band leader, he knew she had the makings of a band singer, who could put over a song without competing with, or distracting from, the orchestra. Belting was not in her playbook, but she could handle a snappy number, as she proved in her film debut, *George White's Scandals* (1934), a lavish but often lackluster musical revue with the numbers periodically interrupted for parcels of plot to remind the audience that they were watching a Broadway show within a movie, in which producer George White, playing himself, turns matchmaker and arranges for Vallee and Alice to be married on stage during the finale. Alice is in love with Vallee, who is pursued by the wealthy Adrienne Ames, eager to make him into a radio star (which is ironic, since Vallee already was one). In the finale, Vallee and Alice reprise "Sweet and Simple," in which an elderly couple (Alice looking convincingly white-haired and frail) relive their courtship and marriage. At the moment the couple exchange vows, White arranged for a real minister to officiate. Earlier, he had both of them sign what they thought were contracts but were actually marriage licenses. Although Alice was third-billed after Vallee and Jimmy Durante, she was never intended for the lead. When the star, Lillian Harvey, quit, White scrambled to find a replacement. When he heard Alice's "Oh, You Nasty Man," which she had already recorded for playback, he knew he need look no further.

GEORGE WHITE'S SCANDALS (1934)

The first time we see Alice in *George White's Scandals*, she is in her silk chemise. Although not particularly voluptuous, she had more than a figure to recommend her. Even in her film debut, Alice showed she had learned a technique that Marilyn Monroe also discovered fifteen years later when she costarred in *Ladies of the Chorus* (Columbia, 1949). To seduce the audience, you must first seduce the camera. "Oh, You Nasty Man," the first number, opens with a fan wipe, a transitional device in the form of a fan adorned with the *Scandals* ladies that closes down the frame, moving from right to left like a foldable fan, as the next shot opens with a close-up of Alice wearing a hat with an enormous feather and dressed in a shimmering white costume. Her hair looks like spun platinum; she rolls her eyes, inviting everyone to enjoy the naughty lyrics. With a beckoning gleam in her eye, she mildly chides the "nasty man/taking your love on the easy plan." White ensured that there would be enough close-ups to guarantee her future stardom, and when Alice's luminous face filled the screen, glowingly front lit, you knew a star was born.

In "My Dog Loves Your Dog," Alice and Vallee are strolling down the street with their dogs, while he courts her with one of the most supremely ridiculous songs ever written, reminding her that while their dogs love each other, "why can't we?" Intercut with the song are shots of dogs doing doggy things, which did not please the Production Code enforcers. True, the dogs get frisky, but what one moviegoer might find offensive, another would find natural. Alice in a snazzy black-and-white outfit neither sings nor speaks. She just walks alongside Vallee with her poodle; or rather, Vallee walks and she struts, flashing a bemused smile suggesting that she gets the subtext which is not about canine affection. Then—and here is another indication that this *Scandals* could only have been performed on a soundstage—dancers stream down staircases with their dogs, show them off, pet them, and jauntily ascend the stairs with them.

There are many examples in screen musicals of offensive blackface routines, but Durante's "Cabin in the Cotton and Cotton in the Cabin," with music and lyrics by Irving Caesar (a sample of which is "I got the South in my mouth"), is close to the nadir. Durante, eyes bulging and lips unnaturally thickened, personifies the racism inherent in the blackface tradition. African American farm workers enter, bent over from carrying bales of cotton. Suddenly the cotton pickers become rejuvenated, frolicking around like Stephen Foster's "darkies," which no doubt made some moviegoers think that plantation life was free and easy, and Old Black Joe was the family retainer.

Alice only had one big number in the film, "Oh, You Nasty Man," which showed how she could play with lyrics, scolding playboys for their waywardness while at the same time enjoying their attention. More subtle but still suggestive is "Here's the Key to My Heart" in *She Learned about Sailors* (1934), in which she played a singer in a Shanghai nightclub. The lyrics suggest a woman willing to toss her key out the window to a waiting suitor (and at one point to the whole fleet), with one caveat: don't use or abuse it. Singing in a voice that is soothingly clear, Alice adds an extra syllable to "lose" and "abuse" for playful emphasis, implying that if the metaphorical key is lost, there are replacements. "Here's the Key to My Heart" explains why Vallee thought of Alice as the ideal band singer: she could put over a song without putting over herself, letting the song register with the audience while she does the work, subordinating self to song.

Alice could do ballads and blues. In *Now I'll Tell* (1934), she proved she could do torch. *Now I'll Tell* is not so much a musical as a crime movie with two songs about a gambler (Spencer Tracy) and his mistress (Alice) that ends tragically with their deaths. Alice's was pretty much a straight acting role, but as a nightclub performer, she had the opportunity to sing "Fooling with Another Woman's Man." A vision of monochrome (curly platinum hair, silver earrings, and black gown), she wearily makes her way to the piano, standing against it as she describes, with an occasional throb in her voice, her uncontrollable habit of pursuing other women's men, despite the notoriety it causes and the broken hearts, including hers, that it leaves behind. When Alice bows at the end of the number, the close-up of her hair forms a platinum fade-out.

Throughout the 1930s, she would have the opportunity to carry the torch and sing the blues, but less so in the 1940s, when she and Betty Grable were co-queens in Zanuck's kingdom. *Now I'll Tell* proved Faye could act, which she continued to demonstrate in such non-musicals as *Tailspin* (1939) and especially *Fallen Angel* (1945). In his *New York Times* review (May 26, 1934) of *Now I'll Tell*, Mordaunt Hall wrote that "Miss Faye does very well by her role." Quite a compliment for a performer with no acting experience who, at the time, had made only one other film.

GEORGE WHITE'S 1935 SCANDALS

Alice achieved top billing in her fifth film, *George White's 1935 Scandals*, which must have pleased her, despite the film's mediocrity. Since the merger with Twentieth Century was a little more than three months away when *George White's 1935 Scandals* was released in late March 1935, the credits read "Fox Film Presents." Later releases, however, were preceded by the Twentieth Century-Fox trademark. It was probably Winfield Sheehan's idea to soften Faye's image, making her hair less eye-blinkingly platinum, perhaps realizing that she would never be a sex symbol like Jean Harlow; and while she could play tough, she was wholesome tough but never earthy or crass. The *1935 Scandals* begins on the closing night of the 1934 revue. White, playing himself, is on his way to Palm Beach when, during a brief stopover in a small Georgia town, he notices a poster adverting White's *Scandals*. The White is Elmer White (the perpetually unsmiling Ned Sparks), and the *Scandals* is a variety show that includes, among other attractions, a dog act and a dance contest. What intrigues White is not the show's unapologetic amateurism but Honey Walters (Alice), dressed in gingham, her hair looking naturally curly, performing "It's an Old Southern Custom" with Eddie Taylor (James Dunn). Believing that New York audiences would be interested in a fresh face, White offers Honey a chance to appear in his revue, even if it means bringing Eddie and the other White along—a clever way of keeping Dunn, Faye, and Sparks in the plot. Honey and Eddie become stars, but the high life leads to lateness and lackluster performances, which so infuriate White that he fires them but brings them back from Scranton when Honey's "Aunt Jane" (the excellent character actress Emma Dunn) comes to New York, hoping to see the show. White cannot disappoint "Aunt Jane," and Honey and Eddie are spirited back to the theatre in time to reprise "According to the Moonlight" atop a pumpkin-faced moon, which, for some reason, is grimacing, with the chorus creating a flood of chiffon from their frilly costumes.

Apart from Alice, the other attraction in *George White's 1935 Scandals* is a brief bit by the great Eleanor Powell in high-waisted iridescent black pants, white shirt, and bow tie, tapping away furiously as if she were awaiting a better occasion to display her art, which came a year later when she joined MGM. In one respect, *George White's 1935 Scandals* is an historical artifact. Audiences had a chance to see the famous producer dance. White was no Fred Astaire, but he was a great showman. The *1935 Scandals*, however, was not a great show.

SING, BABY, SING (1936)

By 1936, the Alice Faye persona had been created. She could be perky and saucy, showbiz brassy, or fresh-faced wholesome. In *Sing, Baby, Sing* (1936), she was all three. By the time the film went into production early in 1936 (it was released that August), Zanuck was fully in charge at the newly merged studio as the credits attest: "Darryl F. Zanuck in charge of production." His imprimatur did not always appear at the bottom of the screen in the main title, but when it did, it was an indication that he had a personal interest in the film. The show-business plot was one of Zanuck's favorites, going back to his years at Warner Bros. (*The Jazz Singer, My Man, Gold Diggers of Broadway, Honky Tonk*) and Twentieth Century (*Broadway Thru a Keyhole, Moulin Rouge, Folies Bergère*). So was the main character's obscurity-to-celebrity route (*The Jazz Singer, My Man, 42nd Street*). Add a media blitz subplot with a scoop hungry reporter, a type familiar to audiences from *The Front Page* (1931), *Five Star Final* (1931), *Love Is a Racket* (1932), and *Front Page Woman* (1935), and you have *Sing, Baby, Sing.*

Alice plays a nightclub performer fired from her job to make room for a debutante who fancies herself a chanteuse. Her agent (the magnificent Gregory Ratoff) tries every trick to get her on the air. He is about to admit defeat when he encounters a drunken Hollywood star (Adolphe Menjou, doing a perfect imitation of a tipsy John Barrymore), who takes one look at Alice and envisions her as his Juliet. The press has a field day with this Romeo and Juliet "romance" until the star's cousin arrives and refuses to let him perform on a radio show that will establish Alice as a star. The plot had been tripping along smoothly until this snag, which adds another complication to an already complicated plot. But the show manages to go on, and watching it requires a true suspension of disbelief, since much of it could only have been experienced visually (e.g., a magic act with pigeons and a parody of *Dr. Jekyll and Mr. Hyde*). Radio, as Jack Benny described it, is "the theater of the imagination," and this "radio show" could only have been possible on television, then in its embryonic stage.

Alice had two good numbers in *Sing, Baby, Sing*: the title song and "You Turned the Tables on Me." In the first, which she sings at the beginning, she is wearing a costume with sequin-studded ruffles, but her look is different. Her eyes have not been widened with eyeliner, nor does she roll them like Jean Harlow. What is truly remarkable is the way she transforms "You Turned the Tables on Me" into a wistful memory of the end of a relationship that she caused but cannot forget even though her ex-lover has moved on. Alice starts the number slowly in her lower register, hinting at a torch song and then moves up, delivering the rest of the song with prismatic clarity and a finely spun tone, as if it were a ballad. There is no self-pity, only short-lived hurt ("Just like the sting of a bee / You turned the tables on me"). But she makes it clear that although she has removed the stinger, she still misses the bee.

Sing, Baby, Sing is typical of the kind of musical for which Zanuck became famous, which featured performers from other branches of show business. In *Sing, Baby, Sing*, he introduced the Ritz Brothers (think of the Marx Brothers lite), who clowned their way from vaudeville and nightclubs to the *Scandals* and the *Vanities*, combining shtick with classy dancing. If they had toned down the antics, they might have fared better in Hollywood. Also appearing in the film was the former vaudevillian Ted Healy, whose "Ted Healy and His Stooges" included Moe Howard and his brother,

Shemp, who later became two of "The Three Stooges," the third being Larry Fine. Healy died the year after *Sing, Baby, Sing* was released. An alcoholic, he suffered kidney failure after being seriously injured in a fight which he instigated while drunk.

ON THE AVENUE (1937)

By the time *On the Avenue* (1937) began shooting in fall 1936, Alice had made eleven films, receiving top billing in *George White's 1935 Scandals*, *Music Is Magic* (1935), and *Sing, Baby, Sing*. Otherwise, it was second billing opposite George Raft in *Every Night at Eight* (1935), a Walter Wanger production released by Paramount; Warner Baxter in *King of Burlesque* (1936); and Shirley Temple in *Poor Little Rich Girl* (1936). In *Stowaway* (1936), Temple's name was above the title, with Robert Young's and Alice's below. By now, Alice was familiar with the vagaries of billing. First one day, second or even third the next. Alice's role of Mona Merrick in *On the Avenue* was really supporting; the star was Dick Powell, the lead in a revue with the same title as the film. On the theater marquee, his name was above the title and Alice's below, which pretty much corresponded to the film's main title, with Powell and his costar, the ethereally blonde Madeleine Carroll, above the title and Alice below it, heading the supporting cast. While Zanuck would no doubt have wanted Carroll to become one of his blondes, it was as a Hitchcock blonde that she became famous after appearing in *The 39 Steps* (1935) and *Secret Agent* (1936).

On the Avenue (1937), with six new songs by Irving Berlin (three others were cut), is a screwball musical derived from the screwball template (man and woman from different classes) with a runaway bride resolution inspired by Frank Capra's *It Happened One Night* (1934). When a Park Avenue heiress (Carroll) and her father attend a performance of Powell's revue, they are grossly offended by one of the sketches, "The Richest Girl in America," in which Powell impersonates the father as an indulgent dotard, and Alice, his daughter, as a vacuous spendthrift who makes a grand entrance descending a staircase brandishing a cigarette holder and followed by a pack of hounds. Carroll is outraged by the sketch while at the same time drawn to Powell, who is similarly attracted to her to the extent that he agrees to tone down the sketch. When Alice learns about the changes, she ignores them, even substituting a herd of pigs for the dogs. Furious, the heiress buys the show from the producers and sabotages one of the performances by hiring people to walk out during one of Powell's numbers while the Ritz Brothers wreak havoc on stage. Powell tears up his contract, ending their romance and sending Carroll back to a stuffy explorer (Alan Mowbray), whom she agrees to marry. On their wedding day, Alice tries to make amends by telling Carroll that she was responsible for the pigs scampering down the staircase. Just as the Bridal Chorus from *Lohengrin* begins, Carroll's omniscient aunt tells her a taxi is waiting. Still in her wedding gown, Carroll skips the ceremony and climbs into the taxi, finding herself seated to someone who looks like her father but who is really Dick Powell. So Carroll gets Powell, but what about Alice, who seems on the verge of becoming a loose thread? But the writers tie it up by ending the movie with the equivalent of a curtain call. The principals are at a diner, seated at the counter: Powell and Carroll, the aunt and the explorer, the Ritz Brothers, and at the furthest end, Alice and the father, who whispers a request, which happens to be for her phone number. So it's a matter of "all in the family" with Alice as a potential in-law.

Musically, *On the Avenue* was Powell's movie. Carroll sings a snippet of "Slumming on Park Avenue" at the end, but that's it. Powell had two of the best numbers, "The Girl on the Police Gazette," and "I've Got My Love to Keep Me Warm," a duet with Alice, who gets one song to herself, "This Year's Kisses," a ballad of disappointment delivered with the air of subdued stoicism that had become her trademark.

Zanuck keenly studied the films of his competitors. He was particularly taken with *Libeled Lady* (MGM, 1936) and its sleazy newspaper plot that reminded him of the tabloid world of *Five Star Final* (1931) and *Advice to the Lovelorn* (1933), which he produced at Warner Bros. and Twentieth Century, respectively. In *Libeled Lady*, an heiress (Myrna Loy), now a familiar type, is suing a newspaper for libel. To save the paper from bankruptcy, the managing editor (Spencer Tracy) talks former reporter William Powell into wooing her and causing a scandal that will make her drop her suit. Naturally, they fall in love as antagonists do in screwball, despite the difference in social class, which is never a deterrent, as another heiress (Claudette Colbert) and a reporter (Clark Gable) proved two years earlier in *It Happened One Night*. *Libeled Lady* was based on an original story by Wallace Sullivan, who, uncredited, also contributed to the screenplay of

Love Is News (TCF, 1937), another heiress-reporter romantic comedy. Both *Love Is News* and *On the Avenue* went into production in fall 1936; both were released in February 1937. Common to both is the screwball plot of an heiress falling for a man from another class (reporter, actor) and the "true love-can-transcend-social-barriers" resolution. One doubts that *Love Is News* and *On the Avenue* could have existed in their present form if it were not for *Libeled Lady*; or that *On the Avenue* could have ended the way it did without *It Happened One Night*, the original runaway bride movie. *It Happened One Night* ends with Claudette Colbert's father saving her from marrying a playboy by encouraging her to rush off in her wedding gown to a waiting car that will bring her to Clark Gable.

Alice was also featured in films that included a few musical numbers because her character was a performer, although neither critics nor audiences regarded them as musicals. *Now I'll Tell* (Fox, 1934) proved that she could handle a straight dramatic role, as she did in *In Old Chicago* (TCF, 1938), in which she sang a mere three songs that in no way contribute to the progression of the plot. She was supposed to have performed one song, "There'll Be Other Nights," in *Barricade* (TCF, 1939), in which she was a singer in 1930s China. Zanuck, who did not think much of the film to begin with, must have decided that any song would be out of place in a film that was basically a tribute to a China terrorized by Mongolian bandits (but no mention of the Japanese imperialists who were overrunning the country). The main title does not bear Zanuck's name, only "A 20th Century Fox Picture." His name, however, does appear in the main title of *Tailspin* (1939), making it truly a "Darryl F. Zanuck Production." Even though Alice's character is a former hat-check girl turned aviator (or aviatrix, in those days), she was given one number, "Are You in the Mood for Mischief?" which she sang to a navy flyer (Kane Richmond, best known for the Republic serial *Spy Smasher* and Monogram's *Shadow* movies), giving a new meaning to the word "mischief." But the flyer is meant for Constance Bennett, and Alice resigns herself to making mischief with someone else.

IN OLD CHICAGO (1938)

When *In Old Chicago* was released in April 1938, few moviegoers would have considered it a musical, despite Alice's presence, second-billed after

Tyrone Power, with Don Ameche's name under hers. Power and Ameche as brothers, initially on opposite sides of the law, are the main characters, along with their mother, played by Alice Brady, who won a best supporting actress Oscar. *In Old Chicago* was in every sense a Zanuck film as the main title announces: "Twentieth Century-Fox Presents Darryl F. Zanuck's production of *In Old Chicago*." Like every production head, Zanuck made it a point to learn what other studios were planning. After MGM released *San Francisco* (1936), whose climax was the 1906 earthquake that destroyed more than 80 percent of the city, Zanuck decided to make his own disaster flick about the Great Chicago Fire of 1871 that destroyed three square miles of the windy city. As in *In Old Chicago*, *San Francisco* also featured a singer (Jeanette MacDonald), who was given considerably more numbers than Alice, including "Sempre Libera" from *La Traviata* and excerpts from Gounod's *Faust*. But unlike Alice's character, Belle Fawcett, who has to trudge along with the crowds at the end of the film, as buildings erupt in flames and come crashing down, Jeanette has a chance to lead the survivors in "The Battle Hymn of the Republic" during the finale. By the time *In Old Chicago* ends, Alice had already sung her three numbers.

In Old Chicago is a classic example of history refracted through the celluloid prism in which a few facts, like rays of light, pass through history into myth, becoming mythicohistory. The screenwriters, Sonya Levien and Lamar Trotti, working from Niven Busch's original story, knew that they had to provide a plot line for the Great Chicago Fire, falsely attributed to an Irish immigrant's cow that kicked over a kerosene lamp in a barn. But the story making the rounds was that Mrs. Catherine O'Leary's cow was responsible, as was, by implication, Mrs. O'Leary herself. Although the O'Learys had two strikes against them (Irish immigrants and Catholics at a time when nativism and anti-Catholicism were widespread), the writers refrained from introducing the topic of prejudice, which would have politicized the narrative. Other theories had also circulated: the fire was caused by careless gamblers, a milk thief, or even nature itself. But the cow was too good a plot point to ignore. In a bit of foreshadowing, the cow kicks over a bucket of milk early in the film. And to make the cause of the conflagration plausible, the cow knocks over the kerosene lamp while suckling a calf that bites her udder.

Clearly, *In Old Chicago* is not "an Alice Faye movie." The main thrust of the story is the tension between the two O'Leary brothers, Dion (Power) and Jack (Ameche)—the former modeled after the real-life James O'Leary, a saloon owner and gambler. Since the O'Learys only had a son and a daughter, Jack is purely fictitious and designed solely as a foil for Dion. He possesses the integrity that his brother lacks and even runs for Mayor on the reform ticket, winning the election with Dion's help. But Dion had his reasons for backing his brother, who wants to destroy the highly flammable section of Chicago where Dion has his saloon. He persuades Jack to officiate at his marriage to Belle (Alice), a singer in his saloon, after which he informs his brother that Belle cannot be called as a witness because a wife cannot testify against her husband. But with an actor as enviably handsome (really, beautiful) as the young Power, Dion cannot remain a scoundrel for long. Jack dies in the fire, but Mrs. O'Leary (called Molly in the film), Dion, and Belle survive, with Dion proclaiming, "Nothing can lick Chicago." It's not the same as Jeanette singing "The Battle Hymn of the Republic" in *San Francisco*, but Alice's character is a saloon singer, not a lyric soprano.

Alice does well in her three numbers. One would think she would be more decorously attired for "Carry Me Back to Old Virginny," but there she is sending waves of nostalgia over the footlights in spangled black tights with a fringed top. She does a spirited cancan in the title song, and performs "I'll Never Let You Cry" with a barber shop quartet. The first two numbers demonstrate what a fine dancer Alice was. No wonder George White hired her for his 1931 *Scandals*. Unfortunately, she plays second fiddle to a conflagration and a brother vs. brother plot that required her to succumb to Tyrone Power's roughhouse, which is his version of lovemaking. That she convinces you she can love a wastrel who manhandles her indicates that, if the phrase "singing actress" had been in vogue in 1938, it would have been her defining label.

ALEXANDER'S RAGTIME BAND (1938)

Zanuck envisioned *Alexander's Ragtime Band* (1938) as a follow up to *In Old Chicago* minus the fire, with the same trio (Alice, Power, Ameche); one of the same writers, Lamar Trotti; and another triangular plot, this time the familiar backstage trope of two men (Power and Ameche) in love with the same woman (Alice). There was also a generous sampling of the Irving Berlin songbook as interpreted by Alice and trumpet-voiced Ethel

Merman, who could stun the ear with her sound—a revelation to those who did not hear her hold a C for sixteen bars when she sang "I've Got Rhythm" in Gershwin's *Girl Crazy* (1930). This time, Ameche's character, Charlie Dwyer, does not die, but audiences must have wondered how Stella Kirby (Alice) and Roger Grant, aka "Alexander" (Power), would ever get together after Stella marries Dwyer. The answer is simple: divorce, frowned upon by the National Legion of Decency, which classified the film as "B" ("Morally Objectionable in Part for All"). That did not deter audiences from turning out en masse and enriching the studio's coffers by $3.6 million. But Ameche's Dwyer is so self-effacingly sincere when he broaches the subject of divorce that his decision to free Stella so she can marry Grant seems almost virtuous. The Legion thought otherwise.

Alexander's Ragtime Band originated as a story by Irving Berlin, who imagined a film that would trace the evolution of ragtime to jazz as the performing venues changed from saloons and clubs to the concert hall. Berlin's inspiration was the real-life Alexander's Ragtime Band, whose leader, Alex "King" Watzke, was also a violinist, as is the band leader (Grant/Alexander) in the film. But here the resemblances end. Watzke's band was a New Orleans mainstay, while the one in the movie starts out in San Francisco, eventually reaching New York City and performing at Carnegie Hall, achieving the kind of respectability Watzke's group never did.

Once the writers created a "meet rude" (a bartender gives Grant a copy of "Alexander's Ragtime Band" that had been earmarked for Stella), the plot can take off. Grant begins playing the song on the violin, treating it as if it were a classical composition. Realizing that he is ruining the song, Alice (forget her character for a moment)—her eyes accentuated with eyeliner, a beauty mark on her cheek, a feather boa draped around her shoulders, and sporting the curly platinum wig from *Now I'll Tell*—starts singing the number in ragtime as she makes her way around the room. The sequence is an excellent example of the way "ragging" works. Alice understood that the rhythm was syncopated, with stresses on syllables where they would not ordinarily fall. In the opening words, "Come on and hear, come on and hear," the stress falls on "hear," whereas in ordinary speech the stressed syllables would be *both* "on" *and* "hear." Without the music, the line would scan short/long, short/long, short/long, short/long: Set to music, it becomes short/short/short/long, short/short/short/long. When Alice reaches "Oh, my honey," she not only rags it ("Oh, m'honey") but also gives is a subtle

African American inflection, which links ragtime to its true origins. The number is such a hit that Grant is dubbed "Alexander," and Stella signs on as lead singer.

The screenwriters of *Alexander's Ragtime Band* stitched together a series of tropes common to the backstage musical genre at that time:

The Pygmalion Syndrome. Grant calls Stella's attention to her flashy wardrobe and gives her a makeover, pulling the feathers from her gown to make her look more ladylike and less avian. Suddenly, the platinum wig has gone into storage, and Stella's hair is ash blonde again, parted in the middle like Alice's. The transformation plot line recurred in *Coney Island* (TCF, 1943), in which George Montgomery pulled off Betty Grable's feathers (repeated by Victor Mature in the 1950 remake, *Wabash Avenue*) and handcuffs her so that she would be forced to sing "Cuddle Up a Little Closer" like a ballad, not a saloon song. Usually, it is a female who is ruining the song. However, In *Alexander's Ragtime Band*, a male starts playing the title song as if it were the opening of a string quartet until a female teaches him otherwise.

Breaking Up the Act. When a New York producer wants Stella but not the others, Stella faces the band vs. Broadway dilemma, choosing the latter. She becomes a star, and Grant joins the army in time to see action in World War I. The same plot point was used in *Ziegfeld Girl* (MGM, 1941), in which Ziegfeld wanted Judy Garland for his *Follies*, but not her father.

Let's Put on a Show. Grant convinces his commanding officer to authorize a Broadway musical with a cast of recruits. There was such a musical, a revue called *Yip Yip Yaphank* (1918), produced and composed by (then Sergeant) Irving Berlin, at the request of his commanding officer to raise money for a community center at Camp Upton, then a boot camp in Yaphank in Suffolk County, Long Island. The revue ran for almost a month on Broadway and was notable for Berlin's rendition of "Oh, How I Hate to Get Up in the Morning," which he reprised in *This Is the Army* (Warner Bros., 1943). When it was time to perform "We're On Our Way to France," Berlin had the cast march off the stage and up the aisle, as if they were going off to war, which is what happens in the film, with World War I reduced to a montage of newsreel footage.

Fade-Out/Fade-In. Still carrying a torch for Grant, whom she thinks is in love with Jerry Allen (Ethel Merman), Stella abandons Broadway at the height of her popularity, making a living performing in clubs. Meanwhile, Grant and his band become internationally famous and are scheduled to play at Carnegie Hall. Desperate to get Stella back, Grant and Dwyer concoct a scheme with a taxi driver (beautifully played by John Carradine), who is listening to the concert broadcast on his radio when he picks up Stella, Overcome with nostalgia, she rushes out of the cab (which, conveniently, is in front of Carnegie Hall) and somehow manages to get backstage in time to join the company in the finale, which, naturally, is "Alexander's Ragtime Band," bringing the movie full circle.

More than any other film, *Alexander's Ragtime Band* revealed Alice's musical range. She had a natural feel for rag as she revealed in both the title song and "That International Rag." Her voice was made for syncopated music, and her lower range, warm and smoky, was perfect for jazz. In the Oscar-nominated "Now It Can Be Told," Alice dressed in a gleaming white satin gown exhibited the sophistication of a Mabel Mercer or Julie Wilson, paying full attention to the lyrics, in which the singer claims that her love story makes others pale in comparison. Her voice took on a whispering, almost confessional quality, rising to a silvery climax making "Now It Can Be Told" a cabaret song; the singer was not just a vocalist but a chanteuse. When she gets to the line, "The great love story has never been told," her voice quivers a bit, as if she is uncertain. But then she brings the voice down to her comfort zone, so that the song can end on a note of quiet affirmation.

HOLLYWOOD CAVALCADE (1939)

In *Hollywood Cavalcade* (1939), Alice did not sing a note. If there is any film that would convince skeptics that Alice Faye could do more than musicals, it is *Hollywood Cavalcade*, even though she claimed that an uncut *Fallen Angel* (1945) would have afforded a better example of her acting ability, if Zanuck had not eliminated some of her best scenes. Despite the billing, with Alice's name followed by Don Ameche's, *Hollywood Cavalcade* is, as the credits attest, "a Darryl F. Zanuck Production" or rather, Zanuck's tribute to the movie industry as it moved inexorably from the silent to the sound era. It is very much of an intertextual film, not unlike Peter Bogdanovich's *Nickelodeon* (Columbia, 1976), a feast of Hollywood lore best appreciated by those with some knowledge of film history.

Ernest Pascal's screenplay for *Hollywood Cavalcade* is filled with authentic touches that came from writers with a firsthand knowledge of film history. Pascal worked from an original story by Hilary Lynn and Brown Holmes, the basis of which was "an original idea" by Lou Breslow. Pascal had been in the business since 1923; Lynn, since the early 1930s. Holmes, the author of such excellent screenplays as *The Strange Love of Molly Louvain* (1932) and *I Am a Fugitive from a Chain Gang* (1933), worked at Warner Bros. and Universal Pictures before coming to Twentieth Century-Fox in 1936. Breslow wrote the screenplay for one of Alice's early films, *Music Is Magic* (Fox, 1935). If *Hollywood Cavalcade* has the ring of authenticity, it is because everyone involved in the creation of the screenplay knew the territory.

Significantly, the credits of *Hollywood Cavalcade* are in the form of a screenplay that opens page by page with the names of the cast and creative personnel, making it seem that the film is a movie script brought to life. Naturally, the final page has two words: "The End." The writers knew their Hollywood, and Zanuck made certain that the film could be enjoyed by both the knowledgeable and the neophytes. The former would flash a smile of recognition at inside references; the latter would regard the film as the equivalent of a basic course in silent comedy with no prerequisites, with the references so embedded in the plot that they seemed to flow naturally from it like a text without footnotes. And for those unfamiliar with "the star is born" template, *Hollywood Cavalcade* becomes the story of an understudy (Alice) who attracts the attention of a would-be film director (Don Ameche). He offers her twice her weekly salary if she abandons Broadway for Hollywood. Ameche plays the director as if he were making a sales pitch; and Alice is so convincing in changing from skeptic to convert that you accept her decision to quit the theater because she falls for the pitch, not from any knowledge of Hollywood history, which is filled to surfeit with examples of stars being discovered sipping a Coke at a soda fountain, toiling in the chorus until spotted by a producer, and appearing in a college play or in a stock production when a talent scout is in the audience.

Alice Faye herself was such a discovery. It was Rudy Vallee who, after watching her perform in the 1931 *Scandals*, made it possible for her to be cast in *George White's Scandals* (Fox, 1934). And when Lillian Harvey left the film, George White himself gave her role to Alice. Although the circumstances surrounding Alice's film debut seem like the plot points for a "star is born" movie, they are historically accurate, proving that being in the right show at the right time, and on the right set on the right day, can send a career into orbit.

It is tempting to think of the director and his protégée as stand-ins for Mack Sennett (1880–1960) and Mabel Normand (1894–1930), the "King of Comedy" and one of the best female comedians of the silent era, respectively. Ameche's character, Michael Linnett Connors, was probably suggested by Sennett's real name, Mikall Sinnott, just as Alice's character, Molly Adair, was by Mabel Normand's. Sennett was in love with Normand and even went so far as to purchase an inexpensive engagement ring in 1911, the year that she started in pictures at a time when Sennett was just an actor at Biograph. It seems to have been love at first sight, but it never led to marriage, even though a wedding had been planned for July 4, 1915. But the couple could not agree on the ceremony. Sennett preferred a civil one, while Normand insisted on a traditional church wedding. The situation was complicated by Normand's growing suspicion of Sennett's fidelity, which precluded any possibility of marriage. Sennett and Normand remained as they were: director and star. The Broadway musical, *Mack and Mabel* (1974), with a book by Michael Stewart and a glorious score by Jerry Herman, is a partly fictionalized version of their relationship, which ended when Normand became attracted to director William Desmond Taylor, who allegedly introduced her to heroin. The writers would never have thought of making Molly a drug addict; the Production Code forbade scenes "which show the use of illegal drugs." Nor would they have even considered introducing William Desmond Taylor into the plot, especially since Normand was supposedly the last person to see him alive before his still-unsolved murder.

Michael Linnett Connors and Molly Adair are really composites. Molly is Normand as if she were a silent star as virtuous as the roles she played. Just as Mabel Normand married actor Lew Cody, Molly marries actor

Nicky Hayden (Alan Curtis). But because Molly is destined to end up with Connors, Pascal disposed of Hayden by having him killed in an automobile accident that left Molly hospitalized. The incident was inspired by a similar accident in January 1934 that killed the driver, Charles Sellers, known professionally as blackface performer Charles Mack, and severely injured his second wife. Interestingly, Sennett was also a passenger in the car and sustained some injuries.

Connors is similar to Sennett in the sense that he, like Sennett, started making movies in Edendale, California, now known as Echo Park, where many of the studios (Selig-Polyscope, Fox, and Tom Mix's studio, "Mixville") were located in the early years of the movie industry. Sennett's Keystone Studios began production there in 1912. *Hollywood Cavalcade* opens in 1913, the year of *The Bangville Police*, a comedy short with Mabel Normand, acknowledged as the film that made the Keystone Cops—bumbling policemen who are always colliding with each other—famous. Sennett had a reason for making cops bumblers. No one would laugh if a homeless person slipped on a banana peel, but if a man in top hat and tails does, it's hilarious. If the steering wheel came off a car in real life, the driver would panic; if it comes off in the hands of a Keystone cop, audiences laugh. Sennett began in burlesque, which "taught him that deflation of authority was a positive manner in which to get laughs." Connors made the same innovations as Sennett: clumsy cops, bathing beauties, pie throwers. But just when you're counting the similarities between Connors and Sennett, you're thrown off the track when Connors develops delusions of grandeur, embarking upon an epic set in ancient Egypt with hundreds of extras. Connors is clearly aiming to be another Cecil B. DeMille, but only succeeds in making a flop by moving out of his element. And to prevent any further identification with Sennett, the king of comedy himself makes a cameo appearance in the film. One should think of Connors as a self-dramatizing dreamer with the comic sense of Sennett, the grand vision of DeMille, the arrogance of Erich von Stroheim, and the adaptability of John Ford, Raoul Walsh, and Allan Dwan, all of whom made the switch from silents to sound.

At the end of the film, Connors attends a screening of *The Jazz Singer* (1927), which convinces him that the talkies represent Hollywood's future. He also realizes that *The Jazz Singer* is really a silent film with sound sequences. He rushes to the hospital, where Molly is lying in bed, her head bandaged but her cheeks subtly rouged, suggesting an imminent recovery. It has to be since Connors has stolen the negative of his last film, which seems to have been a courtroom melodrama with Molly on the witness stand (perhaps suggested by the William Desmond Taylor case, in which Mabel Normand was subjected to intense grilling). He informs Molly that he will add some sound and release the film as a part-talkie. And so Connors follows in the footsteps of Ford, Walsh, and Dwan and makes the transition to sound.

Since Zanuck conceived *Hollywood Cavalcade* as a tribute to the Hollywood of yesteryear when he wrote gags for Buster Keaton, among others, a major segment of the film involves a Keystone-like comedy being shot in which Alice gets hit in the face with a so-called custard pie that Keaton had intended for someone else. The impact left her looking like a gooey Mabel Normand, although in Sennett's movies, it was usually the male (Fatty Arbuckle, Ben Turpin) who got the pie in the face. Alice performed like a true Sennett comic, even falling into a muddy pond. Losing one's dignity was common in silent comedy, and Alice was completely in character. *Hollywood Cavalcade* ranks as her best performance as an actor (non-singing), in which she ran the gamut from skeptical understudy to movie neophyte to budding comedian to full-fledged star. Alice herself did not have to go through so many iterations but she behaved as if she had been born in a trunk, awaiting its final destination.

ROSE OF WASHINGTON SQUARE (1939)

Alice's last pairing with Tyrone Power was *Rose of Washington Square* (1939), a thinly disguised semi-biopic with Alice and Power as stand-ins for Fanny Brice (1891–1951) and Nicky Arnstein (1879–1965), the *Ziegfeld Follies* star and the love of her life. Like Brice, Alice, a vaudevillian with higher aspirations, falls in love with a gambler, con artist, and swindler (Power), whom she marries and loves unconditionally, celebrating her masochism in "My Man," a French song ("*Mon homme*") with English lyrics by Channing Pollock, which Brice introduced in the *Ziegfeld Follies of 1921*. Brice's is the most direct version, sung in a plangent mezzo, every word enunciated with a clarity of a Lieder singer. Brice knew "My Man" could be done as a torch song, but she preferred to treat it as a confession by an abused lover ("He isn't true / He beats me, too") who is too self-aware to ask for pity.

Screenwriter and associate producer Nunnally Johnson thought he had circumvented any legal problems by giving the characters antiseptically Anglo-Saxon names, Rose Sargent (Alice) and Barton Dewitt Clinton (Power), and by having Clinton sent to jail only once, unlike Arnstein, who spent time at Sing Sing and later at Leavenworth. But the inclusion of "My Man," which Alice sang with more pathos than poignancy, and the title song, a Brice favorite, made it evident that Johnson's inspiration was the Brice-Arnstein story. Brice first sang "Rose of Washington Square" in 1920 at one of Ziegfeld's *Midnight Frolics*, late-night revues in a rooftop venue above the New Amsterdam Theatre that the producer inaugurated in 1915 for *Follies* patrons who wanted to prolong the evening.

"Rose of Washington Square" is a first-person lament of a young woman from the Bronx who moved to Greenwich Village, languishing there as an artist's model with no further prospects ("I've got no future, but oh, what a past"). One could only imagine what Brice must have done with that line, stripping it of subtlety, while Alice simply flashed a smile of virginal naughtiness and substituted "ooo" for "oh" as she rolled her eyes. The song only inspired the film's title, not the plot. Rose Sargent was not a model, and the closest she came to Greenwich Village was working in vaudeville on East Fourteenth Street, although a Washington Square mockup was constructed on the backlot suggesting that Rose may have lived there after becoming a star. *My Man* would have been a more appropriate title, but it had already been used for the Warner Bros. 1928 part-talkie, written and produced by Zanuck, which marked Fanny (then Fannie) Brice's feature film debut. Unable to use *My Man*, Zanuck wanted a title that in some way was associated with Brice, choosing *Rose of Washington Square*. Even that did not stop Brice from suing the studio. But it didn't really matter. *Rose of Washington Square* was the highest-grossing musical of 1939.

Alice was second-billed after Power, but it was the third-billed Al Jolson, a master of declamatory singing, who walked off with the movie. To deflect attention from the Brice-Arnstein subtext, Johnson created the character of Ted Cotter (Jolson), a stage performer in love with Rose. Since Brice was never romantically involved with Jolson or any other blackface performer, Johnson must have assumed, as the disclaimer said, that "any similarity to persons living or dead is purely coincidental." But Brice did not think so and sued for $750,000, settling out of court. It was probably Zanuck's idea to cast Jolson as Cotter, since the role could have been played by a number of Twentieth Century-Fox contract players. However, Zanuck was awed by Jolson's electric personality in *The Jazz Singer* (1927) and *Say It with Songs* (1928) when he was production head at Warner Bros. Jolson remained a close friend; in 1954, when Zanuck's daughter, Susan, and actress Terry Moore returned from entertaining troops in Korea, Zanuck staged a costume party at Ciro's at which Jolson performed. In *Hollywood Cavalcade*, when Don Ameche drops by the theatre where *The Jazz Singer* is playing, the scene that convinces him of the future of talking pictures is Jolson's powerful "Kol Niedre." In *Rose of Washington Square*, Jolson had five songs, all but one of which, "Pretty Baby," he had made famous: "Rock-a-Bye Your Baby with a Dixie Melody," "Toot, Toot, Tootsie," "California, Here I Come," and, of course "My Mammy." Alice had eight numbers, five of which were solos, including "My Man," which she sang against a lamp post in a black dress and beret as if she were a Parisian *poule*. When Alice sang "Rose of Washington Square," she did not share the spotlight with anyone. While she is singing "My Man" in the *Follies*, director Gregory Ratoff briefly cuts to Clinton (an unshaven Tyrone Power) in the balcony. Realizing that the song is about him, he rushes out. "My Man" should have been the climax of the film, but *Rose of Washington Square* could not fade out on a note of bleak resignation. There is an additional sequence in which Clinton surrenders to the police so that the film can end at Grand Central Station with a clean-shaven and radiant-faced Tyrone Power on his way to serve a five-year sentence in Sing Sing; and Alice at the gate, calling, "I'll be waiting," as the train pulls out. "My Man" does not end on a happy note but a fatalistic one. *Rose of Washington Square* forces a sunshine ending out of material that is intractably dark.

1940 was an auspicious year for Alice: she had three films in release, *Little Old New York* in February, *Lillian Russell* in May, and *Tin Pan Alley* in November. *Little Old New York* was a biopic about Robert Fulton's invention of the steamboat, with Alice barely singing a note, much to the annoyance of her fans. *Tin Pan Alley* was a refitted *Alexander's Ragtime Band* with a song writer in lieu of a band leader and Alice involved with another man to whom humility was an alien virtue.

LILLIAN RUSSELL (1940)

Lillian Russell (1940) was, understandably, one of Alice's favorites. She had vintage songs like "After the Ball" and "The Band Played On" that suited her voice, and period costumes that flattered her form. Screenwriter William Anthony McGuire recreated the life of Lillian Russell (1860–1922), born Helen Leonard, as audiences would have liked it to have been—or rather as Zanuck would have wanted it lived. *Lillian Russell* was "Darryl F. Zanuck's Production," as the main title announced. The early part of the film is fairly factual. Lillian's mother, Cynthia Leonard, was a suffragist who once ran for mayor of New York and was roundly defeated. Lillian herself aspired to a career in opera but settled for operetta, which was more suited to her voice. She went from performing at Tony Pastor's to Broadway and an international career. She enjoyed a long relationship with "Diamond Jim" Brady who courted her with expensive jewelry, only to be gently rejected when he proposed marriage. As Brady, Edward Arnold gave out a hearty laugh when Lillian turned him down, implying that he was only joking, although his eyes told a different story. That much is accurate.

On the other hand, the real Cynthia and Charles Leonard were not the loving parents depicted in the film. They separated when their daughter was eighteen, probably because Charles believed a woman's place was in the home and not in the suffrage movement. The strained relationship between Lillian and her mother is hinted at in the film and seems to have been caused by her mother's disdain for the stage and her daughter's success on it while she pursued a career in politics and failed. Lillian Russell was married four times, but not in the movie which ignores her first marriage to conductor Harry Brahma and the death of their infant son. One death is sufficient in the film, and it is that of her second husband (first in the film), songwriter Edward Solomon (Don Ameche), who dies at the piano after composing "Blue Love Bird." The historical Solomon was a bigamist, which the film does not acknowledge, nor is any mention made of Lillian's third marriage to a tenor. Solomon's death allows McGuire to reintroduce Alexander Moore (Henry Fonda) into the plot, so that *Lillian Russell* could end with wedding bells in the offing. The historical Lillian Russell married Moore, the editor of the *Pittsburgh Leader*, in 1912 and was willing to live in Pittsburgh, as the film implies, although she returned to the stage a few times before she died ten years later.

Alice had one glorious moment in what should have been the finale instead of the final number that had dancers streaming down staircases to the music of Johann Strauss, with Alice at the top of the stairs in a white sequined gown and a silvery walking stick reprising "After the Ball." What should have been the finale was Alice's heartfelt "Blue Love Bird," which Solomon had just finished before he died. It is true that Edward Solomon had been a songwriter, but "Blue Love Bird" was specially written for the film by Bronislau Kaper (music) and Gus Kahn (lyrics). Equally fictitious is Lillian's asking W. S. Gilbert (of Gilbert and Sullivan) if the song could be interpolated in his show. Historical skewering becomes irrelevant when Alice comes on in a black strapless gown, white arm-length-braceleted gloves, a glittering tiara, a choker necklace, and a rope of pearls. Firmly holding on to her walking stick, as if for support, she sang the doleful song ("It seems that love birds die alone"). The contrast between Alice's black gown and her white accessories testified to the beauty of monochrome which had a spectrum of its own.

Alice might have had a fourth 1940 release. Zanuck had planned a big, splashy Technicolor musical for her that he would personally produce. He made *Down Argentine Way* (1940)—but not with her.

Chapter 10

THE LONG GOODBYE

In 1941, Alice Faye could not have known that she would make her last musical in 1943 and leave the studio two years later. The importance of her last five musicals is that the first, *The Great American Broadcast* (1941), need never have been a musical but became one because of the casting (Alice, John Payne, Jack Oakie). The next two, *Week-End in Havana* and *That Night in Rio* (both 1941), were Good Neighbor Policy movies like *Down Argentine Way* (1940), the first of the short-lived series. *Week-End in Havana* was a reboot (boy falling in love with girl whom he is supposed to keep from suing his employer's company, as in MGM's *Libeled Lady* [1936]); *That Night in Rio* was a remake (a Latin American version of *Folies Bergère* [1935]). The fourth was *Hello, Frisco, Hello* (1943), a remake of *King of Burlesque* (1936), in which Alice introduced her signature song, "You'll Never Know"; the last saw Alice at the intersection of high camp and surrealistic kitsch in Busby Berkeley's *The Gang's All Here* (1943).

THE GREAT AMERICAN BROADCAST (1941)

Of the five, *The Great American Broadcast*, the only one shot in black-and-white, is grounded in history. Zanuck wanted to celebrate the twentieth anniversary of commercial radio with a film that would trace the evolution of the medium from amateur operators using Morse code to communicate with each other to transmission by voice to, finally, the first coast-to-coast broadcast in 1924. That the film is a tribute to the pioneers of radio is evident from the main title which includes a montage of radio personalities such as Rudy Vallee, Kate Smith, Jack Benny, and George Burns and Gracie Allen. Two of the stars were also radio personalities. Alice sang on Rudy Vallee's show, and Jack Oakie had his own program, *Jack Oakie's College* (1936–38), which featured celebrities such as the young Judy Garland in 1937, Robert Benchley, and Benny Goodman and His Orchestra. Tenor James Newill, who makes an appearance at the end of the picture, sang briefly on the *Burns and Allen Show*.

The screenwriters—Don Ettlinger, Edwin Blum, Robert Ellis, and Helen Logan—did their research which they incorporated into the first part of the film, using it as a launching pad for another love triangle (Jack Oakie loves Alice Faye who loves John Payne) in which Oakie will clown around, Alice will sing in her sultry and occasionally silvery voice, and Payne will play the alpha male whose ego is bruised when he discovers Alice has asked wealthy Cesar Romero to bankroll his venture in network radio. The film gives the impression that 1921 was the birthday of radio, which is not entirely true, since there were experiments in radio transmission much earlier. But 1920 and 1921 were watershed years in radio history. On November 2, 1920, KDKA in Pittsburgh., located atop the Westinghouse building, broadcast the results of the 1920 presidential election that put Warren Harding in the White House. Later KDKA moved to the top of another building where it was housed inside a tent. "When the tent blew down in a gale, it was reerected inside, providing the necessary acoustic control." Equally—and to some, more—significant was RCA's launching of WDY on December 13, 1921. Five months earlier, RCA transmitted under the call letters WJY the Dempsey-Charpentier fight which was heard by 200,000 listeners. Interestingly, in *The Great American Broadcast*, a Dempsey fight comes over the air, and a variety show is transmitted from a tent atop a New Jersey warehouse that is on the verge of being rained out but continues to the end, thanks to the resilience of the rain-drenched performers—Alice, Payne, Oakie, and some opera singers. In the film, Oakie and Payne cofound station 2WAB (cf. Detroit's amateur station 8MK), which broadcasted the brutal Dempsey-Willard championship fight on July 4, 1919, authenticated in the film with archival footage that validates *The Great American Broadcast*'s contribution to the history of broadcasting and the newsreel.

The first part of *The Great American Broadcast* is more involving than the second, which is the typical boy-girl-breakup-reunion scenario. The film begins with Jack Oakie and John Payne discovering they were in World War I together. Oakie, a ham operator, shows Payne his wireless set, claiming, "I didn't need code, just the voice." The writers must have been thinking of Charles "Doc" Herrold who transmitted news reports and musical programs by voice, not code. Once Payne learns that Alice is a singer, he plans a musical variety show transmitted from a tent on top of a New Jersey warehouse. Envisioning a medium in which classical music and opera would come over the air, Payne hires an opera troupe that arrives in a rainstorm, minus a tenor, for whom Oakie substitutes in the *Lucia di Lammermoor* sextet, singing nonsense as the rain pelts the tent. Alice, Payne, and Oakie are literally singin' in the rain as they perform "I Take to You" but manage to conclude the broadcast despite the lack of cooperation from the elements. When it is time for the climax, the coast-to-coast broadcast, everyone, including Alice, is upstaged by the specialty acts.

There was such an inaugural coast-to-coast broadcast on February 6, 1924, originating from a Chicago banquet hall. Although February 6, 1924, is an important date in the history of radio, only 10 percent of Americans then owned radios. But those who did experienced a moment in history. Such a moment, however, was not material for a musical. *The Great American Broadcast* had to be a variety show which would unite the three principals, two of whom, Oakie and Payne, had a falling out, with Alice about to wed Cesar Romero. To get Payne back into the plot, the writers repeated the climactic moment in *Alexander's Ragtime Band* when Alice, who had left New York, returns in time to join Tyrone Power on stage at Carnegie Hall. This time it is Payne who disappears and returns in time for the finale. When they reunite to reprise "I Take to You," it is anticlimactic compared to what has preceded: the astonishing Nicholas Brothers, whose ability to athleticize dance enabled them to perform such feats as tapping on top of suitcases and up and down a flight of stairs, leaping over a railing and going into a split, and hurling themselves through an open train window; the Wiere Brothers, who appear as the Stradivarians, were classical trained musicians who regaled audiences with their antics, which included balancing their instruments on their chins; the Ink Spots, who displayed their extraordinary sense of rhythm and harmony in "Alabama Bound" and "I've Got a Bone to Pick with You."

Alice will not be particularly remembered for *The Great American Broadcast*, but it is to Zanuck's credit that he sought to showcase the art of Black performers like the Nicholas Brothers and the Ink Spots, even though he knew that their scenes would be excised when the film played in the South.

In Alice's other 1941 films, *That Night in Rio* and *Week-End in Havana*, released six months apart, she was not playing a performer, although, naturally, she had to sing. Both films were structurally the same, beginning and ending with a Carmen Miranda number and a finale in which the principals reprised bits of the songs very much in the tradition of a Broadway musical. Thus neither musical was that difficult to make because the formula was the same: a derivative plot interspersed with song and dance. Once *That Night in Rio* had been cast to Zanuck's satisfaction (Paulette Goddard, Rosalind Russell, Joan Bennett, and Madeleine Carroll had been considered for the Baroness Duarte, suggesting that Zanuck originally thought of the female lead as a non-singing role, like Madeleine Carroll's in *On the Avenue*), filming began in the fall of 1940 with Alice and Don Ameche in their sixth and last film together.

THAT NIGHT IN RIO (1941) AND *ON THE RIVIERA* (1951)

That Night in Rio was a remake of Fox's *Folies Bergère* (1935) that followed the same plot line: to prevent guests at a reception from discovering that their host, a philandering baron, has flown to Buenos Aires to secure a loan for a failed business venture, entertainer Larry Martin (Don Ameche, in the dual role of the baron and Martin) agrees to impersonate him. When the baron returns unexpectedly, confusion erupts with the baron being mistaken for his lookalike and vice versa. The baroness (Alice) had been informed of the deception earlier, as had the baron shortly after his return. When the baron enters his wife's bedroom, she senses the difference between her husband and Martin, but decides to teach the errant baron a lesson by lavishing him with affection, so that he would think she found Martin more attractive than himself. The baron retaliates by calling her the next morning, informing her that his plane has just landed. The baroness panics, wondering with whom she spent the night. Making one last attempt to win the battle of the sexes, she asks Martin to make passionate love to her as the baron comes through the door. Instead, Martin informs the baron, who sweeps his wife up in his arms and carries her up the stairs in "me, Tarzan, you, Jane" fashion, recalling Clark Gable's doing the same to Vivien Leigh in *Gone with the Wind* (1939).

The Production Code Administration (PCA) frowned upon the script, and the National Legion of Decency gave *That Night in Rio* a "B" rating ("Morally Objectionable in Part for All") because of a "suggestive scene." The PCA and the Legion were in a bind. If the baron and baroness had sex the night of his return, it was not adultery. Alice played the "suggestive scene" splendidly. Wearing a white fur-trimmed robe, she is preparing to retire when the baron walks in. When they embrace, Alice implies with her "gotcha" eyes in an over-the-shoulder shot that she knows that the man in her arms is her husband. Leading him to think she believes he is Martin, she puts an orchestral arrangement of "Good Night," one of Martin's songs, on the phonograph, asking him to supply the lyrics. When he demurs, she begins singing them in bed. He turns off the record player, she smiles, and the scene fades out on the baroness in bed and fades-in on her the next morning, looking radiant. Was the turning off of the record player a metaphor for the end of musical foreplay and the beginning of *grand amore*? It's anybody's guess as to what transpired between the baroness's retiring and her waking up. The writers wrought a good deal of sly humor out of the situation, particularly when the baron asks his perplexed wife the next morning, "Didn't you sleep well?" throwing her into a state of confusion.

In both *That Night in Rio* and *Week-End in Havana*, Alice sang very little. Playing a baroness and a sales clerk, respectively, she only had a few occasions to show off her voice. Although Carmen Miranda was third-billed, it was really her movie despite Ameche's tour de force performance. In *That Night in Rio*, Miranda had three numbers; Alice sang "They Met in Rio" and "Good Night ("*Boa Noite*"), reprising a bit of the latter at the end with Ameche and Miranda. That Alice sings "Good Night" was at least motivated, since the baroness is providing the lyrics to a song that the baron should have known if he were Larry Martin. But in the scene with the baron and baroness at a nightclub watching Martin do his impersonation, she sings—for no apparent reason except to prove to audiences that she had not lost her voice—"That Night in Rio" in English after Ameche had sung it in Portuguese.

It is Miranda who opens the film and pretty much closes it. In the opening number, "Chica Chica Boom Chic," Miranda is wearing a two-piece outfit with bare midriff and her signature *biana*, a basket hat bursting with fruit, or in this instance, flowers with a few dangling cherries. She later performs one of her best known songs, "I, Yi, Yi, Yi, Yi" ("I Like You Very

Much"). She moved like an undulating mechanism, sultry but sexless, primitive yet sophisticated. She was the embodiment of multicolored artifice, every detail rehearsed to perfection and impeccably executed.

If Zanuck had problems with the PCA with *That Night in Rio*, he could not possibly have thought that things would be any different with *On the Riviera* (1951), the second remake of *Folies Bergère*, with Danny Kaye, Gene Tierney, and Corinne Calvet assuming the roles that Don Ameche, Alice Faye, and Carmen Miranda played in the 1941 version; and Maurice Chevalier, Merle Oberon, and Ann Sothern in the 1935 original. *On the Riviera* is almost a scene-by-scene dupe of *That Night in Rio*, with a few changes: Cannes instead of Rio, and an aviator in lieu of a baron, with the entertainer-impersonator (Kaye) as the constant, bearing the same surname, Martin, as Ameche's character, now Jack instead of Larry. The film opens with the traditional establishing montage, this time of swimmers, surfers, and sunbathers, suggesting a decidedly hedonistic milieu.

Zanuck may have been motivated to offer Danny Kaye the part after seeing him in *Wonder Man* (Goldwyn, 1945), in which he played identical twins with distinctly different personalities. *That Night in Rio* was essentially a Carmen Miranda movie with a deft turn by Ameche; *On the Riviera* was Kaye's movie, with room for no one else, not even Gene Tierney as the wife who does not know if she spent the night with her husband or his lookalike. There are five numbers in the film, all sung by Kaye, since both Gene Tierney and Corinne Calvet were non singers. Kaye was the whole show, beginning with his opening number, the title song, which he performed as if he had been reincarnated as Maurice Chevalier, the boulevardier with dancing eyes and rakish charm. From that point on, it's *That Night in Rio* redivivus, but considerably more risqué with the aviator's philandering a recurring plot point; Kaye's second number, "The Rhythm of a New Romance," celebrates the joys of partner changing; and Tierney's beaming face after what was more than just a good night's sleep is a telltale sign of fulfillment.

PCA czar Joseph Breen rejected the temporary script, which he found "unacceptable" because of "suspicion of illicit relationships between various characters," meaning Henry Duran (Kaye), the aviator, and his many loves as well as the possibility of a liaison between Duran's wife, Lili (Tierney), and Martin. The script was still a problem four months later: "If there is the slightest suggestion that Duran came into Lili's bedroom, the script would be unacceptable." There didn't have to be any suggestion: Tierney's face said it all. Throughout the film, she had been tolerant of his errant ways but now felt that he was hers alone. For once, the finale does not include a reprise but rather a closing number for the prodigiously talented Kaye, which summed up the movie, "Happy Ending," and a close-up fade-out with Kaye and Calvet. The National Legion of Decency was even more critical of *On the Riviera* than it had been of *That Night in Rio*, relegating it to category B (Morally Objectionable in Part for All) because of "suggestive costuming, sequences, and dialogue; low moral tone." The "suggestive costuming" was the abbreviated outfit worn by the great Gwen Verdon (uncredited) that had feathers spouting from it, as she did some bumps (no grinds) in her brief minute or two of screen time.

WEEK-END IN HAVANA (1941)

If the storyline of *Week-End in Havana* sounds familiar, it is because it is reminiscent of the delightful screwball comedy, *Libeled Lady* (MGM, 1936), in which a managing editor (Spencer Tracy) persuades a former reporter (William Powell) to woo an heiress (Myrna Loy) who is suing the paper for libel and then arrange for the two of them to be in a compromising situation when the reporter's "wife" arrives, charging the heiress with alienation of affection. Since the reporter is unmarried, the managing editor's fiancée (Jean Harlow) is cajoled into marrying him. Naturally, reporter and heiress, deceiver and deceived, fall in love, and the plot gets increasingly knotted until it unwinds in an "all's well that ends well" resolution.

In *Week-End in Havana*, Alice plays a salesperson whose vacation plans are thwarted when her cruise ship runs aground. The company sends one of its executives (John Payne) to persuade the passengers to sign waivers, offering them passage on another ship. Alice is the only holdout, which poses a problem for Payne after Alice informs him that she will testify that the captain was not on deck when the accident occurred. Alice agrees to sign the wavier if the company guarantees that she will have a memorable time, which Payne arranges by booking her into a suite at a boutique hotel and showing her the sights. Since watching sugar cane being harvested is not Alice's idea of fun, Payne enlists the help of Cesar Romero, agreeing to pay off his gambling debts if he will provide Alice with the excitement she is seeking. Romero agrees, infuriating Carmen Miranda, whose career he is "managing," a word that the PCA found "sex-suggestive."

Alice gradually warms to Payne, who responds in kind, and signs the waiver. Complications arise when Alice discovers Payne is engaged. When his fiancée (the boss's daughter) arrives with a $1,000 check in return for the signed waiver, she reluctantly signs but then throws the check in the waste basket. Since it has only been crumpled, Romero can use it to pay off more gambling debts. The denouement quickly follows with Payne ditching his duplicitous fiancée in Miami and returning to Havana in time to join Alice, Romero, and Miranda in a reprise of the title song which Miranda sang at the beginning.

What made *Libeled Lady* such a brilliant screwball comedy was its cynicism and "end justifies the means" plot. There is not even a whiff of cynicism in *Week-End in Havana* because everyone is so damned likeable, even the philandering Romero and the fiery Miranda, both of whom steal the movie. Alice has one solo, "Tropical Magic," which she sings against a column dressed in a blue gown with silver applique and holding an orchid. Her voice is sultry, and she has a far-off look. But it's a number that has nothing to do with the plot, unless you interpret it as an interior monologue to which Romero has access. As soon as he hears it (or plugs into her unconscious), he's on the make, and she's receptive. In their duet, "Romance and Rhumba," Romero is the surprise, his body all curves as if it were an oscillator. Alice keeps up with him, but his height and flair for the sensual make him the focus of attention. But it is Carmen Miranda in her third American film (she made several in Brazil) who has the best numbers, four to be exact. In her florid costumes, her *biana*, a display of floral effusion, and her platform shoes, which give her totemic stature, she turns her songs into primitive rituals, gesticulating sinuously as if she were delivering an incantation. When Carmen Miranda is on the screen, you can no more take your eyes off her than you can avoid the gaze of a mesmerist.

It may seem hard to believe, but the Production Code Administration found the first draft screenplay of *Week-End in Havana* unacceptable because of "the inference of an illicit sex relationship" between Romero and Miranda and, surprisingly, between Alice and Payne. The PCA was especially concerned about "manage" as double entendre, which was understandable from the way Miranda told Romero, "No one can manage me like you do." When she turns her attention to Payne, she also wants him to "manage" her instead of Romero. Zanuck did not change or delete the "manage" references, and the National Legion of Decency rated the film "A-II" ("For Adults and Adolescents").

If Alice looked particularly radiant in *Hello, Frisco, Hello* (1943), it was not merely the result of Helen Rose's ravishing gowns and Charles Clarke and Allen Davey's flattering cinematography. It was also motherhood. In 1942, Alice and her second husband, Phil Harris, whom she married in 1940 after her divorce from Tony Martin, had their first daughter, also named Alice. She also had a script that revolved around her character, with no competition from Carmen Miranda. John Payne's was primarily a straight acting role (he sang in two numbers with Alice, Jack Oakie, and June Havoc but had no solo). Oakie and Havoc were secondary characters, who did vaudeville shtick, with Havoc proving herself a skilled dancer who could execute a high kick and go into an effortless split.

Mel Gussow wrote that "Zanuck's formula films fell into two major categories, Remakes and Sequels." He might have added a third: films with recycled plot points. *Hello, Frisco, Hello* was both a remake and a recycling with a reunion finale (*Alexander's Ragtime Band*, *The Great American Broadcast*). One of Twentieth Century-Fox's first productions was K*ing of Burlesque* (1936), in which a burlesque producer (Warner Baxter) becomes infatuated with a socialite (Mona Barrie) whom he marries, oblivious to the fact that his star (Alice) is in love with him. Encouraged by his trophy wife, he gives up musicals for serious drama, produces a succession of flops, loses all his money, and eventually returns to his roots, his former partner (Jack Oakie), and the woman who loves him (Alice).

HELLO, FRISCO, HELLO (1943)

Hello, Frisco, Hello adheres to the same plot (upwardly mobile male, mercenary female, true love waiting in the wings) with some changes. The setting is no longer New York but San Francisco's raffish Barbary Coast at the turn of the twentieth century, a milieu that director H. Bruce Humberstone recreated in a thrilling tracking shot as the camera traversed Pacific Street with its saloons, musical halls, and what looked like bawdy houses. Alice is part of a vaudeville act consisting of herself, John Payne in the Warner

Baxter role, Jack Oakie, and June Havoc (replacing Arline Judge from the original). Payne envisions a Pacific Street lined with his own theaters and even a Rollerdome, with performers on roller skates. The predatory socialite (Lynn Bari) now hails from Nob Hill rather than Park Avenue. After she loses the family fortune, her possessions are put up for auction. In the original, the producer bids on a model ship, which she at first refuses to sell. In the remake, Payne bids on her father's opera scores, which Bari will not allow him to buy but agrees to send them on with his other purchases. In *King of Burlesque*, Baxter was persuaded to forsake musicals for the legitimate theater. In the remake, it's for opera. In both films, Alice goes off to London and becomes a sensation; in both, Baxter and Payne go bankrupt, with Payne reduced to working as a barker at a Pacific Street attraction.

The *Hello, Frisco, Hello* denouement is more of a reflection of what audiences expected of a successful woman when her man has hit the skids than a sensible ending with the proud male getting back on top through his own ingenuity, and the successful woman finding a man she does not have to raise up. To have Payne return to producing shows in his own theater, Alice bribes the parasitic Laird Cregar, who is always cadging Payne for goldmining money, to convince him that he has struck it rich by flashing a roll of bills that Alice had given him. When Payne learns where the money came from, he programs himself into the "I-don't-need-anyone" mode (cf. *The Great American Broadcast*). But it is Oakie who forces a finale out of a female largesse-male vanity impasse and gets them on stage for a reprise of the title song and "You'll Never Know," which only Alice can sing with such poignant sincerity. It is small wonder that "You'll Never Know," which won an Oscar for best song, was so popular during World War II, when GIs needed reassurance that they were loved by the ones they left behind. Like so many songs of the period ("Apple Blossom Time," Don't Sit Under the Apple Tree (with Anyone Else but Me)," "I Can't Begin to Tell You," and "We'll Meet Again"), the lyrics were simple and direct without striking images or clever turns of phrase.

In *King of Burlesque*, Alice's eighth film, she was still Zanuck's idea of a Jean Harlow clone. In *Hello, Frisco, Hello*, she is her unalloyed self. Helen Rose dressed her in a succession of ravishing costumes: a lavender jacket decorated with shiny purple applique and a lavender striped white skirt; a black-and-white gown with matching hat and muff; a pale yellow gown with a floral bodice; a blue hoop skirt gown with ruffled sleeves and a silvery bodice that complemented her rendition of "By the Light of the Silvery Moon." But most memorable of all was that smashing black hat she wore at the end with an upturned brim on the left side and topped with a spray of feathers. Alice never looked more glamorous or sang such a variety of songs, among them a jaunty "Ragtime Cowboy Joe," in an anachronistic cowgirl outfit, and "Has Anybody Here Seen Kelly?" in which she looked like an Irish colleen with an accent to boot.

She probably had no idea that she would make one more musical for Twentieth Century-Fox, which would be added to the National Film Registry of the Library of Congress for its cultural significance. *The Gang's All Here* (1943), released nine months after *Hello, Frisco, Hello* and in time for Christmas, is remembered for two reasons, neither of which has to do with Alice: Busby Berkeley and Carmen Miranda.

As if anticipating America's entry into World War II, Zanuck accepted a commission in the Army Signal Corps reserves as a lieutenant colonel in January 1941 and was promoted to full colonel a month after Pearl Harbor. Although Zanuck was away for seventeen months, no one had to make any decisions about the studio's 1942 releases. Zanuck had put together the entire slate before he left. In late April 1942 he was granted a leave to see how the studio was faring in his absence and how the 1943 product was shaping up. Zanuck had put William Goetz in charge of the studio, even though he was well aware of Goetz's limitations. Since Louis B. Mayer had contributed financially to the creation of Twentieth Century, he expected that, in return, Zanuck would find a place for his son-in-law at Twentieth Century-Fox. Zanuck, who claimed that "Goetz couldn't recognize a good script from a roll of toilet paper," gave him the nebulous title of "vice president and executive assistant to Mr. Zanuck." Knowing that he could easily keep tabs on Goetz while he was away, Zanuck left him in control. Empowered, Goetz put his name under *The Gang's All Here*'s title—"William Goetz in charge of production," an imitation of the way Zanuck signed his films when he began as production head at the studio.

Zanuck returned to civilian life in May 1943 in time for *The Gang's All Here* shoot. Impressed by Busby Berkeley's creation and staging of the dances in *42nd Street*, and his direction of such MGM musicals as *Babes in Arms* (1939) and *For Me and My Gal* (1942), he signed Berkeley (1895–1976) to direct, and William LeBaron (1883–1958), a major producer at Paramount before coming to Twentieth Century-Fox in 1940, to produce. After passing on the screenplay, Zanuck moved on to more pressing matters: getting the right scripts for *Laura* and *Wilson* (both 1944), believing that the latter would be his supreme achievement. At first, Berkeley and LeBaron got along. But LeBaron could not compete with Berkeley's unfettered imagination, which roamed freely through the spectrum, extracting colors so visually intoxicating that they could leave you dizzy.

Then there was his erotic geometry in "The Lady with the Tutti Frutti Hat": six recumbent women forming various configurations within a semi-circle of dancers brandishing giant bananas, followed by shots of feet and hands moving from one side to the other. This arrangement of hands and feet is consistent with Berkeley's brand of surrealism in which disembodied heads sing, and extremities are meant for more than mobility. Carmen Miranda's platform shoes do more than increase her height; they look as if they are part of a tribal priestess's regalia. The 5', 8 ½", double-jointed Charlotte ("Lady Longlegs") Greenwood dances a jitterbug with a teenager, swinging her legs from one side to the other as he darts under them. *The Gang's All Here* opens with a disembodied head singing "Brazil" and ends with the heads of the principals, enclosed within small circles like mini iris shots, against a blue background. Forget Goetz and LeBaron. *The Gang's All Here* was a Busby Berkeley production.

The main title of *The Gang's All Here* ends in darkness, out of which emerges the face of a man (Aloysio de Oliveira), spotlighted within a circle, singing "Aquarela do Brasil" (better known in English as "Brazil") in Portuguese. The singer's face expands into a medium shot before receding as rows of slanted lines appear, suggesting waves. We are not in Brazil but at the gangplank of the SS *Brazil*. The passengers disembark, and the cargo is unloaded. An enormous basket of fruit is lowered over Carmen Miranda, who is wearing a hat that looks like a fruit plate. Miranda sings "Brazil" in English, doing a samba in one of her less outrageous costumes: a purple-and-red top festooned with pompoms and a skirt with a V-shaped opening at the waist. When Phil Baker arrives to present Miranda with a key to the city in gratitude for being the embodiment of the Good Neighbor Policy, she switches from "Brazil" to "You Discover You're In New York," with typical wartime lyrics about the butter shortage and restaurant prices. Finally, the camera tracks back, revealing a nightclub. What we have just witnessed was the floor show at the Club New Yorker, which could not have been put on anywhere but a soundstage.

A Carmen Miranda number had opened other movies before (*Down Argentine Way, Week-End in Havana, That Night in Rio*), but this time it makes narrative sense. In the club are Sergeant Andy Mason (James Ellison), his father (Eugene Palette), and the father (Edward Everett Horton) of the young woman (Sheila Ryan) to whom Mason is presumably engaged. The film's working title was "The Girls He Left Behind," which, provocative as it sounds, reflected the storyline: once Mason gets a glimpse of Edie Allen (Alice), a member of the chorus, he calls her "his target for tonight," as if she were his quarry. Following her to the local canteen where she dances with service men between shows, he continues his unorthodox courtship, much to her gradually expressed delight. Screenwriter Walter Bullock knew that wartime morality is fluid. The girls the men left behind were not always the ones to whom they returned, and the men who left often received a "Dear John" letter from a childhood sweetheart. When Mason is dancing with Edie, he asks if any of the men ever got out of line. She replies, "You can't blame them if they get off the beam once in a while." Mason has already gone "off the beam." Loath to tell her about his so-called fiancée, he even lies about his name, saying it's "Casey." The plot then becomes the familiar two women-same man triangle, and it is only a matter of time before Edie learns who "Casey" really is.

But before the plot can progress any further, it's time for another number, the notorious "Lady in the Tutti Frutti Hat," which is pure artifice, the grand bourgeois as kitschy surrealism. We are back at the Club New Yorker—or rather on Twentieth Century-Fox's Stage Sixteen that doubled as the nightclub. An organ grinder with a monkey wends his way through the tables and onto the stage. The monkey climbs up a banana tree, one of several occupied by monkeys. Berkeley uses the banana both as image and prop, and yellow as a banana-inspired color. Past the rows of banana trees is a revolving disc representing an island. Women in purple tops and yellow shorts lie supine on this synthetic island. Suddenly, they rise and begin waving in delight. The object of their attention comes into view: it is Miranda arriving on a wagon laden with bananas, wearing a banana bunch hat with a string of artificial strawberries dangling from it and encircling her neck. She is wearing another costume with a V opening at the waist covered in beige. The women carry in baskets of bananas that look as if they were either made of plastic or were heavily waxed, arranging them in the shape of a xylophone for Miranda to play. But this is one of the tenets of surrealism. Nothing is what it should be. Bananas are meant for eating, not for xylophone bars. For those who find the bananas phallic, one can only say that if sometimes a cigar is just a cigar, a banana is just a banana. When the women raise and lower the giant bananas, they do it with awesome precision. After Miranda departs, the women rush back to their island and fall down, as if in exhaustion. The organ grinder and his monkey leave the stage and stand alongside other organ grinders and their monkeys, with Miranda at the end of the line singing the concluding verses of "The Lady in the Tutti Frutti Hat" against a backdrop dominated by a sunburst of bananas. The dreamlike show is over. The bananas are in the heavens, and all's right with the world.

The finale is a masterpiece of giddy surrealism, like Chagall's *Le cheval ivre* (*The Drunken Horse*). The parents of Mason's fiancée are sponsoring a war bonds drive at their estate with entertainment provided by Benny ("The King of Swing") Goodman and His Orchestra and performers from the Club New Yorker, including Edie. Mason, meanwhile, has been fighting in the Pacific, scoring victory after victory as newspaper headlines attest (historically inaccurate in mid-1943) and returning home a war hero. Naturally, he encounters Edie, who has already met his fiancée, Vivian Potter (Sheila Ryan). Walter Bullock had to find some way to remove Vivian from the triangle. Ryan had been playing Vivian as a superficial socialite rather like the "dizzy dame" of screwball comedy. When Tony De Marco loses his dancing partner, he spots Vivian and asks her to dance with him. She does, and quite professionally. It's ballroom dancing, and Ryan/Vivian has the required poise and litheness. What is refreshing about the number is the absence of studied elegance and faux sophistication that has often made ballroom dancing an exercise in art rather than an art itself.

De Marco and Vivian will also perform at the war bonds show that opens with "A Journey to a Star," which Alice had sung earlier when Edie and Mason were on the Staten Island ferry. It's a charming moment, with Edie setting the mood. "Hear the orchestra?" she asks. "Where's it coming from?" he replies. "Where's your imagination?" she answers, providing the best rejoinder to skeptics who claim that musicals are not realistic. She sings it dreamily, as if an astral trip is one that only lovers can take. This time, Alice, in a silver-sprinkled strapless blue gown with a mesh top. performs the song dispassionately, still believing that she has lost Mason to Vivian. Then Vivian, all in white, and De Marco dance to a different orchestration of "A Journey to a Star." The tempo has now changed, and the once relaxed, almost languid music becomes a feverish waltz as De Marco and Ryan/ Vivian, caught up in its propulsive rhythms, glide and swirl on the circular floor. (Circles dominate the final sequence.) At a break in the show, Vivian informs Edie that De Marco has asked her to appear with him in a Broadway revue, adding that the "engagement" was their parents' idea, not theirs. Alice can go back to being her old self again for the finale, for which words are inadequate. It's a reverie dreamed by a surrealist of the cinema, who can take an image—in this case, a circle—and weave it throughout the sequence. It's as if the collective unconscious were saying: "Forget linearity and plot points. Think image and color."

For reasons known only to Berkeley, the finale involves children dancing a polka—the girls in polka-dot jackets and white dresses with ruffled wrist cuffs; the boys in dress coats and white pants. They behave like adults, with the boys playing model gentlemen and the girls, perfect ladies. Alice moves among them singing "The Polka Dot Polka," noting that while the polka may be passé, "the polka dot is here to stay." The red circle around a girl's wrist cuff detaches itself and moves into space, multiplying as it goes and forming a concatenation of circles. Women in bluish gray bodysuits gracefully raise and lower the circles to music that has a Ravel-like lushness. The circles then become colored discs, which the women again raise and lower, as the faux islanders did with bananas in the "Lady in the Tutti Frutti Hat" number. A face that bears an uncanny resemblance to Alice's is all that is visible from a swirling mass of blue silk that forms the first in a kaleidoscopic array of images, zooming in and out with such an outpouring of changing colors and patterns as to leave the viewer dumbstruck or woozy. Berkeley has not finished with his circles. The faces of the principals on different colored discs zoom onto the screen, each singing a snippet of "A Journey to a Star"; and to prove the polka dot lives on, the screen becomes a blue firmament, literally dotted with a miniature of the entire cast, as jets of water shoot up, signaling THE END. To the right of the end title is a pitch for buying war bonds in the lobby, a common addition in the studio's wartime movies and quite applicable in this case since *The Gang's All Here* ended with a bond drive.

Busby Berkeley has created the greatest sound and light show in movie history, upstaging everyone except perhaps Carmen Miranda. The movie was not vintage Alice, who has nothing equivalent to "You'll Never Know."

"No Love, No Nothin'" comes close. It's a wartime lament from a woman's point of view, intimating that lovemaking has been rationed for the duration. Alice sings it while ironing a slip—an erotic touch, perhaps, but more in keeping with how a lonely woman manages while waiting for Johnny to come marching home. *The Gang's All Here* was the last of Alice's musicals until the disappointing remake of *State Fair* (1962), in which she had little to do. *Fallen Angel* (1945) might have marked her emergence as a serious actress, but Zanuck apparently reduced her role, knowing that audiences would only be interested in Linda Darnell. Disappointed with the final cut, Alice left Twentieth Century-Fox, but she also must have figured out that, in 1943, when she had two films in release, Betty Grable had the same number, *Sweet Rosie O'Grady* and *Coney Island*. Grable was Zanuck's new golden girl. She was also the top box-office attraction of 1943. Alice didn't make the top ten. She knew it was time to go, and *Fallen Angel* gave her an excuse.

Chapter 11

THE ZANUCK MUSICAL AS WOMAN'S FILM

Critic Molly Haskell observed that "in the woman's film, the woman—*a* woman—is at the center of the universe." That is generally true of the Twentieth Century-Fox musical, which is a different type of woman's film: generally, a woman sets the plot in motion, controls it, or resolves it. There are exceptions, such as *Hollywood Cavalcade* and *That Night in Rio*, but even in these examples, the woman never loses her centrality. In the former, Don Ameche may have made Alice a star, but she made him a fortune by starring in his films. In the second, both Alice and Ameche score points as they test each other's fidelity. In *Alexander's Ragtime Band*, Alice teaches Tyrone Power how to rag the title song, thus launching his career. In *Rose of Washington Square*, her heartfelt delivery of "My Man" causes Tyrone Power to turn himself in. In *Week-End in Havana*, Alice's refusal to accept a waver triggers the narrative. In *Hello, Frisco, Hello*, her fame and wealth makes it possible for John Payne to go back into show business. In *The Gang's All Here*, it is Sheila Ryan's decision to become Tony De Marco's dancing partner that clears the way for Alice and James Ellison. That is not the case in MGM musicals, which tend to revolve around a male protagonist:

In *For Me and My Gal* (MGM, 1942), how will Gene Kelly redeem himself in the eyes of Judy Garland after trying to dodge the draft?

In *Anchors Aweigh* (MGM, 1945), how will Gene Kelly and Frank Sinatra get José Iturbi to hear golden-voiced Kathryn Grayson?

In *The Pirate* (MGM, 1948), how long can Gene Kelly go on deceiving Judy Garland into believing that he is Mack the Black?

In *An American in* Paris (MGM, 1951), how will Gene Kelly win Leslie Caron when she is promised to George Guitary?

In *Singin' in the Rain* (MGM, 1952), how will Gene Kelly make the public know that Debbie Reynolds is Jean Hagen's singing voice?

In *Brigadoon* (MGM, 1954), how will Gene Kelly find Brigadoon again so he can spend eternity with Cyd Charisse?

As for Fred Astaire:

In *Easter Parade* (MGM, 1948), will Fred Astaire relinquish Ann Miller for Judy Garland, so Peter Lawford will not be the odd man out?

In *The Band Wagon* (MGM, 1953), will Fred make a hit out of a troubled musical?

In *Silk Stockings* (MGM, 1957), will Fred succeed in converting Marxist Cyd Charisse to capitalism?

Even in the much-admired *Meet Me in St. Louis*, the plot points are male-driven. Will Lucille Bremer's boyfriend call her from New York? Will Tom Drake catch the trolley so he can sit next to Judy Garland? Will he get his tux back in time to dance with Judy at the Christmas ball? And most important, will Leon Ames uproot his family and take the job offered him in New York?

In Twentieth Century-Fox's musicals, especially those with Betty Grable, it is mostly the opposite.

In *Down Argentine Way* (1940), Betty Grable succeeds in ending a family feud with a disclosure about Don Ameche's father.

In *Moon Over Miami* (1941), Betty succeeds in getting the next best thing to a millionaire: a former millionaire who in time will be in the money again.

In *Footlight Serenade* (1942), Betty radiates such integrity that hot-tempered pugilist Victor Mature acts civilly toward her when he learns she has married John Payne.

In *Song of the Islands* (1942), the combination of a tropical paradise and Betty, who does a mean hula, brings feuding fathers together.

In *Springtime in the Rockies* (1942), for a while, it's a toss-up as to who is navigating the plot: is it Betty or John Payne, who needs her to get backing for a show? By the end, everyone involved (Betty, Payne, Carmen Miranda, Charlotte Greenwood, Cesar Romero, Edward Everett Horton) decide to produce the show themselves: plot resolution through group effort.

Coney Island (1943) is an exception. George Montgomery begins the process of turning brassy Betty into a class act, but she has the talent to develop into an artist on her own.

In *Sweet Rosie O'Grady* (1943), Betty mocks journalist Robert Young in her stage act in retaliation for his exposé of her past.

In *Pin Up Girl* (1944), Betty plays a prim stenographer capable of impersonating a musical comedy star.

In *The Dolly Sisters* (1945), Betty does not allow marriage to John Payne to interfere with her career.

Mother Wore Tights (1947) is unusual in the sense that the story-line revolves around a vaudeville team (Betty and Dan Dailey) who must convince their daughter and her skeptical classmates that they are more than hoofers.

In *The Shocking Miss Pilgrim* (1947), Betty will not give up being a suffragist to marry Dick Haymes, who must come around to her way of thinking.

In *When My Baby Smiles at Me* (1948), Betty succeeds in getting an inebriated Dan Dailey through a performance by indicating that she still loves him.

In *That Lady in Ermine* (1948), Betty saves her ancestral castle from destruction by Douglas Fairbanks Jr. with some help from her great-great-great-grandmother who has a habit of stepping out of her painting when needed.

In *My Blue Heaven* (1950), Betty does not allow "other woman" Mitzi Gaynor to take Dan Dailey from her.

In *Meet Me After the Show* (1951), Betty is at the apex of another triangular plot in which she feigns amnesia to extricate her husband from the clutches of the "other woman." Although he falls for her act, the situation is complicated by Eddie Albert's mooning over her, but he doesn't stand a chance.

The Farmer Takes a Wife (1953) has Betty and Dale Robertson each scoring a win. Betty succeeds in getting farmer Robertson to operate her barge but then decides to be the farmer's wife.

In *Three for the Show* (Columbia, 1955), a musical retread of *Too Many Husbands* (Columbia, 1940), Betty, assuming husband Jack Lemmon is dead, marries Gower Champion and then must decide whom she prefers when Lemmon turns up alive. With Gower's dancing partner, Marge, in the cast, the pairing off is obvious. Although made at another studio, *Three for the Show* is very much a "Betty Grable musical."

In her last film, *How to Be Very, Very Popular* (1955), Betty and Sheree North play singers who witness a gangland murder and hide out at a college fraternity where they both find romance.

If women navigated the plot in so many Twentieth Century-Fox musicals, it was because Zanuck had stars who were often playing variations of themselves: singers and dancers equally at home in vaudeville, burlesque, clubs, and the Broadway stage. And when they were cast in roles as other than performers (Betty in *The Shocking Miss Pilgrim, The Farmer Takes a Wife*; Alice in *Tailspin, Week-End in Havana, That Night in Rio*), they still could take command of the film ether because they were given the right material or because the script was slanted in the direction of their character.

So many of Zanuck's Twentieth Century-Fox musicals were variations of the woman's film because he selected writers who could tailor the story to the star, making it an "Alice Faye movie" or a "Betty Grable movie." Lamar Trotti, one of Twentieth Century-Fox's most versatile screenwriters and Oscar winner for *Wilson* (1944), wrote the screenplays for two Alice Faye movies, *In Old Chicago* (1938) and *Alexander's Ragtime Band* (1938); and three for Betty Grable, *Mother Wore Tights* (1947), which he also produced, *When My Baby Smiles at Me* (1948), and *My Blue Heaven* (1950). George Seaton wrote the Betty Grable vehicles *Coney Island* (1943), *Billy Rose's Diamond Horseshoe* (1945), and *The Shocking Miss Pilgrim* (1947), the last two of which he also directed. He also did the adaptation of *Moon Over Miami*. Walter Bullock wrote the lyrics to the songs Alice Faye sang in *Sing, Baby, Sing* (1936) and *Sally, Irene and Mary* (1938), in addition to the screenplay of *The Gang's All Here* (1943). Ken Englund was the screenwriter for Betty Grable's *Springtime in the Rockies* (1942) and *Sweet Rosie O'Grady* (1943). Screenwriter Helen Logan was one of the writers responsible for one of Alice Faye's best remembered musicals, *Hello, Frisco, Hello* (1943). Logan also contributed to the dialogue of one of Alice's early films, *Music Is Magic* (Fox, 1935) and scripted *Four Jills in a Jeep* (1944), in which Alice made a cameo appearance, singing the GI favorite, "You'll Never Know." For Betty Grable, Logan wrote *Tin Pan Alley* (1940), the first and only time Alice costarred with Betty; *Footlight Serenade* (1942), *Song of the Islands* (1942), and *Pin-Up Girl* (1944).

Both Alice and Betty profited by having sympathetic directors. Alice was especially fond of Henry King, who directed her in *In Old Chicago*, *Alexander's Ragtime Band*, and *Little Old New York*. She also worked well with Irving Cummings (*Poor Little Rich Girl* [1938], in which Shirley Temple was the star; *Hollywood Cavalcade* [1939]; *Lillian Russell* [1940]; and *That Night in Rio* [1941]); Gregory Ratoff (*Barricade* and *Rose of Washington Square*, both 1939); and Walter Lang (*Tin Pan Alley* [1940] and *Weekend in Havana* [1941]). Betty worked mostly with Walter Lang (*Tin Pan Alley*, *Moon Over Miami*, *Song of the Islands*, *Coney Island*, *Mother Wore Tights*,

When My Baby Smiles at Me) and Irving Cummings (*Down Argentine Way, Springtime in the Rockies, Sweet Rosie O'Grady, The Dolly Sisters*). She made two musicals with Henry Koster (*Wabash Avenue* and *My Blue Heaven*); two with George Seaton (*Billy Rose's Diamond Horseshoe, The Shocking Miss Pilgrim*); and one each with Ernst Lubitsch and Preston Sturges (*That Lady in Ermine* and *The Beautiful Blonde from Bashful Bend*, respectively). There were a few others, but Lang and Cummings were the directors who created the Betty Grable who was one of the top ten box-office attractions in the 1940s.

Except for King, Lubitsch, and Sturges, these directors were not auteurs whose films bore their distinctive signature. Walter Lang aspired to be a painter and turned to film after a trip to Paris convinced him he would never be a great artist. Irving Cummings was a stage and screen actor before becoming a director. Each had amassed an impressive filmography before working with two of Twentieth Century-Fox's most popular stars in material that had been carefully tailored to their specifications, which meant singing and some dancing for Alice; and singing and a great deal of dancing for Betty, who could do the rhumba (*Down Argentine Way*); hula (*Song of the Islands*); soft-shoe, tap, jitterbug, and sleekly sophisticated ballroom dancing with Cesar Romero (*Springtime in the Rockies*).

Zanuck made certain that that he had songwriters who could compose for his stars' voices, not necessarily their characters, which meant using the same teams as much as possible. Harry Warren and Mack Gordon were assigned to the Alice Faye films *Little Old New York* (music and lyrics by Gordon), *Tin Pan Alley* ("You Say the Sweetest Things," music by Warren, lyrics by Gordon, and sung by Jack Oakie, John Payne, and Alice), *That Night in Rio* and *The Great American Broadcast* (both Warren and Gordon), *Week-End in Havana* (Warren and Gordon, except for "Romance and Rhumba," with lyrics by Gordon and music by James V. Monaco), *Hello, Frisco, Hello* (Warren and Gordon's "You'll Never Know," which will always be associated with Alice), and *The Gang's All Here* (eight by Warren and Leo Robin, and one by Warren and Gordon). Warren and Gordon also composed songs for Betty Grable's *Down Argentine Way, Springtime in the Rockies, Sweet Rosie O'Grady*, and *Billy Rose's Diamond Horseshoe*; James V. Monaco provided the music and Gordon the lyrics for *Pin Up Girl* and the best remembered song from *The Dolly Sisters*, "I Can't Begin to Tell You." *Mother Wore Tights* featured four songs by Josef Myrow and Gordon and one by Warren and

Gordon; *When My Baby Smiles at Me*, two by Myrow and Gordon; *Wabash Avenue*, five by Myrow and Gordon; and *The Beautiful Blonde from Bashful Bend*, one by Myrow and Gordon. It certainly enhances a performer's screen personality when she has the same or similar composers who write her kind of songs. Betty could not have invested "You'll Never Know" (*Hello, Frisco, Hello*) with the same plaintiveness that Alice brought to it, nor could Alice have given "Cuddle Up, a Little Closer" (*Coney Island*) the warmth that Betty did.

Alice and Betty could also handle dialogue well and give credible performances, none of which were Oscar worthy but all of which resonated with audiences, which is all Zanuck wanted. For prestige films, Zanuck had Henry Fonda, Gregory Peck, Dana Andrews, Tyrone Power, Cornel Wilde, George Montgomery, Gene Tierney, Dorothy McGuire, and Maureen O'Hara; and directors John Ford, Elia Kazan, Ernst Lubitsch, Otto Preminger, Henry King, and Henry Hathaway. Musicals, to Zanuck, were movies in which there is "no effort to explain the music or prepare for it." Zanuck admitted that his musicals were formula based and "topped all musicals made elsewhere . . . because we have successfully eliminated stage or theatre technique," meaning that in a Twentieth Century-Fox musical, the numbers do not necessarily grow out of a dramatic situation, but "develop before your eyes . . . so naturally that you were not aware of them until you were into them." In *The Gang's All Here*, the first time "A Journey to a Star" is heard is on a moonlit ferry ride. It's a romantic setting, and a soldier on leave (James Ellison) asks his date (Alice) for a song. She obliges, spoofing the convention of the ubiquitous soundtrack by asking if he can hear the orchestra. What does it matter? The audience hears it: a late-night ferry ride with a romantic song that has nothing to do with the story, nor does it matter except to realists who object to "imaginary gardens with real toads in them," Marianne Moore's description of poetry.

Zanuck's blondes were not made of "sugar water," as Regina said of her daughter in Lillian Hellman's *The Little Foxes*. When a role called for someone winsome and virginal, Zanuck would give it to June Haver, who briefly flirted with the idea of becoming a nun and joined the Sisters of Charity in February 1953, leaving eight months later supposedly for health reasons. Alice and Betty could never play demure nor could either be the studio's Judy Garland or June Allyson. As good a dancer as Betty was, she was no Cyd Charisse. Except for Tyrone Power, none of Zanuck's leading men—Don Ameche, John Payne, Victor Mature, Mark Stevens—had typical matinee-idol looks. And there was no one at Twentieth Century-Fox who could dance like Fred Astaire and Gene Kelly. Although Dan Dailey came close, he could not match Kelly's versatility, even though he held his own in *It's Always Fair Weather* (MGM, 1955), with Kelly and the great dancer-choreographer, Michael Kidd. But Dailey could never have danced on roller skates as Kelly did in the film. Louis B. Mayer had his stock company at MGM; Zanuck had his at Twentieth Century-Fox. But Mayer did not have America's favorite movie star of 1943, who remained in the top ten throughout the decade and was named the country's favorite female star of 1950. Betty Grable's movies grossed more than $100 million, and the Treasury Department listed her as the highest salaried woman in America in 1946–47.

Chapter 12

THE MUSICALIZED FILM

Shirley Temple, Sonja Henie, and
Centennial Summer

In *When Broadway Went to Hollywood* (2016), musical theater historian Ethan Mordden coined the phrase "musicalized film" to characterize a movie whose plot would "implode" without musical numbers. The phrase can also be used of a movie whose plot is either too unsubstantial or commonplace to sustain interest without musical trappings. In *Orchestra Wives* (TCF, 1942), a young bride (Ann Rutherford) discovers what life on the road is like when her trumpeter husband (George Montgomery) goes on tour with Gene Morrison's Orchestra (really Glenn Miller's). Lynn Bari plays a band vocalist who has two numbers, voiced by Pat Friday. None of the principals—Rutherford, Montgomery, Bari—was a singer. But add a renowned orchestra with soloists like Ray Eberle, Tex Beneke, and Marion Hutton, and songs by Mack Gordon and Harry Warren ("At Last," "People Like You and Me," "I've Got a Gal in Kalamazoo," danced spectacularly by the Nicholas Brothers), and audiences will think they are watching a musical, while they have really been seeing a movie about a wife's adjusting to her husband's profession that has been musicalized.

In a true musical, dialogue, song, and dance combine to tell a story in which—rarely—the musical sequences advance the narrative but, more often, enliven or embellish it. There are musical numbers in Shirley Temple's Fox and Twentieth Century-Fox films, only a few of which can be called musicals. Shirley 's first costarring role—and one that made her a leading box-office attraction—was Fox's *Stand Up and Cheer!* (1934), which was to Depression America what Aristophanes's *Lysistrata* was to fifth-century BCE Athenians. In *Lysistrata*, the women of Athens succeed in putting an end to war by refusing to sleep with their husbands, thus bringing about an end to the Peloponnesian War which was still being waged when the play was first performed in 411 BCE. Athens had already sustained serious losses, and the possibility of victory was slim. Yet, at least for a time, some Greeks might have felt optimistic about the end of hostilities after seeing *Lysistrata*. Historically, that was not the case; the war ended seven years later in 404 BCE, with the defeat of Athens by Sparta. In *Stand Up and Cheer!*, a president, presumably Franklin D. Roosevelt, appoints a producer to be the president of entertainment for the purpose of sending troupes of performers across the country to inspire optimism in Americans during one of the worst years of the Great Depression. Optimism triumphs, and the Depression is over. And no doubt some moviegoers left the theatre believing the miasma had dissipated.

THE SHIRLEY TEMPLE PLAYBOOK

By the time Twentieth Century merged with the Fox Film Corporation, the Shirley Temple formula film had been established. Although Shirley was a remarkable child who could sing and dance (and do whatever acting the script required), she could not carry an entire picture by herself. Thus

—There must be a plot involving a couple, either married (James Dunn and Claire Trevor in *Baby, Take a Bow* [1934]; John Lodge and Evelyn Venable in *The Little Colonel* [1935]; Joel McCrea and Rosemary Ames in *Our Little Girl* [1935]); or unmarried (Warner Baxter and Madge Evans in *Stand Up and Cheer!* [1934]; Adolphe Menjou and Dorothy Dell in *Little Miss Marker* [1934]; James Dunn and Judith Allen in *Bright Eyes* [1934]; John Boles and Rochelle Hudson in *Curly Top* [1935]). In the latter, the two fall in love, and Shirley becomes part of their lives.

—Shirley's character can be the daughter of a married couple (*The Little Colonel*); motherless (*Stand Up and Cheer!*); or an orphan (*Little Miss Marker, Curly Top, Bright Eyes*).

—Regardless of the storyline, Shirley must sing *something*, even if it's with another character. In *Little Miss Marker*, Dorothy Dell plays a cabaret singer, and Shirley is, literally, a marker that her gambling father left as collateral before he committed suicide. If Dell can sing "Laugh, You Son of a Gun," Shirley can join in—and does.

—If Shirley dances with adults, she must be able to do everything they do. The finale of *Poor Little Rich Girl* is the brilliantly staged "Military Man," with Shirley, Jack Haley, and Alice Faye in uniform and shouldering rifles, doing spectacular precision tapping, at one point without any musical accompaniment. One would never know that the taps had to be synchronized in the sound room. The most original—and, at the time, daring—partnering in any musical of the 1930s was Shirley and the great African American dancer, Bill "Bojangles" Robinson. The staircase tap dance is the highlight of *The Little Colonel*. Robinson begins tapping on the floor to a medley of folk songs ("My Old Kentucky Home," "Carry Me Back to Old Virginny") and proceeds to tap up and down the stairs. Then he and Shirley, hand in hand, tap on the stairs together until they are interrupted by her grandfather (Lionel Barrymore). The rest of *The Little Colonel* is marred by cringe-inducing racism. Robinson and Hattie McDaniel, both plantation slaves (and mighty happy to be so), mangle the English language for easy laughs, and Shirley baptizes a Black boy by the name of Henry Clay in the river, singing "Alleluia!"

With the merger of Twentieth Century and Fox, Zanuck inherited Shirley along with the conventions of her special type of film, most of which he left unchanged except for racial elements, which he drastically reduced in *The Littlest Rebel* (1935) and *Wee Willie Winkie* (1937).

Again, Shirley is

—the daughter of a married couple (John Boles and Karen Morley in *The Littlest Rebel* [1935]; Russell Hicks and Spring Byington in *The Blue Bird* (1940)];
—the adopted daughter of a married couple (*Young People* [1940]);
—motherless (*Poor Little Rich Girl* [1936], *Just around the Corner* [1938], *The Little Princess* [1939]);
—fatherless (*Wee Willie Winkie* [1937]);
—an orphan (e.g., *Captain January* [1936]; *Rebecca of Sunnybrook Farm* [1938]; *Little Miss Broadway* [1938]). If Shirley is an orphan,

someone must adopt her, or adoption must be implied, to resolve the plot (an aunt and uncle in *Captain January*; presumably Robert Kent and Delma Byron in *Dimples* [1936]; George Murphy and Phyllis Brooks in *Little Miss Broadway*; Randolph Scott and Farrell MacDonald in *Susannah of the Mounties* [1939], until Margaret Lockwood enters the plot, suggesting that her new adoptive parents will be Scott and Lockwood; Scott and Gloria Stuart in *Rebecca of Sunnybrook Farm*).

—Shirley must sing *something*. There was no reason for Shirley to sing in *Wee Willie Winkie*, an overlong expansion of Rudyard Kipling's short story with a change of gender (the title character is now a girl, Shirley), except to satisfy audiences who believed that a Shirley Temple movie without a song is incomplete. And so, when Victor McLaglen is on his death bed, Shirley bids him farewell with "Auld Lang Syne," sung a capella.

—Any plot point or routine that worked once can be repeated. If Shirley was a stowaway on a plane in *Bright Eyes* (1934), she can be one on an ocean liner in *Stowaway* (1936). If Shirley can play soldier in *The Little Colonel*, she can do it again in *Wee Willie Winkie*, with Victor McLaglen as her drill instructor. If Shirley and Bill Robinson can dance up and down a staircase in *The Little Colonel*, they can do the same in *The Littlest Rebel* (1935).

In *Rebeca of Sunnybrook Farm*, Robinson is finally off the plantation and working as a farm hand, which means he can be reunited with Shirley for two numbers. In the first, he taps, she imitates him, and they stroll along picking berries as Shirley sings "An Old Straw Hat." For the finale of "Parade of the Wooden Soldiers," Shirley, dressed in military attire, comes down a set of stairs, followed by similarly dressed dancers led by Robinson. And if there are stairs, Shirley and Robinson will dance up and down them. The finale shows Shirley at her most versatile as the orchestration switches from marching band to swing and jive, with Shirley adapting easily to the changes in rhythm.

Shirley's last pairing with Robinson was in *Just Around the Corner*. Shirley begins singing "This Is a Happy Little Ditty." Then Joan Davis turns the number into a duet. Robinson, now a doorman, enters. Since there are no stairs, he and Shirley tap joyously around the apartment, joined by Davis and Bert Lahr, so that what began as a solo finishes as a quartet. In the variety show finale, Shirley, dressed in rain gear, sings the movie's best known song, "I Love to Walk in the Rain." Robinson joins her, playing a farmer in overalls, and they literally sing and dance in the rain. One wonders if "I Love to Walk in the Rain" inspired Gene Kelly's classic interpretation of the title song in *Singin' in the Rain* (1952). Since there are no stairs in the sequence, Shirley and Robinson cannot reprise their famous routine. But they still get a spectacular send-off. A circular platform rises from below, elevating them above the stage as if they were heading toward deification, which, in a sense, they were. Shirley Temple and Bill "Bojangles" Robinson were the most unique dancing team in the history of the American film.

Variety (December 23, 1936) described *Stowaway* as "a nifty Shirley Temple comedy with musical trimmings." A movie with musical trimmings is the perfect description of a Shirley Temple film.

THE SONJA HENIE PLAYBOOK

At least Shirley Temple could sing and dance. Sonja Henie, the three-time Olympic and ten-time World Champion figure skater from Norway, could do neither. But after Zanuck saw her ice show in Los Angeles in 1936, he knew he could make her into a star by reversing the Shirley Temple formula. Shirley needed a plot that would let her weave in and out of it, doing what she did best: sing and dance. Sonja needed one that would allow her to skate with comics, singers, and orchestras picking up the slack: the Ritz Brothers in *Once in a Million* (1936), Joan Davis in *Thin Ice* (1937), Ethel Merman and the Raymond Scott Quintet in *Happy Landing* (1938), Glenn Miller and His Orchestra in *Sun Valley Serenade* (1941), Sammy Kaye and His Orchestra in *Iceland* (1942), and Woody Herman and His Orchestra in *Wintertime* (1943). Sonja Henie's films were also movies with musical trimmings.

Unlike Shirley, Sonja was not especially adept at line readings, as Zanuck realized. At a story conference (August 1, 1936), he outlined the format for a Sonja Henie film: "Be sure she has as little and simple dialogue as you can get by with. Give her only questions and answers, questions which are questions, answers which are direct statements." He did not have to add, "Throw in an ice capade finale," which was a given, except for *Everything*

Happens at Night (1939), a world-on-the-brink-of-war melodrama, in which Sonja was miscast as the daughter of a Nobel Prize winner who has escaped from a concentration camp. While Shirley's films had some neatly plotted screenplays (especially *Poor Little Rich Girl, Little Miss Marker,* and *Rebecca of Sunnybrook Farm*), Sonja's were simply excuses for her virtuoso skating. Writers hauled out the old templates: "a star is born" (reporter helps Sonja become a famous skater in *Once in a Million*); mistaken identity (Sonja mistakes a prince for a reporter in *Thin Ice*); the romantic trio (Sonja is caught between two men in *Happy Landing, Second Fiddle, Everything Happens at Night, Iceland,* and *Wintertime*).

Sun Valley Serenade (1941), in addition to being her best film, is also her most atypical. It includes a non-skating production number with Phil Coney and the Dartmouth Troubadours (actually, Glenn Miller and His Orchestra) rehearsing, "Chattanooga Choo Choo," one of the big song hits of the period. The orchestra plays it, and Tex Beneke whistles and sings it—first to the men of the Modernaires and then to the sole woman of the popular vocal group which, in 1941, consisted of Ralph Brewster, Bill Conway, Harold Dickinson, and Paula Kelly. After the Modernaires make the song into a mellow quartet, a quick pan to the left reveals a mockup of the title train, before which Dorothy Dandridge and the Nicholas Brothers do some fancy tapping. Dandridge was an astonishingly good dancer, and the Nicholas Brothers had no peers when it came to doing a round of splits. Sonja actually had to do some acting as a war orphan sponsored by John Payne, who expected to find a child at Ellis Island but instead found a nubile Norwegian. When band singer Lynn Bari senses a rival in Sonja, she announces that she and Payne are engaged. Determined to have Payne for herself, Sonja fakes an injury, requiring her to spend the night with Payne at a ski lodge. Naturally, Sonja ends up with Payne, who would also be her costar in *Iceland*. But Sonja's mischievous smile and her seemingly guileless nature made her character a devilishly interesting refugee.

Except for *Sun Valley Serenade*, Sonja's nine films for Zanuck have some thrilling skating sequences that leave one in awe of her art, but in no way do they have the charm and staying power of Shirley Temple's.

CENTENNIAL SUMMER (1946):
A MUSICAL WITH NON-SINGERS

The oddest musicalized film that Twentieth Century-Fox—or any studio—produced during Hollywood's Golden Age is *Centennial Summer* (1946), which was Zanuck's answer to *Meet Me in St. Louis* (MGM, 1944). If MGM could make a musical set at the time of the Louisiana Purchase Exposition of 1904, commonly known as the St. Louis World Fair, Zanuck could make one about the Centennial Exposition of 1876 in Philadelphia. But there is nothing in *Centennial Summer* comparable to the thrilling "Trolley Song" number in *Meet Me in St. Louis* or to Judy Garland singing "Have Yourself a Merry Little Christmas" to the misty-eyed Margaret O'Brien.

At least Garland could sing. None of the principals in *Centennial Summer*—Jeanne Crain, Linda Darnell, Cornel Wilde, William Eythe, Constance Bennett—were known as singers. Although Bennett sang in *Moulin Rouge* (1934), she was primarily regarded as an actress equally adept at drama (*What Price Hollywood?*, *Bed of Roses*, *Sin Town*) and comedy (*Topper*, *Topper Takes a Trip*, *Two-Faced Woman*). Eythe's limitations as a singer were apparent when he was cast as the husband of a woman on whom the god Jupiter has designs in Cole Porter's *Out of This World* (1951), a modern retelling of the Amphitryon myth. Eythe did not have a solo in *Centennial Summer*, and in the ensembles he was dubbed by David Street; Crain by Louanne Hogan; and Wilde by Ben Gage. Supposedly, Darnell sang "Up with the Lark" in her own voice. Avon Long, who played Sportin' Life in the 1942 revival of *Porgy and Bess* and could both sing and dance, enlivened the otherwise static proceedings with his rendition of "Cinderella Sue."

Centennial Summer would have fared better as a non-musical, a period piece like *Heaven Can Wait* (TCF, 1943) or *Margie* (TCF, 1946), but Zanuck was determined to musicalize Albert E. Udell's novel of the same name, with a score by none other than Jerome Kern (1885–1945), who received $100,000 for ten songs, which eventually became six. The first title to appear on the screen was "Jerome Kern's *Centennial Summer*," which made it seem as if it were the composer's film, which must have come as a surprise to Otto Preminger, who directed and produced it. Kern was an interesting choice of composer. In the 1940s, he wrote the scores for two popular Columbia Pictures musicals, *You Were Never Lovelier* (1942), with Fred Astaire and Rita Hayworth; and *Cover Girl* (1944), with Gene Kelly and Hayworth; and one for Universal Pictures, *Can't Help Singing* (1944), with Deanna Durbin. Zanuck knew that MGM was planning a Kern biopic, *Till the Clouds Roll By*, which began filming in September 1945, around the same time as *Centennial Summer*, which was nearing completion when Kern died of a cerebral hemorrhage on November 11, 1945. Since *Till the Clouds Roll By* was planned as a musical biopic, producer Arthur Freed halted production so that the script could be rewritten. *Centennial Summer* premiered in August 1946; *Clouds*, in January 1947. The latter grossed well over S6 million; *Centennial Summer*, which cost $2.275 million, made just $3 million. Although both films featured Kern's songs, *Centennial Summer*, the composer's last score, had a paltry six, only one of which became popular, "All Through the Day," recorded by Frank Sinatra, Doris Day, and Margaret Whiting. *Till the Clouds Roll By* had about twenty-five, including, in addition to the title song, "Who?," "Look for the Silver Lining," "Make Believe," "The Last Time I Saw Paris," "They Didn't Believe Me," "All the Things You Are," "The Way You Look Tonight," and "Ol' Man River," the last sung by Frank Sinatra.

The *Centennial Summer* main title sequence is in the form of a colorful sampler with the film's title given, auteur style, as "Jerome Kern's *Centennial Summer*," followed by members of the cast. The embroidered credits suggest a piece of Americana, which the film is to some extent, particularly in its stylish production and period costumes. The plot is another matter. The first scene suggests political satire. The US president, unnamed but obviously Ulysses S. Grant, is delivering a prepared speech on July 4, 1876, at the Centennial Exposition. As the camera tracks back into the crowd, his voice becomes increasingly less audible, annoying Jesse Rogers (Walter Brennan), who expresses his displeasure, insisting that he and his wife Harriet (Dorothy Gish) and their daughters, Julia and Edith (Jeanne Crain and Linda Darnell, respectively) leave after being shushed by a man whom he calls a Republican. When Philippe (Cornel Wilde), a handsome French man arrives from Paris with Harriet's sister, the worldly Zenia (Constance Bennett), he and Julia are immediately attracted to each other. Although Edith is engaged to Ben Phelps, an obstetrician (William Eythe), she informs her sister that she intends to steal Philippe from her. Such pettiness is not the stuff of musicals, but rather of the women-as-rivals film (Norma Shearer and Joan Crawford in *The Women*; Bette Davis and Mary Astor in *The Great Lie*; Bette Davis and Miriam Hopkins in *Old Acquaintance*). When Edith deceives Philippe into believing that Julia is engaged to Ben, Julia and

Ben retaliate by pretending to be in love, infuriating Edith and confusing Philippe. To complicate matters, Harriet thinks her husband is becoming infatuated with Zenia, who is more interested in snaring the president of the railroad where Jesse works. At the end, Zenia and Edith redeem themselves to ensure a happy ending. Zenia convinces the president of the railroad to buy Jesse's invention, a clock that indicates the different time zones. Edith apologizes to Ben, and the whole family sees Zenia off at the train station. The president of the railroad has already boarded as Zenia waves goodbye, and the final shot of the Rogers family and the daughters' prospective husbands freezes into a framed picture complementing the sampler-like main title.

The few songs do not so much "drop" into the film, as Zanuck would say, as arrive at certain points. At a nightclub, an entertainer (Larry Stevens) sings the ballad, "All Through the Day," during a magic lantern show and leads the patrons in a singalong. It is a lovely moment but adds nothing to the plot except to introduce one of the last songs Kern wrote, which was nominated for a best song Oscar, losing to "On the Atchison, Topeka and Santa Fe" from *The Harvey Girls*. But the most unusual number in *Centennial Summer* occurs in a saloon where Philippe and Jesse are commiserating with each other over jiggers of whiskey—when suddenly a Black man in a brown suit and white top hat struts in followed by some children. It's the great Avon Long, who launches into "Cinderella Sue," a girl from the other side of town with "patches on her gown." He moves sinuously, raising his hat as the children tap with him. Then, just as mysteriously, he exits followed by the children who scramble for the coins the patrons throw on the floor. The liberal Preminger may have wanted to give the multi-talented Long a cameo appearance, although he obviously knew that the number would be cut when *Centennial Summer* was shown in the South. Preminger himself had little to say about the film, except that he would never make it "today" since "neither the story nor the characters would interest me today [i.e., 1970]." *Centennial Summer* resembles a Twentieth Century-Fox musical only because it has a finale with a reprise ("Up with the Lark"), a curtain call in the form of a group picture of the cast, and a symmetrical plot (two women paired off with the right men, and their aunt with her latest conquest). Otherwise, it is just a movie with six songs set during America's centennial.

Chapter 13

REPLACEMENT BLONDE
Betty Grable

If Zanuck saw Betty Grable (1916–73) in any of her unmemorable 1930s movies, including *Pigskin Parade* (1936), best remembered as Judy Garland's feature film debut, she left no impression. It was not until three years later, when Betty appeared in the supporting cast of Cole Porter's delightfully bawdy *Du Barry Was a Lady* (1939), that he took note. Betty and Charles Walters, a superb dancer who went on to become a major director at MGM, sang the witty duet, "Well, Did You Evah," which Frank Sinatra and Bing Crosby made famous in *High Society* (MGM, 1957). The influential drama critic Brooks Atkinson wrote favorably of Betty and Walters (less so of the show) in the *New York Times* (December 7, 1939), noting that they "dance and sing with remarkable dash," which was impressive enough to bring them to Hollywood.

DOWN ARGENTINE WAY (1940)

Betty's first starring vehicle was *Down Argentine Way* (1940), which was never planned for her. Zanuck had originally intended Betty and Alice Faye to costar in *Tin Pan Alley* (1940), perhaps to find out which of the two the public preferred. Alice had been slated for *Down Argentine Way*, but for reasons that have never been satisfactorily explained (appendicitis or an altercation with Zanuck), the role went to Betty, who was better suited to it. At any rate, *Down Argentine Way* made Betty a star. She did not have to risk comparison with Alice; her only competition was Don Ameche's seductive baritone and some magnificent racehorses. And those who saw *Down*

Argentine Way after *Tin Pan Alley*, released within a month of each other (the former in October 1940; the latter in November), might have wondered what Betty was doing in a black-and-white movie like *Tin Pan Alley* after being photographed to great—and glamorous—advantage in Technicolor.

Down Argentine Way is a strangely disjointed film. The billing is also askew: the names of Don Ameche, Betty Grable, and Carmen Miranda appear above the title. At least, Betty and Ameche play characters: she, an American horse lover; he, the son of a horse breeder; and together they not only fall in love, get a horse trained as a jumper to run a race, and win over Ameche's father who bears a longtime grudge against Betty's.

CARMEN MIRANDA PLAYS HERSELF

After Miranda, "the Brazilian Bombshell," opened on Broadway in the musical revue, *The Streets of Paris* (1939), Zanuck immediately signed her, realizing that she and her band, Banda de lua, were what the studio needed to promote President Franklin D. Roosevelt's Good Neighbor Policy, which the president implemented to ensure friendly relations between the United States and Latin America, especially important in 1939 after Hitler invaded Poland, setting off a world war. *Down Argentine Way*, Miranda's first film, was released several months after the fall of France and Norway. The war in Europe made American isolationism problematic. If the United States should be forced to enter a conflict that was becoming increasingly global, it would need all the allies it could get, including Latin America, which had previously suffered from the United States' involvement in its political affairs.

Except for a brief return to Broadway in *Sons o' Fun* (1941), with Olsen and Johnson, to which she added some class to a pedestrian revue, Miranda remained in Hollywood for the rest of her movie career, which ended with *Scared Stiff* (Paramount, 1953), starring Dean Martin and Jerry Lewis. Many Latin Americans found Miranda overdressed and over-accessorized and felt she was projecting an image that was not representative of their culture. Others believed she had betrayed her heritage, exchanging it for fame as outsized as her persona. Still, she was extremely popular during the war years. While she was appearing in *The Streets of Paris*, she was invited to the White House, probably because someone believed she would be a good advertisement for the Good Neighbor Policy. In *Springtime in the Rockies* (1942), when John Payne sees Miranda in her signature costume, he exclaims, "Good neighbors!" In *The Gang's All Here* (1943), Phil Baker referred to her as the "Good Neighbor Policy." Since *Down Argentine Way* was planned as Miranda's debut, once Alice dropped out, it became Betty's film, with Zanuck personally taking credit as producer: "Produced by Darryl F. Zanuck, Associate Producer Harry Joe Brown." Brown had worked at several studios both producing and directing before coming to Twentieth Century-Fox in 1938, producing *Alexander's Ragtime Band*, *Tailspin*, and *Hollywood Cavalcade*, among other films. Since *Down Argentine Way* was Zanuck's project, Brown, best known in the next decade for producing a series of Randolph Scott westerns, functioned as line producer, keeping the film on budget and on schedule.

There was another reason *Down Argentine Way* appealed to Zanuck: horses, specifically one horse, Furioso, who is a character in his own right. Horses and sex were Zanuck's great passions besides filmmaking. He grew up with horses and treated them as equals, and sex was a relaxant he required in the afternoon to alleviate the tensions of the day. Zanuck conceived of *Down Argentine Way* as a musical retread of *Kentucky* (TCF, 1938), also a Darryl F. Zanuck production, which provided the writers, Darrell Ware and Karl Tunberg, with the basic plot points: lovers from horse-breeding families (Loretta Young and Richard Greene), one of which (Greene's) is the sworn enemy of the other; a climactic Derby race in which the dark horse wins the cup; and the removal of the obstacle (Walter Brennan) in the way of true love.

Since *Kentucky* has tragic overtones (a murder and a death from heart failure), the plot had to be altered to work as a musical, keeping the same opposing families theme and setting the action in the present (1940), minus *Kentucky's* 1861 prologue. In performing a *Kentucky* makeover, the writers retained the plot points (lovers from feuding families, a vengeful patriarch, a prize-winning dark horse) and achieved a successful resolution not by killing off the patriarch but by disclosing the real reason for his animosity. In *Down Argentine Way*, Glenda Crawford (Betty) is on the verge of buying a prize steed from Ricardo Quintano (Don Ameche), when his father learns her identity. Years ago, their fathers became estranged for reasons that are explained at the end. Meanwhile, Glenda and Ricardo fall in love. Glenda, who seems to know more about horses than Ricardo, believes that the beloved Furioso (the renamed Bluegrass from *Kentucky*) is a born racehorse, not a jumper, as Ricardo's father maintains. They secretly enter Furioso in a horse race, and despite some Machiavellian meddling (a substitute jockey), Furioso wins, and Glenda produces a document, showing that her father saved Ricardo's father from scandal when he became involved with a disreputable woman. End of film proper and beginning of finale with reprises of some of the songs.

It is clear that Zanuck thought of *Down Argentine Way* as a new type of musical, at least for Twentieth Century-Fox. Zanuck told William Goetz, his executive assistant, to solicit associate producer Harry Joe Brown's opinion on John O'Hara's first thirty-five pages of the *Down Argentine Way* script. Zanuck was put off by the direction the script was taking. It had a sophistication that was out of place in a movie in which the characters, despite their wealth, were unsophisticated. (Whatever O'Hara had written was never used.) Zanuck did not want Noël Coward-like dialogue that was witty, urbane, and aphoristic. The movie is "a musical comedy [which] should have the pace of a show like *The Man Who Came to Dinner*," referring to Kaufman and Hart's 1939 hit comedy that would be filmed by Warner Bros. the following year. Zanuck admired the playwrights' "frank" dialogue, meaning that it was direct, without subtext or nuance, as opposed to O'Hara's, in which "no one says what they mean."

Zanuck wanted the musical numbers in *Down Argentine Way* to be similarly honest—not so much advancing the plot as enhancing it: "We don't want to make any effort to explain the music or prepare for it." In other words, the numbers just *happen*. Periodically, Betty and Ameche will sing either alone or together, and Betty will also dance. Although Zanuck claimed that his approach differed from that of a Broadway musical, essentially it was the same: people sing sometimes, speak at other times, and dance when they are doing neither. In a musical, stage or screen, anyone can express him- or herself in song and dance: cowboys and farm hands (*Oklahoma!*), a barker and a mill worker (*Carousel*), a planter and a nurse (*South Pacific*), or even a leprechaun and an Irish lass (*Finian's Rainbow*). Why not a horse seller (Ameche), a horse buyer (Betty), and her aunt (Charlotte Greenwood)? To Zanuck, the musical numbers must seem natural, rising out of the action either because, at certain points, the characters apparently prefer to express their feelings through song rather than words; or because the movie needs a song or a production number either to create a mood or fill in the hollows of the plot. When Betty and Don Ameche (let's dispense with their characters' names) are becoming serious about each other—she in a white blouse and a red-and-blue striped skirt (very American) and he in a gleaming white tux (very continental)—they sing "Two Hearts Met," in which they affirm their love. Because Charlotte Greenwood needed a song, she is given one, "Sing to Your Senorita," at a festival, which she sings while dancing around in a circle and doing her specialty kicks. The idea of a middle-aged American woman in a long skirt, surrounded by Argentinians and dancing up a storm, makes no narrative sense, but who cares? Everyone is in an exuberant mood which Greenwood reflects in her uninhibited performance.

The first musical number is also unrelated to the plot. After the color-ful main title with the credits in yellow against a blue background with a horse and dancer motif at opposite ends of the frame—metonyms for the film itself—Carmen Miranda comes on all in red: ruffled top, red skirt, and red bandana headband, and moving her hands expressively as if she were casting a spell. She sings "South American Way" (she pronounces "south" as "souse"), gyrating discreetly. The song isn't even a prologue; it's a scene-setter, whose only purpose is to tell the audience, "You're not in North America any longer." But the song works because Miranda performs it so naturally that you accept her unusual dress and delivery as part of her persona. Miranda, who at the time was appearing on Broadway in *The Streets of Paris*, was unable to travel to Los Angeles. Instead, Zanuck sent a crew to New York where they spent five weeks filming her three numbers, which were edited into the film. If the studio could also release *Tin Pan Alley* in 1940, it is because the *Down Argentine Way* exteriors had already been filmed in Buenos Aires. *Tin Pan Alley*, shot in black-and-white, was a soundstage creation.

The next musical sequence, a three-part one, is a typical Twentieth Century-Fox production number. Ameche has invited Betty for a drink. When she arrives at the club in a beaded light blue top and black skirt, he is seated at the piano in a tux singing the title song in Spanish as if he were part of the entertainment, which he clearly is not, even though he is dressed like a pianist in a cocktail lounge. But Ameche looks so much at home that you might think it's his nightly gig. Betty listens and then sings the song in English, after which she dances a rhumba to the same music, tapping in heels and creating ripple effects in her hips. Couples move onto the dance floor, as the camera cranes up to provide an overview of the room. Ameche joins Betty, and the tempo changes. It's waltz time, and when the music is over, the two of them move dreamily onto the terrace. A production number that had nothing to do with the plot ends in romance, which has everything to do with it.

Another such production number occurs in a nightclub where Miranda is the star attraction. She sings "Bambu Bambu" and the better known "Mamãe Yo Quero." But Miranda was upstaged by the extraordinary Nicholas Brothers, who sing the title song in Spanish and then perform a routine that combines tap, flips, twists, and splits. They can also go into a split and remain in that position while sliding around the floor. Always a pleasure to watch, the Brothers briefly return for the finale, in which Betty, in a red-and-gold gown with a ruffled top, does a brief rhumba. Charlotte arrives as if on stage to repeat her signature kicks, and Betty and Ameche in profile reprise "Two Hearts Met." The finale was similar to the ending of a stage musical, in which the entire cast would often reprise some of the songs after the last bows. Zanuck recreated the essence of a Broadway musical. Even in Twentieth Century-Fox's non-show-business musicals, the format was generally the same: the characters switch from speech to song so casually that what they sing is really a continuation of the scene; and instead of a simple denouement, there is a finale with reprises (*Down Argentine Way*, *Week-End in Havana*, *That Night in Rio*).

The typical Broadway musical is in two acts; so are Zanuck's musicals. The first half of *Week-End in Havana*, ends with John Payne agreeing, and then regretting, to become Carmen Miranda's manager. Alice, who has grown attracted to Payne, assumes he is more interested in Miranda than in her. On the stage, this would be the cue for the lights to dim on a despondent Alice and a slow curtain. Zanuck had brought Broadway to Hollywood. He did it again in *Tin Pan Alley* (1940) when John Payne tells Alice he has given *her* song, "America, I Love You," to the famous Nora Bayes. Cue for slow curtain coming down on a crushed Alice.

TIN PAN ALLEY (1940)

In *Tin Pan Alley*, Alice and Betty are a sister act, with Alice getting the best songs. Betty may have had second billing, but hers was really a supporting role. Although John Payne was third-billed, he was Alice's costar. If Betty could have two films in release in 1940, it was because she had comparatively little to do in *Tin Pan Alley* both in terms of plot and production numbers. Both *Down Argentine Way* and *Tin Pan Alley* were relatively short: 89 and 94 minutes, respectively. When *Down Argentine Way* went into production on Stage 9 in June 1940, the Buenos Aires footage and Carmen Miranda's numbers had already been filmed. It was an easy shoot, as was *Tin Pan Alley*, which started filming on the same soundstage two months later.

Shot in black-and-white, *Tin Pan Alley* was a revamped *Alexander's Ragtime Band*, with song publishers (Payne and Jack Oakie) instead of a band leader (Tyrone Power). Payne, who specialized in playing career-driven chauvinists, is a song publisher in search of a hit song and so determined to get one plugged that he deliberately spills wine on Betty's gown in a nightclub so that Alice could go on in her place and introduce "On Moonlight Bay," which she sings as if she were taking a stroll down memory lane. To keep Alice from going to Chicago with her sister to star in a show, Payne has Oakie run off with her luggage. By now, Alice had mastered the art of playing women sacrificed to a man's monomania: her eyes turn misty, and she suffers in silence—until the unforgivable occurs when Payne gives her song, "America, I Love You," to Nora Bayes. End of act one. Alice joins her sister in London, where they attain stardom in record time, as one would expect in a movie that runs a little over ninety minutes.

In *Alexander's Ragtime Band*, it was Power who went abroad and turned his band into an orchestra, while Alice went into oblivion. In both films, the leads (Power and Payne) join the army and see action in World War I, which flies by in a montage, culminating with "ARMISTICE" and a victory parade. Since there are two sisters, each will end up with a potential mate: Alice with Payne, as if the film could end any other way, although anyone following the plot closely might question the permanence of a marriage between a star and a failed song publisher; and Betty with a Brit (John Loder). Oakie will continue as Payne's sidekick in *The Great American Broadcast* (1941) and eventually pair off with June Havoc in *Hello, Frisco, Hello* (1943) and *When My Baby Smiles at Me* (1948).

Alice had the best material and made the most of it. She does a bouncy "You Say the Sweetest Things," which she and Payne later sing as a duet. In 1940, Archie Gottler and Edgar Leslie's "America, I Love You" (1915), with its flag-waving lyrics ("It's your land, it's my land / A great do or die land"), seemed more suited to the present, when it was only a matter of time before belief in a "do or die land" would be put to the test, than to the past, when that belief had been tested in the Great War and found wanting. The song, which begins softly and swells into a march, was perfect for Alice's lower register that was a dusky contralto. Others join in: Payne at the piano, an accordionist and three teenage girls, a quartet of three string players and a pianist, and four female trumpet players, ending with the return of Alice and Payne in full voice, singing with patriotic fervor. You had the feeling you were at a recruitment rally rather than in a music publishing house.

Alice and Betty appear twice as a sister act. The first was a Hawaiian number in which they wore tinsel-like grass skirts; the second, in a London revue performing "The Sheik of Araby" in a tacky harem setting dressed in equally tacky billowy pants and golden tops. The poor Nicholas brothers, bare chested, did some spectacular leaps and splits, but the sequence itself was so supremely vulgar that it seemed more appropriate to a house of burlesque than a theater in London's West End. Betty had one solo, "Honeysuckle Rose," with a segue into "Moonlight and Roses" wearing a daring split gown that showed off her million-dollar legs. Anyone seeing *Tin Pan Alley* before *Down Argentine Way* would have seen a star in the making. And anyone who saw *Down Argentine Way* first would have seen a star.

There is a running plot line in the film that became a trope in songwriter musicals: the quest for the right title (for example, MGM's *Lady Be Good* [1941] and *Three Little Words* [1950]). Oakie is constantly trying to come up with the opening lyrics to a song that celebrates a country—Hawaii, Alaska, Bermuda—which would in turn determine the title. Nothing seems to be working until the end when Payne calls Alice by her character's name, Katie. Eureka! The song title becomes the pentasyllabic "K-K-K Katie," which forms the finale, with Alice marching alongside Payne, and Betty alongside John Loder.

After her success in *Down Argentine Way*, there was no doubt that Betty would star in *Moon Over Miami* (1941), although for a time her costar was rumored to be either John Payne or Dana Andrews. Since Betty and Don Ameche were such a compatible team in *Down Argentine Way*, Ameche not only became the male lead but was also top-billed. It was the same in *Moon Over Miami*, but after that, and throughout the 1940s, it was Betty's name that came first in the credits.

MOON OVER MIAMI (1941)

Like *Tin Pan Alley* and *Down Argentine Way*, *Moon Over Miami* was a derivative; its source was the 1938 Twentieth Century-Fox comedy, *Three Blind Mice*, in which three sisters from Kansas (Loretta Young, Pauline Moore, and Marjorie Weaver) use their inheritance to hunt for rich husbands in Santa Barbara. One finds a millionaire as well as love; the other two, just love. In the remake, two sisters (Betty and Carol Landis), who work at a Texas drive-in where their aunt (Charlotte Greenwood) is the cook, take what is left of their inheritance and fly to Miami for the same purpose. Betty passes herself off as an heiress, with Carole as her secretary and Charlotte as her maid. As in *Three Blind Mice*, one (Carole Landis) finds a millionaire (Robert Cummings); the other two, love—in one case, with a twist. That Betty would end up with Ameche is a foregone conclusion. The twist is that he once was wealthy and might be again in five years. Meanwhile, he will be selling refrigerators in Brazil, where Cummings will be managing one of his father's businesses. Since Charlotte and Jack Haley provided the comic relief, they naturally pair off, like Marjorie Weaver and the lovable buffoon, Stu Erwin, in the original.

The *Moon Over Miami* screenwriters, Vincent Lawrence and Brown Holmes, replicated the structure of *Down Argentine Way*. The main title functioned as an overture comprised of music from the score, in this case "Miami (Oh Me, Oh Mi-Ami)" and "You Started Something." The musical numbers adhered to what had now become the Zanuck principle: insertion at various points in the narrative either as a response to a cue that is really a set up for a song, or as a spontaneous occurrence, as if the characters simply decided to sing, but doing it so naturally that song becomes an alternative form of speech. To paraphrase Archibald MacLeish's "Ars Poetica," a musical number should not mean but be. When Betty and her entourage enter their Miami hotel suite, the manager says effusively, "You have made Miami so happy," prompting Betty to sing a bit of "Miami (Oh Me, Oh Mi-Ami)," joined by Landis and Greenwood. If there is to be a scene with Ameche and Betty in a boat gliding down a flower-banked stream at Cypress Gardens, the setting is too romantic to be without music, so Ameche sings "Loveliness and Love" so enticingly that although Betty would prefer Cummings for his money, she realizes that Ameche has something money cannot buy.

There should be an occasion for a production number, such as a victory at a racetrack (*Down Argentine Way*) or a party celebrating the engagement of Betty to Cummings (*Moon Over Miami*), at which Cummings discovers he is really in love with Landis, leaving the field open for Ameche. Since Betty had demonstrated the art of the rhumba in *Down Argentine Way*, she moves on to the conga in *Moon Over Miami*. Wearing a two-piece outfit, shimmering white top and matching skirt with a silver stripe, she launches into "Kindergarten Conga," sung to nursery rhymes ("Ring Around the Rosey," "Goosie, Goosie Gander"). There is no logical reason for the conga, except the logic of reverse repetition: a rhumba in one film, a conga in another. Betty does both with such finesse that it does not matter who her character is. You're not watching Glenda Crawford (*Down Argentine Way*) or Kay Latimer (*Moon Over Miami*). You're watching Betty Grable. Similarly, Charlotte Greenwood may be playing a maid, but no maid could do high kicks like Greenwood and also extend one of her legs so Jack Haley could pass under it. Although Alice had two films in 1941, *Week-End in Havana* and *That Night in Rio*, neither showed her at her best. *Moon Over Miami* was a triumph for Betty, who was on her way to becoming Twentieth Century-Fox's movie musical queen.

Chapter 14

ZANUCK'S BROADWAY

S tage musicals end in several ways, sometimes dramatically (the return of Emile de Becque in Rodgers and Hammerstein's *South Pacific*; the death of the King in Rodgers and Hammerstein's *The King and I*); others with a finale, sometimes a grand one. Although the title song in Jerry Herman's *Hello, Dolly!* (1964) is not the last number in the show, it feels like it is, coming so close to the end and done with such great style, as Dolly in an iridescent red gown descends the staircase at the Harmonia Gardens, that you tend to forget that the last song in the show is the lilting "It Only Takes a Moment." No musical ended as shatteringly as Jule Styne's *Gypsy* (1959) in which Momma Rose goes into meltdown as she rails against her burlesque queen daughter, boasting that she could have been a star if she had someone to goad her on as she did Gypsy.

TWO ACTS, REPRISES, AND CURTAIN CALL

Once the denouement occurs, there is often a reprise before the final curtain. Although the movie version of *Guys and Dolls* (1955) ends with a double wedding (Sky and Sarah, Nathan and Adelaide), the last scene in the original has Sky already married to Sarah and now, a reformed gambler, banging the drum in the mission band. Finally, Nathan and Adelaide are about to marry—and at the Save-a-Soul mission, no less. Once the plot is resolved, the cast reprises the title song, and the curtain falls. There were reprises at the end of the three South American musicals: *Down Argentine Way*, *Week-End in Havana*, and *That Night in Rio*. In *Moon Over Miami*, the three couples are at Miami Beach—Betty in a white bathing suit—a preview of the one she wore in the famous 1942 pinup that was taped to many a GI's locker during the war. Betty and Ameche sing a bit of "You Started Something," as do Landis and Cummings. Greenwood and Haley reprise a few lyrics from their big number, "Is That Good?" The end credits are the equivalent of exit music. In many stage musicals, the orchestra remains in the pit, playing a medley of the show's songs as the audience files out. It is the same with movie musicals with end credits. Those in *Moon Over Miami* come on the screen accompanied by "Miami (Oh Me, Oh Mi-Ami)"; the ones in *Springtime in the Rockies*, with the movie's hit song, "I Had the Craziest Dream."

Although the traditional screenplay follows the three-act (situation-complication-resolution) principle, the stage musical, for the most part, is a two-act creation. The first act advances to a point where a reversal or a new development is imminent. At the end of act one of *Guys and Dolls* (1950), Sky Masterson and Sarah Brown return from a trip to Havana, where, after too many *dulces de leche*, she becomes amorous, and both discover they are in love, the gambler and the "Mission Doll." When they return to New York, they learn that, in Sarah's absence, the Save-a-Soul mission had been used for a crap game. Sarah blames Sky, who is innocent, and their relationship is in jeopardy as the curtain falls. The shorter second act has Sky making amends by offering the gamblers a proposition: $1,000 to each if he loses, but if he wins, they must all show up at the mission for a prayer meeting. Sky wins, marries Sarah, and joins the mission band. Nathan is about to marry Adelaide, and the cast reprises the title song.

In *Tin Pan Alley*, there is a break in the action when Alice's character discovers that John Payne has given her song, "America, I Love You," to Nora Bayes and decides to join her sister in London. If this were a stage musical, you could imagine the curtain slowly descending as Alice fights back tears, perhaps singing a few lines of *her* song in a broken voice. The second act adheres to the "star is born" template (male's star wanes, female's waxes). Act one of *Springtime in the Rockies* ends with Betty Grable throwing John Payne's engagement ring out the window after learning that he had come up to Lake Louise to lure her back to Broadway. Act two picks up with Betty searching for the ring and discovering Payne doing the same. There are some more misunderstandings, followed by a question of "will they or won't they do another revue?" and ending with the revue, this time a team effort without interference from producers.

Like *Down Argentine Way, Week-End in Havana,* and *That Night in Rio,* the finale of *Springtime in the Rockies* also includes a curtain call of sorts. In the other musicals, the leading players return to reprise excerpts from their numbers. In *Down Argentine Way,* it was Charlotte Greenwood doing her signature kicks, and Betty and Ameche reprising their duet. In *Week-End in Havana* and *That Night in Rio,* the reprises featured the principals standing alongside each other—Alice Faye, John Payne, Cesar Romero, and Carmen Miranda in the former; Don Ameche, Alice Faye, and Carmen Miranda in the latter—as if they were on a stage. The *Springtime in the Rockies* finale, "Pan American Jubilee," is the concluding number of both the revue and the film, a combination common in backstage musicals. The grand finale of MGM's *Broadway Melody of 1938* is both the final number of a lavish revue and the movie's conclusion. The *Springtime in the Rockies* (TCF, 1942) finale is different for uniting all of the principals: Betty, John Payne, Cesar Romero, Carmen Miranda, Charlotte Greenwood, Harry James, and Edward Everett Horton. Harry James blows his trumpet; the chorus demonstrates the difference between a rhumba and a samba; Miranda in a white gown trimmed in purple fur dances a samba with Romero; Betty and Romero do a sexy jitterbug; Charlotte does some kicks; and Edward Everett Horton does some clowning. At the end, the stars advance toward the camera as if they were walking toward the footlights for a curtain call. "I Had the Craziest Dream" is heard during both the main title and the end credits. Helen Forrest also sang it with Harry James and His Orchestra. Forrest, perhaps the best vocalist of the swing era, was sadly underutilized. She sang the song in long shot, walking through a crowd and onto the band stand without ever receiving a close-up. Helen Forrest may not have been glamorous, but few band singers could equal her in warmth and expressiveness.

Although using music from the score for both the main title and end credits had now become commonplace in musicals, the curtain call finale had not, perhaps because it was considered a theater convention. Zanuck seemed to be looking for some way to make the Twentieth Century-Fox musical unique, knowing it could never match the quality of MGM's best. The classic MGM musicals—*The Wizard of Oz, Meet Me in St. Louis, Singin' in the Rain, Seven Brides for Seven Brothers, It's Always Fair Weather*—were truly movie musicals. Even when some of them were converted into stage musicals, they became the equivalent of an adaptation, a version of the original. On the stage, *Meet Me in St. Louis* (1989) emerged as a family musical, not a work of art. The work of art was created for the screen. What Zanuck had to offer was Broadway-style entertainment, musicals without any depths to plumb or ideas to ponder. No one in a Zanuck musical would ever react the way Judy Garland did at the end of *Meet Me in St. Louis* when she attends the Exposition: "I can't believe it. Right here where we live. Right here in St. Louis." "Naiveté" was not in Zanuck's lexicon.

It was probably Zanuck's idea to replicate the form of a two-act Broadway show, although he must have had the encouragement of William LeBaron, who joined Twentieth Century-Fox as a producer early in 1940 after a highly successful stint at Paramount. LeBaron had the most diverse background of any producer on the lot. At New York University, he wrote the lyrics, and Deems Taylor the music, for four varsity shows. LeBaron's first stage credit was *The Echo* (1910), for which he wrote the book with Deems Taylor. LeBaron was also the librettist and lyricist of *The Half Moon* and *The Yankee Princess* (1922). Two of his plays were made into movies: *The Very Idea* (1917), filmed under the same title in 1929, and *Something to Brag About* (1925), filmed as *Baby Face Harrington* (1935), directed by Raoul Walsh.

At Twentieth Century-Fox, LeBaron produced such musicals as *Week-End in Havana*, *Song of the Islands*, *Footlight Serenade*, *Springtime in the Rockies*, *The Gang's All Here*, *Pin Up Girl*, and *Greenwich Village*. As a librettist, lyricist, and playwright, LeBaron probably understood theater better than Zanuck. If it was Zanuck's idea to bring Broadway to Hollywood, LeBaron facilitated the journey. But it does seem that Zanuck was thinking along such lines as early as 1937 with *On the Avenue*, which ends with the principals sitting together in Billy Gilbert's diner and reprising Irving Berlin's "Slumming on Park Avenue," which makes the ending a quasi-curtain call as well. MGM may have been the studio that legitimized the musical as an art form, but it was Zanuck who raised it to the level of theater, creating a type of entertainment that brought Broadway razzle-dazzle to the screen. Generations based their idea of a Broadway show on Zanuck's screen musicals, and seasoned theatergoers understood that the Twentieth Century-Fox musical was soundstage Broadway, the perfect marriage of performance and technology, seamlessly edited into an organic whole.

The reprises in Zanuck's musicals are theatrical in context but at the same time unlike reprises in most Broadway musicals. Basically, a reprise is the recurrence of a song in a musical to indicate that the character has changed since the first time he or she sang it. Ideally, that should be the case—as it is in Jerome Kern's *Show Boat* (1927), when "Ol' Man River" is reprised once in act one and twice in act two, each time after a significant plot development. Joe, the stevedore, sings it after Magnolia asks him for advice about the gambler Gaylord Ravenal, to whom she is attracted. Joe tells her that Ravenal is a familiar type on the river and then remarks that she should really ask the Mississippi, which is oblivious to human emotions and just "keeps rollin' along." He sings a bit of it again when Magnolia and Ravenal become romantically involved, and the stevedores hum it when Ravenal proposes to Magnolia, intimating that this will not be a marriage made in heaven.

Near the end of act two in *Show Boat*, Joe, now a much older man, sings "Ol' Man River" again, making the lyrics more meaningful. The river cannot know, nor would it care, that Ravenal abandoned Magnolia and their daughter Kim. He sings it one last time after a repentant Ravenal returns, and the family is reunited. Such perfect integration of reprise and narrative is exceedingly rare. A character may reprise a bit of his or her song to express a new state of mind. But a reprise is not an encore, just a portion of the original number. At the end of Rodgers and Hart's *Pal Joey* (1940), Vera Simpson has discovered how unprincipled Joey is and says so, reprising the end of "Bewitched, Bothered and Bewildered" but with different lyrics—not "Bewitched, bothered, and bewildered am I," which she sang when she was infatuated with him, but "Bewitched, bothered and bewildered no more." There are all kinds of reprises in Broadway musicals. In the classic 1952 revival of *Pal Joey*, the cast reprised "I Could Write a Book" at the end; in Cole Porter's *Out of this World* (1951), the company reprised the show's only hit song, "Use Your Imagination." In Jerry Herman's *Hello, Dolly!* (1964), music associated with the characters was played during the curtain call: "Put On Your Sunday Clothes," when the chorus comes on; "It Only Takes a Moment," when the romantic leads do; and, of course, the title song, when the actress playing Dolly parades across the runway. In *The Gang's All Here*, Alice Faye sings "Journey to a Star" twice—first feelingly as a romantic ballad when James Ellison asks for a song, then ruefully when she believes Ellison and Sheila Ryan are engaged. She sings "You'll Never Know" twice in *Hello, Frisco, Hello*—first as a number in John Payne's show, then at the opening of his new music hall, suggesting that, despite her fame, she is willing to return to her roots on the Barbary Coast. In each case, the reprise was a sign that the character had undergone a change of heart. Zanuck's reprise-curtain call finales were his attempts to bring the Twentieth Century-Fox musical into the Broadway orbit.

If Zanuck's musicals exude a theatrical aura, it is partly because the performers had worked on Broadway (Alice Faye, Betty Grable, Carmen Miranda, Dan Dailey, Charlotte Greenwood, Sheree North); in straight plays (Tyrone Power); as band singers (June Haver, Vivian Blaine); in stock (Don Ameche, John Payne); in ballet (Mitzi Gaynor); and in radio (Perry Como). Zanuck was partial to the big bands and often featured them in his movies: Harry James and His Orchestra (*Springtime in the Rockies*, *Do You Love Me?*, *If I'm Lucky*, *I'll Get By*); Benny Goodman and His Orchestra (*The Gang's All Here*); Glenn Miller and His Orchestra (*Sun Valley Serenade*, *Orchestra Wives*); Sammy Kaye and His Orchestra (*Iceland*); Woody Herman and His Orchestra (*Wintertime*); and Charlie Spivak and His Orchestra (*Pin Up Girl*). In a class by herself was Marilyn Monroe, who had no theatrical background. But as a model, she understood the camera and knew how to put her body to maximum use when she appeared in her first starring vehicle, *Ladies of the Chorus* (Columbia, 1949), in which she played the daughter of a burlesque star who became one herself. When Marilyn performed "Every Baby Needs a Da-da Daddy" strutting down the runway, it seemed as if she was a regular on the Minsky circuit. It took Zanuck a while to see that Marilyn had a natural affinity for musicals, which she proved in *Gentlemen Prefer Blondes* (1953) and especially in *There's No Business Like Show Business* (1954).

Zanuck, more than any other studio head, brought the Broadway style to the film musical and hired producers like William LeBaron and George Jessel to authenticate it with a two-act structure, musical numbers inserted at the right moments in the plot, reprises, and, in some cases, a group curtain call. Zanuck may not have had the same feeling for musicals as Arthur Freed, but he understood the appeal of "naughty, bawdy, gaudy, sporty Forty-Second Street." He should know. At Warner Bros., he "supervised" one of the best.

Chapter 15

THE LADY WITH THE MILLION DOLLAR LEGS

In 1942, Twentieth Century-Fox released three Betty Grable musicals: *Song of the Islands* in February, *Footlight Serenade* in August, and *Springtime in the Rockies* in November. There was no Alice Faye movie that year; Alice gave birth to her first daughter on May 19, 1942. When she returned to the studio later that year, it was business as usual. In 1943, two Betty Grable musicals were released: *Coney Island* in June and *Sweet Rosie O'Grady* in October; and two with Alice: *Hello, Frisco, Hello* in March and *The Gang's All Here* in December. Betty had one film in 1944, *Pin Up Girl*, released in April. Alice had nothing, unless you count her cameo in *Four Jills in a Jeep* (1944), in which she sang "You'll Never Know"; and Betty, "Cuddle Up a Little Closer, Lovey Mine." By the time that *Fallen Angel*, Alice's last film for Zanuck, opened in late fall 1945, she had left the studio.

For a time, Zanuck was thinking of Betty as the flip side of Alice, able to do any picture Alice could. The plot could remain intact, although the production numbers, especially the dance sequences, would have to be cut to the specifications of the Grable persona: lavish, a bit bawdy, leggy whenever possible, skirts slit up the side, and costumes that conjured up images of exotic plumage. Zanuck would have agreed with Billy Flynn in Kander and Ebb's *Chicago* (1975): "Give 'em the old razzle dazzle/Razzle dazzle 'em." And Zanuck did.

CONEY ISLAND (1943)

Zanuck considered *Coney Island* and *Hello, Frisco, Hello* bookend attractions, the former set at the turn of the twentieth century and the latter, around 1915. Both were period pieces, in which a performer graduates from saloon singer (*Coney Island*) or vaudevillian (*Hello, Frisco, Hello*) to musical comedy star. *Coney Island* was an original screenplay by George Seaton, although it was another obscurity-to-fame musical on the order of *Rose of Washington Square* and *Alexander's Ragtime Band*, and a two-men-competing-for-the-same-woman plot like *Springtime in the Rockies*. *Hello, Frisco, Hello* was a remake of *King of Burlesque*, with Alice recreating her original role. *Coney Island* would be remade as *Wabash Avenue*, with Betty playing the same role but with a different name. Just as *Down Argentine Way* was planned for Alice but became a breakthrough film for Betty after Alice bowed out, *Coney Island* seems to have been originally planned for Alice, according to the *Hollywood Reporter* (January 20, 1941), with Laird Cregar and Pat O'Brien in the roles that eventually went to Cesar Romero and George Montgomery, who were far more suited to them.

Zanuck was uncertain about what form the *Coney Island* script would take. At one point, he seemed to see it as a piece of Americana rather than a musical, an authentic recreation of the famed amusement park during the "gay nineties." The *Hollywood Reporter* (September 28, 1942) then announced that Ann Rutherford would be starring in the film, which would make sense since she was neither a singer nor a dancer. By that time, Alice was about to go into *Hello, Frisco, Hello*, leaving Zanuck no other choice but to rethink the project as a musical with Betty. Oddly, the *Los Angeles Times* (February 6, 1943) reported that Betty and Carole Landis were to have been in *Hello, Frisco, Hello*. That, of course, never happened, and the roles in question were played by Alice and June Havoc. Zanuck realized that the characters in both films were practically interchangeable and that either actress could play them. Yet it was to Zanuck's credit as a creative producer that he sensed, in the way that only a true production head can, that Alice would have been better in *Hello, Frisco, Hello* than Betty, who would have been more believable in *Coney Island* than Alice. Yet he thought of *Hello, Frisco, Hello* and *Coney Island* as companion pieces, each opening with an establishing sequence—the former, with a tracking shot of the main attractions of the Barbary Coast; the latter, with a montage of various attractions at the amusement park.

Of Betty's two 1943 movies, *Coney Island* is considered the better, although Betty herself preferred *Sweet Rosie O'Grady*. In *Coney Island*, she was caught up in a tug-of-war between two men (George Montgomery,

Cesar Romero) who have been double-crossing each other since boy-
hood—cheating at cards, undermining each other's business ventures, and
using their star attraction (Betty) as a pawn, with Romero going so far as
to ruin her wedding day. Yet when Romero inadvertently admits what
he had done, the disclosure is just another example of the men's ongoing
chicanery, which leaves Betty in the middle as each tries to outdo the other
in treachery. Betty only demonstrates she has a will of her own when she
signs with Willie Hammerstein, who stars her in a musical revue at the
Victoria Theatre owned by his father, Oscar. Petty cavil: the historical Willie
Hammerstein was not a producer but a theater manager, and the Victoria
at the turn of the century was a vaudeville house.

When Montgomery takes over Romero's saloon, he also takes over Betty,
who can't seem to perform any number standing still. To transform her
from a saloon singer into an artist, he cuffs her ankles and wrists, covering
the manacles with the feathers he has plucked off her dress. As a result, she
has to stand without moving and render "Cuddle Up a Little Closer" as a
warm ballad, not as the jazzed-up ditty she was singing as she bounced
around the stage during rehearsals. From that point on, Betty is a class act,
except for one flagrant lapse of taste. In "Miss Lulu from Louisville," Betty
is tarted up in a gaudy blouse, purple skirt, slit up the side (naturally), and
shiny black wig. She is also in brownface, dancing as if her last gig was in a
Caribbean dive with male dancers who looked as if they had just dropped
in from a minstrel show.

Except for the love ballad "Take It from There," the other numbers are
pleasantly forgettable. The three-part finale, which is the same as the one at
the Victoria Theatre, is oddly entitled "There's Danger in a Dance," although
peril is not lurking anywhere. In the first segment, Betty dances elegantly
in a gold gown; then the scene changes to the Old South, with Betty as a
Southern Belle, complete with hoop skirt and pantaloons, dancing with
the great Hermes Pan, who again becomes her partner in the concluding
sequence with Betty back to her old self in an anachronistic red ruffled
dress, feathered headdress, and boa, doing a tango and then some real jive
with Pan, which was more 1943 than 1899. At this point, the plot trickles
in for the denouement. The crowd demands an encore, and Betty with
an armful of roses glances into the pit and notices that Montgomery has
replaced the conductor. (She always sings better when he conducts.) He
smiles up at her, she smiles back, and Romero's machinations give way to

true love. *Coney Island* ends with a Twentieth Century-Fox specialty: a reprise-curtain call, with Betty reprising "Take It from There" and, in the final close-up, acknowledging her audience both at the Victoria Theatre and wherever the film is shown.

SWEET ROSIE O'GRADY (1943)

For most of *Coney Island*, Betty was an object of manipulation by two men. In *Sweet Rosie O'Grady*, she is her own woman, free to choose between a muckraking journalist (Robert Young) and a duke (Reginald Gardiner).

Sweet Rosie O'Grady was not exactly a musical remake of *Love Is News* (1937), but instead a musical setting of a similar plot. In *Love Is News*, a reporter (Tyrone Power) has written a series of unflattering articles about an heiress (Loretta Young), who retaliates by falsely announcing that they are really engaged. With two such attractive performers in the roles, the battle of the sexes could only end with a fade-out embrace.

In *Sweet Rosie O'Grady*, the heiress became the darling of the English musical stage, Madeleine Marlowe, née Rosie O'Grady from Brooklyn, who began her career in burlesque. She presumes her past has been buried until reporter Sam Magee (Robert Young) unearths it and turns it into tabloid copy. To even the score, Madeleine/Rosie informs the press that they are engaged and that she will be supporting him since he cannot do the same for her on his salary. When Magee suggests they declare a truce and meet for lunch at Delmonico's, Madeleine makes a diva's entrance and plays Juliet to his Romeo, much to the amusement of the patrons. He then has a song composed about her, "Sweet Rosie O'Grady," sung all over New York. In the battle of the sexes, each party keeps scoring points until the final round, which ends in a tie. But just when it seems that love has conquered pettiness, the duke, who had been courting Madeleine in London, arrives unannounced and is appalled at the news stories about his intended. The feud starts up again with Madeleine introducing a number in her show, making fun of Magee by singing to an actor wearing a Magee-like mask. Magee could have retaliated by allowing his editor (Adolphe Menjou) to publish Madeleine's love letters to the duke, but he is too much of a gentle-man and too smitten with Madeleine/Rosie to descend to such treachery. Besides, the duke has found a more compatible future wife in Madeleine's social secretary (Virginia Grey).

Despite the screwball plot, *Sweet Rosie O'Grady* defies—but does not strain—credulity, except for Grey's character, who is said to be fabulously wealthy, although why she's working pro bono for Madeleine is never explained. She is a plot device, a consolation prize for the duke, which turns the trio into a quartet with both couples headed for the altar. While there is no curtain call finale, there is a real stage exit, with Madeleine and Magee departing the newspaper office, as if they were exiting the stage as the curtain is about to descend, which it does cinematically as "The End" appears on the screen. A Twentieth Century-Fox musical would not be complete without a reprise. In *Sweet Rosie O'Grady*, there are four reprises of "My Heart Tells Me." Phil Regan introduces it while Betty is bathing, so she will have some idea of what it sounds like. Then she sings it in her bath. When Magee brings her, unwillingly at first, to the beer garden where her career began, she sings it for the patrons and privately for him. The other musical numbers look as if they were taking place in a theater. The director Irving Cummings maintained the illusion of a live performance by starting the numbers with a view of the orchestra pit and the first couple of rows. Since the time is the 1880s, the footlights were candlelit—an authentic touch in an otherwise conventional musical.

By 1943, Betty had become Zanuck's favorite blonde. But he was also grooming another blonde, Carole Landis, as a possible replacement for Betty, believing that there must always be a successor if the star proves difficult or is no longer an audience favorite. Zanuck tried to showcase Landis as both a musical comedy star (*Moon Over Miami, My Gal Sal*, and to lesser effect in *Dance Hall* and *Cadet Girl*) and a dramatic actress (*I Wake Up Screaming, Manila Calling*). Although Landis was an attractive performer, there was nothing distinctive about her. She could have had a career as a supporting actress or an occasional lead in a B movie since she was always believable, as she proved when she played Betty Grable's sister posing as her mousey secretary in *Moon Over Miami*, blossoming into a desirable woman when Robert Cummings begins to notice her. Landis had a short-lived career. Her despondency over a failed relationship with Rex Harrison drove her to suicide in 1948 at the age of twenty-nine.

By 1943, Betty Grable had no equal on the Twentieth Century-Fox lot. Carole Landis was never a threat, nor was June Haver, who arrived a year later. Haver was Betty's reverse image: fresh-faced and winsome. She could also sing and dance. The two costarred in *The Dolly Sisters* (1945), but it was clear that Betty was the main attraction. Haver held her own in Zanuck's lesser musicals (*Irish Eyes Are Smiling*, *Where Do We Go from Here?*, *I Wonder Who's Kissing Her Now*). When she played Marilyn Miller on loan to Warner Bros. in the musical biopic, *Look for the Silver Lining* (Warner Bros., 1949), it was hard to believe that this was the Marilyn Miller, the queen of musical comedy, whose statue adorned the top of what was once the I. Miller Shoe Company Building at 1552 Broadway. In his *New York Times* review (June 24, 1949), Bosley Crowther delivered his verdict: "The vapid appearance of Miss Haver is a token of the little she has to give." That may have been too strong: she had charm and a modest talent, but if Zanuck thought of her as Betty's replacement, he was soon disabused of that notion. In fact, there was nothing distinctive about her last films. *I'll Get By* (1950) was another Zanuck retread, this time of *Tin Pan Alley* with Haver and Gloria DeHaven in the roles created by Alice and Betty, and William Lundigan and Dennis Day as the songwriters played by John Payne and Jack Oakie in the original. Believing she had a vocation to the consecrated life, Haver joined the Sisters of Charity of Leavenworth (Kansas) early in 1953 and left after eight months, presumably for health reasons. She returned to the studio for one last film, *The Girl Next Door* (1953), with Dan Dailey and Dennis Day. The following year, she married Fred MacMurray and retired from the screen.

Betty's only real competition and possible replacement at Twentieth Century-Fox was Marilyn Monroe, but that would not become an issue until the early 1950s. When Betty was the top box-office attraction of 1943, Marilyn was Mrs. James Dougherty living with her Merchant Marine husband on Catalina Island, where he was stationed. That year it occurred to Zanuck that, although Betty had become America's number one pinup girl after Frank Powolny photographed her in a white bathing suit, looking over her right shoulder with a beckoning smile, he had not starred her in any musical with a World War II setting. All the other studios had gotten on board: Universal (*When Johnny Comes Marching Home*), Paramount (*Star Spangled Rhythm*), Warner Bros. (*Thank Your Lucky Stars*, *Hollywood Canteen*), MGM (*Thousands Cheer*), RKO (*The Sky's the Limit*), and Columbia (*Cover Girl*).

PIN UP GIRL (1944)

Twentieth Century-Fox's contribution was appropriately entitled *Pin Up Girl* (1944), with references to the war effort inserted into the lyrics of any song that could accommodate them, such as Martha Ray's "Yankee Doodle Hayride," a tribute to the farmers of America, lauded as the "soldiers of the soil." The main title showed Betty in her iconic bathing suit with the credits in blue and white, accompanied by "Anchors Aweigh" and "The Marine's Hymn" on the soundtrack, which left no doubt that *Pin Up Girl* was the studio's tribute to the red, white, and blue. The plot was one of Betty's weakest. She played the star-struck Lorry Jones, a former USO entertainer from Missoula, Missouri (Betty was born in St. Louis), now working as a clerk-typist for the government. When she lies her way into a swank nightclub, claiming she is the guest of navy hero Tommy Dooley (John Harvey), she passes herself off as Broadway's Laura Lorraine, a deception that requires Betty to shift back and forth from prim stenographer to glamorous star for the rest of the film. Anyone should have been able to tell the difference, even with Betty's plain hairdo and horn-rimmed glasses, but Dooley can't until the end of the film, which is the only way the masquerade can work as a plot device. As Laura Lorraine, Betty has a chance to do a bit of dirty dancing with the great dancer-choreographer Hermes Pan in "Once Too Often," in which she acts the floozy in a tight skirt and gaudy blouse, telling her lover that he has cheated on her once too often. The number is a Hollywood-style Apache dance, stopping short of parody but showing that Betty and Pan understood that this kind of dancing, which is more music hall than Broadway, is effective only if the dancers take it seriously, even if the audience only considers it a routine. "Once Too Often" prefigures the sexier "Honey Man" in *Wabash Avenue* (1950), the closest Betty ever came to doing bumps and grinds.

Pin Up Girl includes an unusual reprise: a song repeated in its entirety, which was rarely done. To prove to Dooley that she is both Lorry and Laura, Lorry reprises "Don't Carry Tales Out of School," which she sang for the first time at the nightclub. When it's time to wind up the masquerade, Lorry, dressed in a business suit and looking like a schoolteacher, sings it again, so that Dooley will know that the sympathetic stenographer and the woman of his dreams are one and the same. Then it's time for the two-part grand finale, Twentieth Century-Fox's equivalent of a recruitment pitch, which might have had a greater impact two years earlier. In spring 1944, when *Pin Up Girl* was released, the war was winding down, and the drill at the end seems like another production number. Even on that level, the finale is a subtle transition from a song about a merry widow, who gave up night life for war work, to a military exercise involving two platoons of women commanded by a uniformed Betty.

In part one of the *Pin Up Girl* finale, Betty comes on in a black gown singing "The Very Merry Widow," the story of a widow who loved doing the latest dances until the war came. Now "this merry little widow is a busy little widow / Working for the USA." The scene changes to Betty on Stage 14, putting two platoons of women (actual members of the Women's Auxiliary Corp or WAC) through their paces, shouting, "Hip, hip, hip, ho." As she barks instructions, you almost expect her to break into "Sound Off!" any minute. The drill is almost expressionistic in style with its strong horizontals and geometric deployment of the women as they break off into squads, changing direction with awesome precision. Betty did not look like herself in a dull uniform and visored cap with a saber at her side. The pinup girl is now a platoon leader. That sequence said more about the country's military strength than any other musical of the period. And the close-up/ curtain call had Betty holding the saber against her face, as if to say, "Don't worry. Your favorite pin up girl will get you through the rest of the war."

DIAMOND HORSESHOE (1945)

Betty's popularity was at its peak. She might not have been making musicals for connoisseurs, but her appeal to mass audiences was undeniable. *Diamond Horseshoe* (1945), also known as *Billy Rose's Diamond Horseshoe*, might have made a bigger profit if it cost less to make; it came in at $2.6 million but only netted $3 million in rentals. The problem was recreating the ambience of Billy Rose's legendary nightclub in the basement of New York's Paramount Hotel. From 1938 to 1951, the Diamond Horseshoe was one of Manhattan's classiest night spots. Revues featured statuesque women in exotic costumes, reproduced in the film by Charles LeMaire, head of women's wardrobe, who had worked for Flo Ziegfeld and Billy Rose and who urged his designers—Sascha Brastoff, Bonnie Cashin, René Hubert, and Kay Nelson—to strive for authenticity.

Although George Seaton's screenplay seemed to have been original, it was really inspired by (rather than adapted from) Kenyon Nicholson's drama *The Barker* (1927), in which the son of a carnival barker decides to quit law school and join his father in the tent show business. The son falls in love with a performer and marries her much against his father's wishes, but eventually returns to law school. Seaton took the same Oedipal conflict, changing the setting from a carnival to the Diamond Horseshoe, where the father (William Gaxton) is the headliner, and the son (Dick Haymes) is a medical student eager for a career in show business who becomes attracted to a showgirl (Betty). It's not just a father-son-woman as career obstacle script. Seaton added a few more twists and counter twists to a plot that is considerably more complicated than Nicholson's.

The father's lover (Beatrice Kay) offers Betty a mink coat in return for distracting the son long enough so she can get his father to marry her. The plot is too convoluted for a 104-minute movie with seven production numbers, three reprises of "I Wish I Knew" and one of "The More I See You." Betty's character is too decent for such machinations and actually tells Haymes the truth. But when she sees him save a diabetic stage hand from death, she realizes that he is meant to be a doctor, which he eventually becomes. But with Haymes in the role, the doctor will be one of the smoothest crooners in the ER.

The musical numbers feature chorus girls in feathered headdresses and shimmering gowns and two songs that became hits, "I Wish I Knew" and "The More I See You." Betty even sings a chorus of "You'll Never Know" in a sequence intended for 1940s hepcats, with Gaxton and Kay extolling the music of the past ("Play Me an Old Fashioned Melody") and Betty voicing the sound of the present ("A Nickel's Worth of Jive"). "You'll Never Know" is a ballad that will be forever associated with Alice Faye. Betty's version, in a canted shot and backed up with four men in silhouette, seemed to belong somewhere else, perhaps in a musical short. If Alice saw the film, she probably shook her head. The second number in *Diamond Horseshoe* is "Cooking Up a Show," in which Gaxton impersonates a chef extoling various spices and herbs, all represented by women wearing appropriately decorated hats (bedecked with sage, parsley, etc.). In the final number, Gaxton is now a desert chef showing off his specialties with women in hats topped with apple pie, a chocolate cake, and even Jell-O. Then Gaxton steps out of character and says, "Time for a reprise," signaling the end of both the revue and the movie. He and Betty reprise "The More I See You," with Haymes adding his voice off stage. When Gaxton spots Beatrice Kay sitting by herself, he has her join them, and the reprise becomes a curtain call finale, an appropriate touch for a musical that begins and ends at one of New York's fabled clubs.

Diamond Horseshoe was released in May 1945. Five months later, a much bigger hit arrived: *The Dolly Sisters*, with Betty, John Payne, and June Haver. The Dolly Sisters, Jenny and Rosie, were Hungarian-born identical twins who came to America with their parents early in the twentieth century and established themselves as a sister act. They played in vaudeville, toured Europe, and returned to America to appear in the *Ziegfeld Follies*. Eventually they went their separate ways and occasionally reteamed. Jenny's marriage to Harry Fox, a singer and dancer, ended in divorce. Rosie Dolly was married three times, but you would never know it from the film. Jenny developed a passion for expensive jewelry and gambling, fleetingly suggested in the film, and required plastic surgery as the result of an auto accident caused by her driver not through her own recklessness, as portrayed in the film, which also ignores her final years of depression that became so acute that she hanged herself in her Hollywood apartment on June 1, 1941.

The Dolly Sisters was no better or worse than most musical biopics. The writers, John Larkin and Marian Spitzer, were highly selective in their choice of facts, sticking to them when it was safe and resorting to embellishment and invention when it was not—"safe," defined as material suited to a family musical. Actually, they had no other choice. Rosie, who survived her sister by almost thirty years, sold the rights to their story to Twentieth Century-Fox on the condition that no mention be made either of Jenny's adoption of two Hungarian orphans or her suicide. Larkin and Spitzer knew that no matter how they reconfigured the sisters' lives, the final draft had to be one for a Betty Grable movie, with a narrative structure and storylines that would be familiar to her fans. If Alice Faye had played Jenny, as the *Hollywood Reporter* (May 28, 1943) announced, the production would have been tailored to her persona. Betty was not even considered for either sister. The lesser role of Rosie would have been unsuited to America's number one box-office attraction. Zanuck was considering, among other actresses, Vivian Blaine and Janet Blair for Rosie. Since Betty was pregnant with her first child, Victoria Elizabeth, born on March 3, 1944, filming was delayed until Betty completed *Pin Up Girl*. By that time, Alice was ready for *Fallen Angel*, released in October 1945, the same month as *The Dolly Sisters*.

In a biopic, accuracy is important when it matters, which is only occasionally. Betty (Jenny) and June Haver (Rosie) looked and dressed like sisters, blonde and fair, while their historical counterparts were not. And the film's Harry Fox (John Payne) is a triple threat: singer, dancer, and songwriter—an important addition since a song, or rather two songs, are plot points. The writers were fortunate to have a director, Irving Cummings, who began his career on the stage as a member of Lillian Russell's company and had directed Betty in *Down Argentine Way*, *Springtime in the Rockies*, and *Sweet Rosie O'Grady*; and a producer, George Jessel, who, like the Dolly Sisters, began in vaudeville at the age of ten and probably knew them. The result was a musical no different from the other Betty Grable movies (*Down Argentine Way*, *Springtime in the Rockies*, *Coney Island*, *Sweet Rosie O'Grady*, *Pin Up Girl*) that preceded it. But since the Sisters also performed in the *Ziegfeld Follies* and the *Folies Bergère*, the production numbers would be more elaborate than those in any of Betty's previous films.

Any Betty Grable movie had to be consistent not only with the star's screen image but also with the visual style of her—and other Twentieth Century-Fox—musicals, including such elements as:

—An **Establishing Shot** at the beginning to indicate time and place. First, a title: New York 1904. A trolley goes up a colorful New York street. (Compare the opening sequence in *Coney Island* with the various attractions.) Two of the passengers are the preadolescent Dolly sisters and their uncle, who is seeking out a compatriot at the Little Hungary Cafe. While the two men are playing cards, the sisters began entertaining the patrons.

—**Next title:** New York, 1912. The sisters are now the main attraction at the Little Hungary and about to embark upon a career in vaudeville.

—**The Meet Different** (not cute, but rude or embarrassing): John Payne, who boasted to the sisters that he is a headliner, is forced so share billing with them and a trained seal act, much to his embarrassment.

—**Production Numbers:** The swankier the venue, the more elaborate the number. Betty's wardrobe changed when she graduated from saloon singer to musical comedy star in *Coney Island*, as did Alice Faye's in *Hello, Frisco, Hello*. When the sisters appear in the *Ziegfeld Follies*, they are part of a world in which less is never acceptable and more means most. The parsley and chocolate cake hats in *Billy Rose's Diamond Horseshoe* were quaint compared to the high camp of "Powder, Lipstick and Rouge," with showgirls appearing as "Lady Lipstick," "Patricia Powder," "Patty Powder Puff," "Rosie Rouge," and "Mascara" in a white gown decorated with eyes. "The Darktown Strutters' Ball" begins elegantly with African American showgirls gracefully descending a staircase when suddenly the mood is interrupted by the sisters' coming on in blackface, their hair in paper curlers and wearing dresses short enough to reveal their bloomers. Among Hollywood's many blackface numbers, this is one of the most offensive in its portrayal of the Black child as frolicsome "darkie."

—**Marriage vs. Career:** In *Tin Pan Alley* and *Hello, Frisco, Hello*, John Payne proved adept at playing men who expect women to conform to their chauvinist code. If a performer has a chance to go big time, she should forego it. And if she is a star like Jenny Dolly, she must bypass the opportunity to appear in the *Folies Bergère* and remain on Long Island as Mrs. Harry Fox. Betty prefers Paris to the island, and divorce to being a homemaker.

—**Joining the Army:** When Payne broke up with Alice in *Tin Pan Alley*, he joined the army. In *The Dolly Sisters*, Payne enlists without telling Betty and then expects her to give up an opportunity for international stardom while he is fighting to make the world safe for democracy. Rarely has a musical been as sexist as *The Dolly Sisters*. A husband can sign up even before he is drafted without telling his wife, whom he expects to keep the home fires burning until he returns even if it means breaking her contract.

—**The Big Song:** In *Hello, Frisco, Hello*, it was "You'll Never Know," first sung by Alice and reprised at the end; and in *Diamond Horseshoe*, "The More I See You," introduced by Dick Haymes and sung again at the finale. There are two big songs in *The Dolly Sisters*, both sung first by John Payne: James V. Monaco and Mack Gordon's "I Can't Begin to Tell You" and the ever-popular "I'm Always Chasing Rainbows," with lyrics by Joseph McCarthy and music attributed to

Harry Carroll, who adapted it from Chopin's "Fantasie-Impromptu in C minor."

—**The Reunion:** It should take place on a stage: Carnegie Hall in *Alexander's Ragtime Band*, John Payne's new saloon in *Hello, Frisco, Hello*; the title venue in *Diamond Horseshoe*. In *The Dolly Sisters*, it's at the All-Star Benefit, where the sisters find themselves on the same program with Harry Fox/John Payne, now a successful songwriter engaged to Trudy Marshall, who knows to whom his heart really belongs, and it's to Betty. In a typical Twentieth Century-Fox finale-curtain call, Betty, Payne, and Haver reprise the two big songs, and the film ends in a three-shot, as if they are acknowledging applause.

THE SHOCKING MISS PILGRIM (1947)

There was no Betty Grable movie in 1946, although she was active during that year making two films, one of which was a personal favorite, *Mother Wore Tights* (1947); the other, *The Shocking Miss Pilgrim* (1947), a feminist curio atypical of the marriage vs. career dilemma movie that was generally resolved in favor of marriage. Even before *The Dolly Sisters* was released, Zanuck was looking for another vehicle for Betty, which turned out to be *The Shocking Miss Pilgrim*. The film went into production in mid-November 1945, completed the following February, and released in early January 1947. It was neither a critical nor a popular success. Bosley Crowther of the *New York Times* (February 12, 1947) was particularly critical of Betty and Dick Haymes who "are neither given nor deserve a script if the caliber of their performances is a valid criterion," concluding that "there is no more voltage in 'The Shocking Miss Pilgrim' than there is in a badly used dry cell." Budgeted at $2.595 million, it only grossed $2.50 million nationwide.

It might have been different if Zanuck had found another project for Betty and retained the plot of *Miss Pilgrim's Progress* by Ernest Maas and Frederica Sager, which Twentieth Century-Fox purchased in October 1939 and had real melodramatic potential. The Maas-Sager story involved a female typist who inadvertently caused the death of a sexually aggressive male employee. There were various attempts to come up with a suitable screenplay over the years, but it was not until writer-director George

Seaton reworked the story, setting it in 1874 when a typist was known as a "typewriter" (an odd form of metonymy in which the name of a machine becomes the job description of its operator). The typist in question is Cynthia Pilgrim (Betty), a recent business college graduate, reluctantly hired by the manager of a Boston shipping company (Dick Haymes) after being pressured by his suffragist aunt (Anne Revere). Cynthia is persuaded to join the woman's suffrage movement, which has a chilling effect on her employer, particularly after he has fallen in love with her. Insisting that a woman's place is in the home, he alienates Cynthia, who quits her job. Unable to find a suitable "typewriter," he visits a typing school for young women that has just opened and asks to see the manager, who, of course, is Cynthia. Chastened, he agrees that women are men's equal, and Betty and Haymes reprise their innocuous duet, "Aren't You Kinda Glad We Did?"— cue for a fade-out reprise-cum-embrace, even if the more appropriate reprise would have been the only memorable song in the movie, "For You, For Me, For Evermore."

Cynthia Pilgrim was a role that required more acting from Betty than usual. In fact, *The Shocking Miss Pilgrim* might have been better as a non-musical with one of the studio's new actresses (e.g., Anne Baxter, Jeanne Crain, Vanessa Brown) in the lead. Betty did what she could with Cynthia Pilgrim, playing her as a young woman of conviction who believes in gender equality. She did not deserve Bosley Crowther's dismissive review.

The score was quasi-original. Ira Gershwin told Zanuck that he and George had written some songs that were never used and for which he would supply new lyrics, if necessary. That indeed was the case, since one of the songs, "Stand Up and Fight," vigorously sung at a suffrage rally, is defiantly feminist and required appropriate lyrics: "Like it or not, men have got to take the view / That women are people, too." The other songs were minor Gershwin, except "For You, For Me, For Evermore," which Haymes crooned with dreamy sincerity, with Betty responding in kind. Since the film was not a show-business musical, Betty was dressed in period clothes that concealed her million-dollar legs. Seaton made sure that audiences at least got a glimpse of them when she discreetly lifted her skirt and later danced around the bedroom in her night gown. But it was not enough to save the film. Zanuck had learned his lesson. In a memo to Preston Sturges (September 30, 1948), who was directing Betty in *The Beautiful Blonde from Bashful Bend* (1949), he applauded the sketch of a split gown designed for

Betty, noting that the comparative lack of leg exposure in *The Shocking Miss Pilgrim* resulted in "a million letters of protest" that nearly sparked "a national furor."

MOTHER WORE TIGHTS (1947)

There was no dearth of limb in *Mother Wore Tights* (1947), which started filming in mid-October 1946, ended in mid-January 1947, and arrived in theaters that September. When production began, Betty was already pregnant with her second child; another daughter, Jessica, was born on May 20, 1947, four months before the film's release. Betty's pregnancy contributed to both the musical's sunny mood and her sympathetic portrayal of a show-business mom. *Mother Wore Tights* was the studio's third highest-grossing film of 1947, bringing in over $4 million in domestic rentals. Adapted from Miriam Young's novel by Lamar Trotti, one of Zanuck's favorite writers, who doubled as producer, the musical was a loving tribute to a bygone era, vaudeville in the age of the two-a-day, when performers went from city to city, often becoming so confused that they misidentified the city they were supposed to be celebrating. Trotti framed the main action with a prologue and epilogue that showed the team of Frank Burt and Myrtle McKinley (later McKinley Burt), Dan Dailey and Betty, in their golden years. The film proper spans the period from 1900 to 1917, the year of America's entry into World War I, which is evident from the sight of Robert Arthur in uniform at the high school graduation of Iris Burt (Mona Freeman), the couple's older daughter.

Mother Wore Tights is stronger on nostalgia than plot. In fact, not much happens until the Burts enroll their daughters in an exclusive boarding school. An incident on a train involving boorish vaudevillians draws derisive comments from Iris's peers, making her ashamed of her parents' profession. She is mortified when she discovers they will be performing in the same town as her school. The couple, knowing their daughter's classmates will be in attendance, put on a stylish show more suited to a supper club than a vaudeville house—he in a spangled tux, she in a decorous white gown in "Rolling Down Bowling Green," the last of a series of numbers showcasing the dazzling variety of Betty and Dailey. Earlier, Dailey, red-nosed and wearing a loud suit, mocked the British upper class in "Burlington Bertie from Bow," which Betty also performed in a black tuxedo, mimicking Dailey's high-toned delivery. Betty also introduced the film's best number, "You Do," in a white sequined gown, brandishing a fan of white feathers as she glided gracefully across the stage. Together, she and Dailey did a charming soft-shoe, "Kokomo, Indiana." They also complemented each other in height: he was 6', 3"; she, 5', 4". Their rapport was evident, particularly when she smiled at him with a look of respectful affection. *Mother Wore Tights* has an unusual reprise for a Twentieth Century-Fox musical. It is actually part of the ending. At her graduation, Iris sings her parents' favorite song, "You Do." Mona Freeman lip-synced perfectly to Imogene Lynn's voice. In fact, if Freeman did the offscreen narration instead of Anne Baxter, with her unmistakably breathy voice, it would have sounded less theatrical.

WHEN MY BABY SMILES AT ME (1948)

When My Baby Smiles at Me, the first of betty Grable's two 1948 musicals, was the studio's fourth most profitable film of 1948, grossing $3.4 million domestically. It was another remake, the third iteration of *Burlesque*, which ran for 373 performances on Broadway during the 1927–28 season and starred Hal Skelly and Barbara Stanwyck as a performing couple whose marriage crumbles when he goes big time, becomes a spendthrift, hits the bottle, and then the skids. They separate and are reunited, but the future is problematic. (*Burlesque* brought Stanwyck to Hollywood, where she became one of the finest actresses of her generation.) Paramount wasted no time in coming out with a generally faithful movie version, *The Dance of Life* (1929), filmed at its Astoria studio in New York, with Skelly recreating the role of "Skid" Johnson and Nancy Carroll as Bonny King, his faithful wife.

Paramount was not finished with *Burlesque*, which became *Swing High, Swing Low* (1937) directed by the (then-) undervalued Mitchell Leisen, with "Skid" (Fred MacMurray) as a trumpeter and Bonny rechristened Maggie (Carole Lombard). Sid undergoes the same trajectory as his predecessors: sudden fame, profligacy, and alcoholism. Although Maggie initiates divorce proceedings, she is so devoted to him that she gets him through a radio broadcast, suggesting possible regeneration, although neither film version went beyond the comeback resolution. *New York Times* critic Frank Nugent was unimpressed, calling *Swing High, Swing Low* "a thin excuse for a film that requires an hour and thirty-five minutes to trace the rise, the fall, and the potential ascendancy of a trumpet king." But that was also the play's trajectory, which any film version was obliged to follow.

The problem is that the milieu portrayed in *Burlesque* with its basement dressing rooms and dingy corridors is so unglamorous that it resists the glossy overlay of star power and, in the case of *When My Baby Smiles at Me*, Technicolor, which gilds the hard-edged world of lowbrow entertainment with its raucous comics, provocatively dressed chorines, and ogling men. *When My Baby Smiles at Me* was another trip down memory lane with Dan Dailey and Betty as the latest "Skid" Johnson and Bonny King in Lamar Trotti's adaptation, which stayed fairly close to the original, making it clear from the opening number, in which Betty parades down a runway singing "Oui, oui, Marie" in a blue costume that ends at the hips, that we are in a house of burlesque. The National Legion of Decency did not object to the costuming or dancing but gave the film a "B" rating ("Morally Objectionable in Part for All") because it "reflects the acceptability of divorce," even though it is evident that Bonny does not marry her wealthy rancher fiancé (Richard Arlen) but remains with her husband, who seems to sober up when she rejoins him to perform one of their old routines.

When My Baby Smiles at Me revealed the full range of Betty's and Dailey's art both individually and as a team. Betty and Dailey stroll across the stage singing "By the Way" as they crack corny jokes. Alone, Betty does the lowdown "What Did I Do?" in a canary-yellow top, tight purple skirt, and a yellow feathered hat, lamenting her bad luck with men outside a waterfront drive, leaving no doubt that this was her beat. Dailey ranges from playing the bulbous-nosed clown in the checkered suit to performing "The Birth of the Blues" as the consummate song and dance man stylishly dressed in top hat and tails. And what would a Twentieth Century-Fox musical be without THE SONG, which, in this case, is Josef Myrow and Mack Gordon's "By the Way," sung first by Betty and Dailey as part of their act; by Betty as a solo; and by the two of them at the end, where logically it does not belong. Skid is given a chance to redeem himself in a new show but arrives semi-inebriated on opening night. Bonny insists she can get him through "By the Way," hardly a song for a "new show" but one that they had performed on numerous occasions. She succeeds, interspersing the lyrics with patter as she convinces him that there was no divorce. Dailey achieves sobriety in record time, and the film fades out with the familiar embrace. Dailey played a self-loathing drunk to the hilt, receiving a Best Actor nomination but losing to Laurence Olivier in *Hamlet*. But to be in the company of Olivier, Clifton Webb, Lew Ayres, and Montgomery Clift was a testament to his talent as a dramatic actor, which had been on view earlier in *Ziegfeld Girl* (MGM, 1941) where he played an ex-prizefighter who preys upon a down-and-out Lana Turner. The nomination made him doubly valuable to the studio, where he was able to act in such non-musicals as *Chicken Every Sunday* (1949), John Ford's *When Willie Comes Marching Home* (1950), Ford's *What Price Glory* (1952), and *The Pride of St. Louis* (1951), in which he played Hall of Fame baseball pitcher, Dizzy Dean.

THAT LADY IN ERMINE (1948)

Whenever Betty starred in a musical that was not a backstager, particularly one set in the nineteenth century where period costumes concealed her world-famous assets, it showed at the box office. *That Lady in Ermine* was Twentieth Century-Fox's lowest grossing film of 1948. Budgeted at $3 million, it only grossed $1.5 million. The musical had a rather long shelf life. It originated as a German operetta, *Die Frau im Hermelin* (1919); it then became the basis of a popular three-act musical, *The Lady in Ermine*, which ran for 238 performances on Broadway during the 1922–23 season; a 1927 silent film of the same name starring and produced by Corinne Griffith, released through First National Pictures, which was absorbed into Warner Bros. in 1929; and as *Bride of the Regiment* (1930) under Zanuck's supervision when he ran production at Warner Bros.

Zanuck was looking for a property for Ernst Lubitsch, who joined the studio in 1943 as producer-director. Zanuck recognized Lubitsch's genius, his smudge-free touch that he applied to romantic comedy in which he could do more with closing a bedroom door than most directors could by keeping it open. Zanuck give Lubitsch "total autonomy," viewing the rushes as he always did, but otherwise letting him "follow his own lead." Innuendo was Lubitsch's trademark, creating an atmosphere that remained coolly sexy even when it seemed to be heating up. In his first Twentieth Century-Fox film, *Heaven Can Wait* (1943), Lubitsch discreetly implied that the French maid (Signe Hasso) did more than tutor her employers' teenage son in French. Lubitsch needed a property that required his immaculate touch to

Darryl F. Zanuck (1902–79).
Courtesy of Photofest

Eugenie Besserer and Al Jolson in *The Jazz Singer* (1927). Courtesy of Warner Bros. Pictures/Photofest.

Ruby Keeler and Eddie Nugent in *42nd Street* (1933). Courtesy of Warner Bros. Pictures/Photofest.

Fanny Brice (1891–1951) in *My Man* (1928). Courtesy of Warner Bros. Pictures/ Photofest.

Alice Faye (1916–98).
Courtesy of Photofest.

Jack Haley, Shirley Temple, and Alice Faye in *Poor Little Rich Girl* (1936). Courtesy of 20th Century Fox/Photofest.

Carmen Miranda in *Week-End in Havana* (1941). Courtesy of Photofest.

Betty Grable (1916–73). Courtesy of 20th Century Fox/Photofest.

Betty Grable and Dan Dailey in *Mother Wore Tights* (1947). Courtesy of 20th Century Fox/Photofest.

America's Favorite World War II Pin Up Girl: Betty Grable in the iconic white bathing suit (1944). Courtesy of 20th Century Fox/Photofest.

Betty Grable and June Haver as Jennie and Rosie Dolly in *The Dolly Sisters* (1945). Courtesy of 20th Century Fox/Photofest.

Left to right, Vera-Ellen, Vivian Blaine, and June Haver as the trio in *Three Little Girls in Blue* (1946). Courtesy of 20th Century Fox/Photofest.

Vivian Blaine and Dick Haymes in Rodgers and Hammerstein's *State Fair* (1945). Courtesy of 20th Century Fox/Photofest.

Jayne Mansfield and Tom Ewell in *The Girl Can't Help It* (1956). Courtesy of 20th Century Fox/Photofest.

Mitzi Gaynor as Nellie Forbush in
South Pacific (1958). Courtesy of
20th Century Fox/Photofest.

Mitzi Gaynor and James Barton in *Golden Girl* (1951). Courtesy of 20th Century Fox/Photofest.

Marilyn Monroe (1926–62). Courtesy of Photofest.

Marilyn extolling the virtues of diamonds in *Gentlemen Prefer Blondes* (1953). Courtesy of 20th Century Fox/Photofest.

Marilyn in the notorious "Heat Wave" number in *There's No Business Like Show Business* (1954). Courtesy of 20th Century Fox/Photofest.

Gordon MacRae and Shirley Jones as Billy Bigelow and Julie Jordan in *Carousel* (1956). Courtesy of 20th Century Fox/Photofest.

Richard Rodgers and Julie Andrews at the world premiere of *The Sound of Music* (1965). Courtesy of Photofest.

Julie Andrews as Gertrude Lawrence in *Star!* (1968). Courtesy of 20th Century Fox/Photofest.

Sheree North (1932–2005). Courtesy of Photofest.

Yul Brynner as the King and Deborah Kerr as Anna in *The King and I* (1956). Courtesy of 20th Century Fox/Photofest.

Rex Harrison as the title character with the two-headed llama in *Doctor Dolittle* (1967). Courtesy of 20th Century Fox/Photofest.

Barbra Streisand performing the title song with the waiters in *Hello, Dolly!* (1969). Courtesy of 20th Century Fox/Photofest.

Ethel Merman and Donald O'Connor performing "You're Just in Love" in *Call Me Madam* (1953). Courtesy of 20th Century Fox/Photofest.

turn a bedroom into a boudoir and passion into verbal and visual foreplay. Remembering *Bride of the Regiment*, Zanuck realized it was a perfect match for Lubitsch: a Hungarian colonel occupying the castle of a countess, whose ancestor dealt with a similar invader three centuries earlier by engaging in an action that saved her kingdom. Would the countess be willing to pay the same price? In short, a will she or won't she movie, Lubitsch's specialty.

By 1946, Zanuck was thinking of the newly titled *That Lady in Ermine* as a non-musical with Gene Tierney—one of his favorite actresses, whom he admired for her excellent work in *Heaven Can Wait, Laura* (1944), and *Leave Her to Heaven* (1945)—in the dual role of the countess and her ancestor, and either Cornel Wilde or Rex Harrison as the Hungarian colonel who lays siege to her castle and falls under her spell, with an assist from her ancestor who steps out of her portrait to save the castle and the countess from having to do what she had done. Lubitsch saw the project as the operetta it originally was and should remain, with Jeanette MacDonald as the countess, whom he had directed in *Monte Carlo* (1930), *One Hour with You* (1932), and *The Merry Widow* (1934). Even if MacDonald were free (she was making *Three Daring Daughters* at MGM), she would have been too mature for the role, particularly if her costar was Douglas Fairbanks Jr., who had been cast as the colonel. Zanuck wanted Betty, even though he knew she could never give the movie the airiness and high style of European operetta. And although the action is set in 1861, there had to be at least one scene in which Betty shows her legs.

Eight days into production, Lubitsch died of a heart attack, and Otto Preminger took over the direction, preferring to remain uncredited in honor of Lubitsch. It showed. Fairbanks claimed Preminger "ruined everything," and that "everything light in the Samson Raphaelson script had been squeezed out." Raphaelson had written two of the most sophisticated comedies of the 1930s, *Accent on Youth* (1934) and *Skylark* (1939), which Paramount bought and made into equally sophisticated movies in 1935 and 1941, respectively. He also understood that an operetta is like a soufflé: lightness is all. Preminger did not have a light touch, and even if he did, Betty could not respond to it. She could be brassy and tender, but the high style eluded her, as it would the studio's other musical stars, June Haver and Vivian Blaine. Since Zanuck purchased the rights to the operetta in 1942, the picture should have been made as a romantic comedy sans music right after *Heaven Can Wait* with Gene Tierney and perhaps Tyrone Power, both of whom would have understood that the script was drawing room comedy transferred to the boudoir. After the failure of *Viennese Nights* (Warner Bros., 1930), Zanuck knew operetta would never be a specialty at Twentieth Century-Fox as it was at MGM. Perhaps Lubitsch could have saved the film from turning into a musical fantasy, but he still would have had to deal with Betty, who understood musical comedy but not operetta.

The opening scenes do not portend well. When the Hungarian troops are advancing on the castle, the paintings in the gallery, which includes one of the Countess Angelina's ancestor Francesca in an ermine robe (Angelina and Francesca are both played by Betty), come to life and, led by Francesca, romp around the hall singing "Ooh! What I'll Do (To that Wild Hungarian)," which does not allow for easy rhyming except with "barbarian." For a musical, there are very few songs. Betty as Francesca sings "The Melody Has to be Right" to Betty as Angelina; and Betty and Fairbanks sing and dance to "This Is the Moment," the film's working title. *That Lady in Ermine* is one of Betty's more plot-heavy musicals, a sign that it might have been better as a non-musical.

Most operettas involve deception and disguise, which is also true of *That Lady in Ermine*. Angelina's husband (Cesar Romero) passes himself off as a violin-playing gypsy to keep tabs on his wife while the colonel and his troops are occupying the castle. When the servant Luigi (Harry Davenport) learns of the colonel's fascination with Francesca's portrait, he tells him that three centuries ago Francesca, barefoot and in an ermine robe, arrived at the tent of the duke who was about to lay siege to the castle. Whatever transpired within caused him to relent. Francesca leaves, and the duke collapses with a dagger in his back. Then the film becomes a "will history repeat itself, and will Angelina give herself to the colonel and then kill him?" kind of story. When the colonel proposes a late supper, Francesca uses her (apparently) preternatural powers to conjure up a dream for the colonel in which she will appear as Angelina. But will she kill him? Spying a carving knife on the table, she throws it at the clock instead of plunging it in his back, thus stopping time as the two of them perform the only decent number in the movie, "This Is the Moment." There have been several sight gags in this sequence, including a screen that moves across the balcony where the musicians are seated, preventing them from seeing what is happening. After the exhilarating "This Is the Moment," the couple is about to ascend the grand staircase, when Betty picks up Fairbanks and carries him to the top where they levitate and crash through the ceiling, as if to suggest that passion knows no bounds.

To satisfy the Production Code Administration, something had to be done about Angelina's marriage. At the end, she comes to the colonel's quarters with a priest; speaking hurriedly, and not very convincingly, Betty/ Angelina informs the colonel that her marriage was annulled (there was no time for consummation) and thus there is no impediment to their union. Not knowing how to end the film, Preminger repeats the "Ooh! What I'll Do" scene with the ancestral chorus prancing around the hall. At least the ending was in the tradition of the reprise/fade-out.

The PCA was satisfied with the resolution, but the National Legion of Decency objected to the film's "light treatment of marriage," which is odd, since in the eyes of the Church, the marriage had been annulled because it was never consummated, as if that mattered. Bosley Crowther, who wrote a favorable review in the *New York Times* (August 25, 1948), did not seem to know that Otto Preminger directed most of the film, which he called "a glittering and mischievous romp," with Betty bringing to the title role "a certain attractiveness of person," while noting that "she isn't as agile with the wit and glance"—understandably. She was used to Walter Lang and Irving Cummings, not a martinet like Preminger.

THE BEAUTIFUL BLONDE FROM BASHFUL BEND
(1949)

Betty did not have any better luck with her next film or with her director, Preston Sturges, who wrote, directed, and produced *The Beautiful Blonde from Bashful Bend* (1949), another musical in name only in which Betty did more acting than singing. She is Freddie, a saloon singer, who also happens to be a sharp shooter with a short fuse. When the bullet intended for her cheating lover (Cesar Romero) hits a judge (Porter Hall) in the butt on two occasions—first in the saloon, then at her trial—she and her Mexican sidekick (Olga San Juan, whose signature expletive is "Go suck an egg") run off to Snake City, where Betty masquerades as a grade school teacher. (Her geology lesson is one for the books.) Two of her students, the mentally challenged (to be euphemistic) Basserman boys, trigger one of Sturges's familiar descents into screwball farce. Wrongly believing that they have been killed, the boys' father demands justice, which gives Freddie a chance to show off her shooting skills, at one point getting the train of her dress pulled off. Her way with a gun is sufficient evidence that she is not a schoolmarm. Back in court, Freddie is about to be cleared when she senses her lover is still playing the field, this time with a French woman (an elegantly dressed Marie Windsor). Again she aims at him, misses and shoots the judge in the butt for the third time. The judge, furious, starts saying something beginning with an "s" and ending in an extended "iss," an unusual pronunciation of the four-letter vulgarism. Since *The Beautiful Blonde from Bashful Bend* wasn't much of a musical, the reprise is the title song sung over the end credits as it was over the main title. Not exactly a commercial failure, the film, budgeted at $2.1 million, grossed $2.889 million domestically.

Always the professional, Betty looked as if she had fun doing the picture, although she reportedly spoke negatively about it to colleagues. Sturges, however, wrote glowingly about Betty, calling her "a splendid actress, capable of any role," and wishing "the story . . . were one-tenth as good as she is." He was right. Since the movie was a farce, it was better suited to her comedic skills than *That Lady in Ermine*, which was a disguised operetta. *The Beautiful Blonde from Bashful Bend* is historically significant for reasons other than Sturges's brief tenure at Twentieth Century-Fox after having made, by Zanuck's standards, two unsuccessful films (the other was *Unfaithfully Yours* [1948]). Sturges worked from an original screen story, "The Lady from Laredo," attributed to Earl Fenton but written by the most famous member of the Hollywood Ten, Dalton Trumbo. Since Trumbo had been blacklisted, Fenton fronted for him. The story in the Twentieth Century-Fox archives at the University of Southern California (USC) and the University of California at Los Angeles (UCLA) is pure Trumbo, writing as a cheeky ironist. It begins with a description of what it was like in 1865 with everyone swindling everyone and settlers "frequently scalped by their passing brothers, the Red men." If Sturges had maintained Trumbo's tone, *The Beautiful Blonde from Bashful Bend* would have been the most politically incorrect film of 1949 if, for no other reason, than the presence of Olga San Juan playing a Mexican impersonating a Native American with a feather sticking out of her headband. When asked about her heritage, she says, "I ain't pure."

The next decade began promisingly with *Wabash Avenue* (1950), a literal remake of *Coney Island* (1943) and even better than the original, which is rarely the case. There would be a few more musicals, none of major importance, and a CinemaScope non-musical, *How to Marry a Millionaire* (1953), with Betty costarring with Lauren Bacall and Marilyn Monroe. Betty's name preceded the others in the credits, but not in the trailer or the ads, where Marilyn's name came first, followed by Betty's and Bacall's. The film seemed to be another iteration of *Three Blind Mice*, which had already been remade twice (*Moon Over Miami, Three Little Girls in Blue*) with the three-women-in pursuit of-wealthy-husbands plot, although the source is more likely the similar-themed Zoë Akins's play, *The Greeks Had a Word for It* (1939). Betty did not sing a note, proving that she did not have to sing or dance to hold her own with two formidable actresses, one of whom was being groomed as her successor—perhaps the most famous Zanuck blonde. Betty probably sensed that her movie career was waning. It would be over in 1955. Then it was on to Las Vegas engagements, summer theater, and finally Broadway in *Hello Dolly!*, as one of the Dolly Gallagher Levis who followed Carol Channing.

Chapter 16

THE POCKET GRABLE

June Haver

She was called the "pocket Grable" either because of her height (5', 2") or because she was the paperback equivalent (paperbacks were then called pocket books) of a bestselling hardcover. All that June Haver (1926–2005) had in common with Betty was a distinct flair for musicals, especially those set in the early decades of the twentieth century. A former band singer, June, blue-eyed and blonde, arrived in Hollywood in 1942 as a Twentieth Century-Fox contract player and, like Jeanne Crain, was given a bit part in *The Gang's All Here* (1943) before graduating to a supporting role a year later. In 1944, Zanuck was looking for an actress of about the same age as Jeanne Crain and Lon McCallister, who were both in their late teens, to play the rival for McCallister's affections in *Home in Indiana* (1944). June, then eighteen, seemed right for the role of the flirtatious "Cri-Cri." The film, with its horse racing plot, meant much to horse-loving Zanuck, who entrusted Henry Hathaway with the direction, resulting in a film of "picturesque abundance," as Bosley Crowther wrote in the *New York Times* (June 24, 1944). As for Jeanne and June: "Neither young lady is a Duse." But then, neither was expected to be anything other than her character: Jeanne, fresh-faced and spunky; June, wholesomely seductive.

Home in Indiana went into production in January 1944 and was released six months later. June was fifth-billed in the ads, seventh in the credits. Zanuck wanted to showcase the trio by giving them their own credit: "And introducing three young players in their first featured role." That was true of Jeanne and June, but McCallister had played a featured role in *Stage Door Canteen* (United Artists, 1943), in which he was unforgettable as the young soldier who confessed to Katharine Cornell, a great Juliet, that he once played Romeo in a high school production. Cornell immediately began enacting the balcony scene with the star-struck McCallister as a touchingly sincere Romeo.

IRISH EYES ARE SMILING (1944)

All Zanuck knew about June was that she was a blonde who had performed with some orchestras including Ted Fio Rito's, in which Betty also sang, but not at the same time. Zanuck saw June as, if not Betty's replacement, then as a mirror image, Betty in reverse: demure even when she had to do a brassy number, attractive without being glamorous, and making up in personality for what she lacked in charisma. He realized he was right when he saw her in *Irish Eyes Are Smiling* (1944), in which she was second-billed. Even Bosley Crowther saw the connection between Betty and June:

> Obviously Betty Grable is not indispensable to those lush Twentieth Century-Fox musical albums in which she has usually appeared. For a new and equally blonde candidate was placed in nomination . . . in "Irish Eyes Are Smiling" and got a surprising hand. . . . Miss Grable has a formidable rival. (*New York Times*, November 8, 1944)

To be fair, June was Betty writ small, schoolgirl sexy, who could play naughty but nice without ever becoming a pin up in a GI's locker. The "pocket Grable" is a good description.

Irish Eyes Are Smiling solidified June's position at the studio once the reviews came out and the money rolled in: $2.250 million. The film was the second of a quintet of musicals about song writers that Zanuck initiated in 1939 with *Swanee River*, a largely fictionalized life of Stephen Foster (1826–1864), with Don Ameche as the composer. Zanuck personally produced it because he associated Foster and his minstrel show music with an America that was still in its Edenic phase, which, of course, it was not. But that did not stop Zanuck from portraying it as such. This was an America where slaves were "darkies"; every Black man, an emanation of Old Black Joe; every young white woman, Jeannie with the light brown hair; and every elderly white couple, the old folks at home, sitting in rocking chairs on their front porch. That was the kind of America that Zanuck longed for when he was a boy, but rarely knew except in the summers that he spent with his grandparents.

Zanuck continued exploring Americana in glorious Technicolor with *My Gal Sal* (1942), suggested by the career of Theodore Dreiser's brother, Paul, who changed his surname to Dresser when he was twenty. Paul Dresser (1857–1906) became a singer-songwriter ("On the Banks of the Wabash"), portrayed by Victor Mature in the film. When Alice Faye turned down the role of the fictitious title character, Sally Elliott, Zanuck approached Columbia's Harry Cohn about loaning out Rita Hayworth. Cohn at first refused but eventually relented. Hayworth looked ravishing in color but seemed to have arrived on the Twentieth Century-Fox lot from an alien planet. She was neither a Zanuck blonde nor a Twentieth Century-Fox musical star, but was cast in an Alice Faye musical without Alice, and with a director, Irving Cummings, who worked exceptionally well with Alice (*Hollywood Cavalcade*, *That Night in Rio*). Hayworth's best musicals were made at her home studio: *You Were Never Lovelier* (1942), *Cover Girl* (1944), and *Down to Earth* (1947), although she is probably better remembered as the femme fatale in Orson Welles's noir masterpiece, *The Lady from Shanghai* (Columbia, 1948).

A more representative Twentieth Century-Fox biopic is *Irish Eyes Are Smiling* (1944), a fanciful recreation of the life of Ernest Ball (1878–1927), who, according to the opening title, wrote "the most sentimental ballads the world has ever known." However, except for a few facts (e.g., his musical training at the Cleveland Conservatory), most of the film is a neatly plotted fabrication, as one would expect from a Damon Runyon inspired story. Even though Earl Baldwin and John Tucker Battle are credited with the screenplay, the film is entitled "Damon Runyon's *Irish Eyes Are Smiling*." Runyon was the producer, not the screenwriter, yet anyone familiar with his stories could sense his spirit in the script. The writers were familiar with Runyon's world of touts, bookies, pool sharks, and gamblers.

Zanuck had a particular fondness for Runyon (1880–1946), partly because their youths were similar. Each had his first publication at age eleven in a local paper: Zanuck's was a letter that his grandfather submitted to the *Sentinel*, Runyon's, a poem published in the *Pueblo Chieftain*. Like Zanuck, Runyon, not quite eighteen, was too young to enlist in the army; instead, he joined a contingent of volunteers on route to the Philippines to fight in the Spanish-American War. Unlike Zanuck, he did not see action, but sent back accounts to the *Chieftain*, as Zanuck had to his grandfather, who sent them on to the *Sentinel*. Zanuck was also attracted to Runyon's stories with their Broadway argot ("elbow" [detective], "blat" [newspaper], "kady" [hat], "ducats" [theater tickets]), and characters with emblematic names ("Blind Benny," "Little Joey," "Nicely Nicely," and "Harry the Horse"). As Colonel Zanuck, he was especially grateful to Runyon for writing the foreword to *Tunis Expedition* (Random House, 1943), Zanuck's diary with pictures describing his experiences at the North African front in November and December 1942. Runyon praised it lavishly, even comparing Zanuck to Richard Harding Davis, who was a role model for journalists, not movie producers.

Damon Runyon's spirit hovers over *Irish Eyes Are Smiling*, whose plot pivot is one favored by Runyon: a bet: A Jack-of-all trades manager (Monty Woolley) bets a shady operator (Anthony Quinn) $25,000 that he can make a star out of the first woman to come out of the ladies' lounge who, thanks to the machinations of Dick Haymes (a rather bland Ernest Ball), is June. Although June had some impressive musical numbers, there were not enough of them to make her Betty's rival, despite Bosley Crowther's claim. It was as if Zanuck were testing June by having her do a brownface number, "Strut, Miss Lizzie," whose racial stereotypy is neutralized by June's natural buoyancy, making it one of Hollywood's less offensive excursions into minstrelsy. Zanuck was taking precautions. Uncertain that June could carry a musical, he went big time. Aware that MGM had engaged opera and operetta stars for its musicals (Miliza Korjus in *The Great Waltz*; Grace Moore in *A Lady's Morals*; Marta Eggerth in *Presenting Lily Mars*) and that even Columbia made a series of musicals with Moore, one of the best known Metropolitan Opera sopranos, Zanuck brought in two Metropolitan Opera stalwarts, baritone Leonard Warren and mezzo Blanche Thebom, both in full voice and singing Ernest Ball favorites: Warren, "A Little Bit of Heaven"; and Thebom, "Mother Machree." Both would return for the grand finale—and grand it was.

Irish Eyes Are Smiling ends with the premiere of a fictitious Irish-themed musical, *Kathleen*, with June in the title role. We only see the finale, which begins with a close-up of a volume entitled "My Book of Memories by Ernest Ball." The book opens slowly, and instead of pages, there is Leonard Warren singing "Love Me, and the World Is Mine" as if it were an aria. Next come the reprises, Thebom at a loom singing the treacly "Dear Little Boy of Mine," which Haymes had performed earlier; "Mother Machree" again; and finally Haymes, in an appropriately green-colored vest, crooning "When Irish Eyes Are Smiling" and joining June in a shamrock-decorated skirt in a reprise of "Let the Rest of the World Go By," which had been heard three times previously. Few musicals have had such a wealth of reprises.

I WONDER WHO'S KISSING HER NOW (1947)

June would be cast in another biopic, *I Wonder Who's Kissing Her Now* (1947), about composer-performer Joseph E. Howard (1878–1961), who wrote the title song, as well as "Hello! Ma Baby" and "Goodbye, My Lady Love," the latter interpolated into the score of the original production of *Show Boat* (1927). However, not every song in the film was Howard's; in fact, four had lyrics by George Jessel and music by Charles Henderson. George Jessel (1898–1981), the popular singer-songwriter-actor, also produced the film. Jessel's admiration for Howard is evident in the opening title that bears his signature. *I Wonder Who's Kissing Her Now* is "based on incidents from the early life of Joe Howard, the ageless American troubadour," whose songs have left behind "memories that can never be forgotten. Gad, what a life! George Jessel." It was, however, a life comprised of more fancy than fact. *I Wonder Who's Kissing Her Now* was both a George Jessel production and a typical Twentieth Century-Fox show-business musical.

The film also had the advantage of Lloyd Bacon's direction. Bacon, a former stage and film actor, had directed *42nd Street* and *Footlight Parade* (both 1933) as well as *Wake Up and Dream*, one of June's two 1946 releases. His last two films before his death in 1955 were also musicals: *Golden Girl* (1951), with Mitzi Gaynor, and *The French Line* (1954), with Jane Russell. Since *I Wonder Who's Kissing Her Now* had several production numbers taking place on stage, Bacon made certain that some scenes were filmed from the perspective of patrons in the front orchestra and others from those in the balcony, so that the effect was something akin to live theater.

I Wonder Who's Kissing Her Now is more about June's character, the fictitious Katie McCullem, than Joe Howard (Mark Stevens), which is in keeping with the tradition of the female protagonist's charting the plot trajectory in a Zanuck musical. Originally, Katie (another Irish lass) was not part of the story. Zanuck, seeing a connection between *Irish Eyes Are Smiling* and *I Wonder Who's Kissing Her Now*, had writer Lewis R. Foster—who had inherited a troubled script, including Zanuck's rewrites as "Melville Crossman"—work her into the plot as the niece of Howard's guardian, who grew up in the same household with him and will do anything to further his career. So, in the early scenes, June played another spunky kid who pursues Howard after he has accepted a job as the accompanist of vaudeville performer Lulu Madison (Martha Stewart). Lying that her uncle had died, Katie becomes part of the group, using every opportunity to come between Howard and Lulu, even cutting Lulu's corset strings to keep her from performing so that Howard can do a solo, singing his own compositions. When Howard becomes infatuated with another performer, Fritzi Barrington (Lenore Aubert), Katie becomes her understudy; and when Barrington leaves the show to marry a former lover, Katie takes over her role. Katie becomes a star on her own under the name of Pat O'Dare, and the plot winds up with a fade-out kiss.

There are two delightful numbers and one atrocity. Katie and Howard do a high-stepping "Goodbye, My Lady Love" that revealed Stevens as a dancer of grace and style. Hermes Pan choreographed "Glow Worm," an exquisite pas de deux for June and one of Hollywood's best (and underappreciated) dancers, Gene Nelson, which caught the gossamer quality of the music, visualized by June in red sequined top and pink skirt. The atrocity was a three-part sequence with June as Madame du Barry in a white hoop skirt gown and powdered wig, singing Jessel's limp lyrics ("A king is just a thing"); then as Catherine the Great in an abbreviated black costume with a Cossack hat and riding crop singing equally cringing lyrics ("-ski" or "-ovitch" is added to the end of words in a sad attempt at authenticity); and finally as Lillian Russell in white again and dancing with Theodore Roosevelt.

During much of the film, Howard is struggling to find the lyrics for a melody that haunts him. It's the title song, of course. When the historical William Hough (Reginald Gardiner) hears that Barrington has departed, he says, "I wonder who's kissing her now." Eureka! Hough supplies the words (along with Frank Adams) for Howard's melody, which Katie sings at the end as Pat O'Dare. *I Wonder Who's Kissing Her Now* was the studio's fourth biggest money maker of 1947, grossing $3.2 million.

OH, YOU BEAUTIFUL DOLL (1949)

June's last songwriter musical was *Oh, You Beautiful Doll* (1949), which, although she received top billing, was S. Z. Sakall's movie. It had the most original premise of any of the songwriter musicals: an imagining of the career of German born Alfred Breitenbach (1875–1942), played by Sakall, who changed his name to Fred Fisher and composed some of the most popular songs of the first two decades of the twentieth century such as "Come Josephine in My Flying Machine" (1910), "Peg o' My Heart" (1913), "Chicago" (1922), but not the title song, which was the creation of Nat D. Ayer and A. Seymour.

Part of the reason that *Oh, You Beautiful Doll* seems more of a drama than a musical is its director, John M. Stahl, known primarily for serious films such as Twentieth Century-Fox's *The Keys of the Kingdom* (1944), *Leave Her to Heaven* (1945), *The Foxes of Harrow* (1947), and *The Walls of Jericho* (1948). The main title is in the form of a pop art street in turn-of-the-century New York, similar to the opening scenes in other Twentieth Century-Fox musicals in which the setting is established before the action begins. *Oh, You Beautiful Doll* starts with what seems to be a frame narrative: a bartender explaining to some regulars how Breitenbach and Fisher were the same person—except that the film does not end back at the bar, as expected. That was one of several surprises. First and foremost was Sakall in an affecting performance as a financially strapped opera composer whom a song plugger (Mark Stevens) talks into converting his arias into popular songs under the name of Fred Fisher. Mark Stevens revealed, for the second time, an affinity for musical comedy which was rarely exploited; Charlotte Greenwood as Breitenbach/Fisher's wife, Anna, was shown sewing, knitting, and cooking, but not singing or dancing; and June as their daughter, Doris, plays the piano in the finale like the professional musician June Haver might have become after winning three musical contests in Cincinnati.

Feeling he has betrayed his art, Breitenbach leaves his family, determined to complete his opera. The resolution combines an implausibly happy ending with the grandest of finales. A conductor (Eduard Franz) manages to lure Breitenbach out of seclusion by announcing a concert consisting of Mozart, Beethoven, and not Brahms, but Breitenbach, which includes both his classical and popular works. Doris/June is at the piano, and a symphony orchestra is on stage with a chorus behind it reprising "Dardanella" and

"Peg o' My Heart." June and Stevens join the chorus in reprises of "I Want You to Want Me" and "Chicago." They bow, but their curtain call does not mark the end of the movie, as it had in the past. Stahl cuts over to one of the boxes with Sakall and Greenwood, giving the great character actor the crucial fade-out shot. The movie was about Breitenbach/Fisher and the high culture/pop culture polarity that was at the core of *King of Burlesque*, *Hello, Frisco, Hello*, and *Nob Hill*. Charlotte Greenwood resolved the culture war in one simple sentence: "Good music is good music."

WHERE DO WE GO FROM HERE? (1945)

Although Zanuck knew that June was at her best in costume musicals, he could not feature her exclusively in period films. He decided to cast her in two films set during World War II, neither of which generated much interest or revenues. Third-billed in *Where Do We Go from Here?* (1945) after Fred McMurray and Joan Leslie, on loan from Warner Bros., she only had a few opportunities to display her trademark skills. The film promised much: a time-travel musical with a screenplay by Morrie Ryskind and music and lyrics by Kurt Weill and Ira Gershwin, none of whom were at their best. Ryskind—who wrote the screenplays for such classics as *A Night at the Opera* (MGM, 1935) and *My Man Godfrey* (Universal, 1936) and coauthored the book of George and Ira Gershwin's Pulitzer Prize musical *Of Thee I Sing* (1931)—created the kind of plot in which the humor derives from (1) the main character being transported back in time where he can tell others about things that have already occurred or will occur (e.g., the invention of the automobile), but not in their era; (2) his realization that since the colonists in seventeenth-century New Amsterdam invert English word order ("I thee take"), he would have to do the same; and (3) sight gags (a Broadway and Forty-Second Street signpost in 1626 Manhattan and a return to the present on a magic car ride across the sky with the Twentieth Century-Fox logo looming in the distance).

Weill and Gershwin's score for *Lady in the Dark* (1941) was far superior to that of *Where Do We Go from Here?* In fact, adaptations of Weill's other musicals, *Knickerbocker Holiday* (United Artists, 1944), *Lady in the Dark* (Paramount, 1944), and *One Touch of Venus* (Universal-International, 1948), came to the screen with their scores shamefully reduced. Although *Where*

Do We Go from Here? is Weill's only movie musical, it seemed rooted in the stage. In fact, the New Amsterdam sequence harks back to *Knickerbocker Holiday* (1938), which is also set in the Dutch colony. Before beginning work on *Where Do We Go from Here?*, Weill enjoyed a major success on Broadway with *One Touch of Venus* (1943), in which a statue of Venus comes to life as Mary Martin when a young man tries out an engagement ring on her finger. Weill decided to continue in the fantasy mode when Twentieth Century-Fox beckoned; the result was *Where Do We Go from Here?* Since America was still at war in 1944 when the film was in the planning stage, a wartime theme was inevitable.

The plot pivot—the predicament of draft-age men eager to enlist but classified 4-F and constantly asked why they are not in uniform—may have resonated with 1945 audiences, but with a befuddled Fred MacMurray playing the rejected Bill Morgan, his draft status was a blessing in disguise. June first appears as Lucilla, a USO volunteer, telling every GI that his branch of the service is her favorite. When June sings "All at Once," which sounds somewhat like "This Is New" from *Lady in the Dark*, the film seemed to be coming alive musically. And when June in a flashy red dress, along with the men in uniform and the volunteers, segues into "Morale," doing a really high kick, the movie reaches a level of excitement that does not return until the 1492 sequence.

Morgan is caught between two women: Lucilla, who is attracted to any man in the armed services, and Sally (Joan Leslie), who is only attracted to him. Coming upon an antique lamp at a scrap metal yard, he breaks it, releasing Ali (Gene Sheldon), a genie, and initiating a backward-in-time odyssey with Ali granting Morgan his wish to serve in the army. But through a cosmic fluke, it is George Washington's Continental Army. Ryskind expected audiences to recall their American history when Morgan explains how the Revolution will end and warns Washington to beware of Benedict Arnold. Morgan becomes a spy and infiltrates a tavern where the Hessians are being entertained by the entrancing Gretchen (June in braids) singing the "Song of the Rhineland" in praise of a Germany where everything is superior: "beer is beerier" and "wine is winier"—not exactly the most felicitous of lyrics but suggesting the ideology of a modern Germany.

There is something ominous about the tavern sequence: dark undercurrents in the music that sound like a drinking song gone haywire. Morgan is interrogated by a Hessian colonel, who sports a monocle like the Nazis in the World War II movies. At this point you think you are watching one with references to the master race and Morgan's prediction that Germany will conquer the poles—North, West, South, East—and then, the cruelest of jokes, "the Polish poles." Ali keeps Morgan from being executed but errs again, sending him sailing with Columbus to the New World. The crew threatens mutiny, longing for "vino, bambino, 'O sole mio,' and the sextet from *Lucia*," while Columbus reminds them that failure means that "Isabella, queen of queens / will be a queen without any means." The entire sequence is an operatic spoof with sung dialogue and a great catalog aria for MacMurray, "The Nina, the Pinta, the Santa Maria," in which he enumerates all the benefits that will come from Columbus's discovery, including a day off in October. The lyrics are Gershwin at his wittiest, with "Maria" generating rhymes with "idea," "panacea," and even "Hialeah"; when a natural rhyme is impossible, Gershwin adds a short "a" to "see" (see-a) and "tree" (tree-a).

Neither June nor Joan is in the Columbus sequence, but June appears in the 1626 Manhattan sequence as a sexy Native American. She doesn't sing, and her only function is to be part of a scheme to sell Manhattan Island to Morgan for $24. So much for Peter Minuit. Morgan's "ownership" of New Amsterdam brings him in contact with Katrina (Joan Leslie/Sally) forced to marry the man who owns the deed to her father's farm. Either scripter Ryskind had seen *Knickerbocker Holiday* (1938), set in 1647 New Amsterdam, or Weill suggested it to him as a plot point, since both involve a Dutch colonist about to marry against her will. In *Knickerbocker Holiday*, Tina (cf. Katrina in the film), in love with Brom Broeck, attracts the attention of the governor, Peter Stuyvesant, who plans to marry her. Only a deus ex machina can save Tina and Katrina from marrying men they do not love. In the play, the narrator, Washington Irving, cautions Stuyvesant about his legacy, reminding him that historians will think ill of a man marrying a woman against her will. In the film, Ali whisks Morgan and Katrina back to the States, where Katrina morphs back into Sally, and Morgan gets his last wish. After serving in the army and navy, he is now in the marines, marching proudly with Sally beside him; and June/Lucilla beside Ali, who has also joined up. The narrative sense is not as skewered as it seems: Lucilla is attracted to men in uniform, even an ex-genie. The fade-out music is a reprise of "Morale," and the two couples marching together is the equivalent of a curtain call.

The public was indifferent to *Where Do We Go from Here?* Costing $2.4 million, the film only generated $1.75 million in revenues.

WAKE UP AND DREAM (1946)

When June appeared in a contemporary movie like *Wake Up and Dream* (1946), the charm was there, but the appeal was absent. In the very first scene, she is in a server's uniform tidying up the diner where she works; but whether in a dress, a shirt and slacks, or jeans, she looked no different from any other ingénue. Jeanne Crain, Anne Baxter, or Vanessa Brown could have played the role if the film were a non-musical, which it should have been. Zanuck purchased the rights to Robert Nathan's novel, *The Enchanted Voyage* (1936), immediately after its publication as a vehicle for Shirley Temple. When no one could come up with a script that satisfied him, the project lay dormant until early 1946, when he thought that it could work as a semi-musical set in 1943, with June and John Payne singing a few numbers in keeping with audience expectations.

Payne enlists in the navy; when he is declared missing, his kid sister (Connie Marshall) persuades an eccentric ship builder (Clem Bevans) to take her to the tropical island with white sand that her brother has told her about, convinced that she will find him there. Believing children should hold fast to their dreams, he agrees. June joins the cockeyed odyssey, and along the way, they encounter a dentist (John Ireland), ending up in what looks like the Everglades where they discover a hermit who creates hybrids such as peanut-encrusted cucumbers. All ends well, of course. Bevans, a superb character actor, gave an ingratiating performance as a senior citizen who has not stopped dreaming. Charlotte Greenwood was wasted as his wife, but John Ireland revealed a flair for comedy that, for most of his career, went untapped. June and Payne had to justify audiences' sitting through ninety-two minutes of sentimental whimsy by performing a few songs. Payne sings the movie's credo, "Give Me the Simple Life," reprised by June and played over the end title. To compensate for the dearth of musical material, "We're Off to see the Wizard" from *The Wizard of Oz* (MGM, 1939) was added, but that was not enough to save the film. Released in late November 1946, more than a year after World War II had ended, *Wake Up and Dream* was a box-office failure. Budgeted at $1.590 million, it made a mere $900,000.

THREE LITTLE GIRLS IN BLUE (1946)

A far more representative June Haver musical was her other 1946 release, *Three Little Girls in Blue*, the second reboot of *Three Blind Mice* (1938), now as a period musical, which, except for a new character, is *Moon Over Miami* (1941), with a different score, a different setting (Atlantic City), and a different trio (June, Vivian Blaine, and Vera-Ellen). The sisters are back to what they were in *Three Blind Mice*, owners of a chicken farm, this time in Red Bank, New Jersey, where they use what is left from their estate to travel to Atlantic City in search of wealthy husbands. June inherited Betty Grable's role, the sister posing as an heiress, with Vivian, a Twentieth Century-Fox contract player, and Vera-Ellen, on loan from Samuel Goldwyn, as her social secretary and maid, respectively. Anyone who saw either of the earlier versions will know that June will end up with a man as poor as she (George Montgomery); Vivian with the sole millionaire (Frank Latimore); and Vera-Ellen with a waiter (a delightfully ingenuous Charles Smith). The only surprise in the film is the addition of Latimore's ditsy sister (Celeste Holm in her film debut). Holm was the original Ado Annie in Rodgers and Hammerstein's *Oklahoma!* (1943), whose big number, "I Cain't Say No," pretty much summed up her character. Since Holm is playing a bubbly French-speaking socialite, she was given a similar number, "Always a Lady," which could have been entitled "I Cain't Say Yes." She sings part of it in French, but then goes into her Ado Annie voice from the heartland as she laments all the propositions she had to decline.

The score contains three outstanding songs: "On the Boardwalk in Atlantic City"; "Somewhere in the Night," which Vivian delivers with the intimacy of a cabaret performer; and the standard "You Make Me Feel So Young," sung with disarming innocence by Vera-Ellen and Charles Smith (voices dubbed). Blue is the predominant color, and June, Vivian, Vera-Ellen, and Holm each wear it at some point. The finale, another reprise-curtain call, has the three men pushing a cart, in which the three sisters are seated, along the boardwalk, reprising "You Make Me Feel So Young." *Three Little Girls in Blue* was not a huge hit. Costing $2.595 million, it only brought in $3 million.

Zanuck then realized June could never be Betty's replacement. Betty did not have to appear in a period musical to generate big box office. Her contemporary musicals—e.g., *Down Argentine Way*, *Springtime in the Rockies*, *Footlight Serenade*, *Billy Rose's Diamond Horseshoe*, and *Pin-Up*

Girl—also attracted audiences and performed well: $2, $3.5, $2.5, $3, and $2 million, respectively. Moviegoers did not flock to a June Haver movie as they did to a Betty Grable one. The highest-grossing June Haver film was *The Dolly Sisters*, which cost $2.510 million and did $4 million worth of business domestically. The draw was Betty, not June, whose role was really a supporting one.

It might have been different if June had made her Twentieth Century-Fox debut the same time as Betty. But Betty arrived first, and if there was any movie star that personified the kind of glamour GIs were missing when they were pining for home in their barracks or foxholes, it was Betty Grable. June arrived too late on the scene to be a pinup girl, although Zanuck wanted the public to think of her as one. She made the cover of *Modern Screen* (July 1945) in a colorful two-piece bathing suit. It was not exactly a warm smile, but rather one that was probably coaxed from her. The accompanying piece, "Memo on June," included some other cheese cake shots, along with ones of June dabbing perfume behind her ear and studying a script. To dispel any notion that she and Betty were rivals, the reader is informed that "she's teaching Betty Grable's [daughter] Vicky to call her 'Auntie.'"

When Warner Bros. asked to borrow June for two period musicals, the Marilyn Miller biopic, *Look for the Silver Lining* (1949), and *The Daughter of Rosie O'Grady* (1950), Zanuck immediately agreed to a loan-out. He had no costume musical for her. *I Wonder Who's Kissing Her Now* (1947) cost $2.650 million and did well ($3.2 million); *Oh, You Beautiful Doll* (1949), which was budgeted at $1.965 million, only made $1.95 million. Perhaps the Marilyn Miller biopic would be the musical that would redefine her image. It wasn't. In his *New York Times* review of *Look for the Silver Lining* (June 24, 1949), Bosley Crowther, once June's champion, criticized her for failing "to give vitality to the leading role," adding that her dancing "would never be mistaken for the brilliance of the lady she's supposed to be." Crowther was prejudiced; he had seen Miller on stage when she reigned as the queen of musical comedy. That was the problem. Marilyn Miller (1898–1936) was too well known, and June was clearly not her embodiment, even though there was a physical resemblance. She also had a director with whom she was unfamiliar, David Butler; and a script by Phoebe and Henry Ephron that was a copy of the Twentieth Century-Fox vaudeville-to-Broadway template.

Look for the Silver Lining received lukewarm reviews and made a small profit. *The Daughter of Rosie O'Grady* (1950) did better. But at the time,

Warner Bros.' leading musical stars were Doris Day and Virginia Mayo, so it was back to Twentieth Century-Fox for three films between 1950 and 1953, none of which had much distinction. *I'll Get By* (1950) was a remake of *Tin Pan Alley* (1940), updated to the World War II era, with June in Alice Faye's role and Gloria DeHaven in Betty Grable's. The studio apparently didn't know how to generate interest in a film that was better suited to an earlier era than the 1940s except by featuring some of its contract players as themselves: Jeanne Crain, Dan Dailey, and Reginald Gardiner, with a special appearance by trumpeter Harry James. June had a chance to sing the title song and team up with DeHaven in "I've Got the World on a String." The songs made the movie, not the stars. *Love Nest* (1951) was a non-musical, remembered, if at all, for Marilyn Monroe as a model whom June perceives as a marital threat.

Unlike Betty Grable's career, June's barely lasted a decade. She was the kid sister, the girl next door going with the boy down the street. Her last film was appropriately entitled *The Girl Next Door* (1953). Her name was no longer first in the credits; Dan Dailey's was. In June 1954, she married Fred MacMurray, whom she had met a decade earlier during the filming of *Where Do We Go from Here?*, and left the business for good.

Chapter 17

THE CHERRY BLONDE
Vivian Blaine

Like June Haver, Vivian Blaine (1921–95) also began her career as a much beloved band singer discovered by a Twentieth Century-Fox talent scout. She arrived in Hollywood in 1942, only to find herself cast in a series of B movies until she was given the female lead in the Laurel and Hardy comedy, *Jitterbugs* (TCF, 1943), with her name appearing first among the featured players. Since the studio already had three blondes—Alice Faye, Betty Grable, and June Haver—Vivian was touted as the "cherry blonde" with the reddish blonde hair. "Strawberry blonde" would have been just as accurate, except that it was also the title of a Warner Bros. 1941 semi-musical.

When Alice Faye's pregnancy prevented her from making *Greenwich Village* (1944), Zanuck replaced her with Vivian, since Betty was preoccupied with *Pin Up Girl*, and June with *Irish Eyes Are Smiling*. Vivian was rushed into the film, a three-month shoot (November 4, 1943–January 5, 1944) and released in September 1944.

Five months later, Vivian went into *Something for the Boys* (1944), released two months after *Greenwich Village*, affording audiences a chance to see her in her first two Twentieth Century-Fox musicals before the year came to an end. *Greenwich Village*, budgeted at $1.830, only brought in $1.85 million. *Something for the Boys* did even less business: production cost, $2 million; domestic rentals, $1.25 million. Yet Vivian's films are significant for different reasons: (1) *Greenwich Village*, for the aborted debut of the Revuers, a trio of satirists consisting of Betty Comden, Adolph Green, and Judy Holliday, who, after their spoof of a Viennese operetta was cut, returned to New York where they had better luck—Comden and Green with the book and lyrics for Leonard Bernstein's first musical, *On the Town*

(1944), and Holliday as the irrepressible Billie Dawn in Garson Kanin's *Born Yesterday* (1946), which she recreated on the screen in 1950, winning an Oscar for Best Actress; (2) *Something for the Boys* (1944), as a textbook example of how not to adapt a Cole Porter musical; (3) *Doll Face* (1946), for the author of the original story and later a play, Louise Hovick, better known as Gypsy Rose Lee; and (4) *Something for the Boys*, *Doll Face*, and *If I'm Lucky* (1947), for Zanuck's attempt to make another popular singer, Perry Como, into a star on the order of Dick Haymes.

GREENWICH VILLAGE (1944)

The credits for *Greenwich Village* attest to Zanuck's high expectations for Vivian. Carmen Miranda is top-billed in what is really a supporting role. Next come Don Ameche and William Bendix, whose characters are more central to the plot than Miranda's; finally, "and introducing Vivian Blaine in her first featured role," which was not entirely accurate since she had also been featured in *Jitterbugs* (1943), *Greenwich Village* is a synthesis of two familiar plot lines: "mounting a show" and "high art vs. popular culture," a Zanuck favorite (e.g., *Alexander's Ragtime Band*, *King of Burlesque*, *Hello, Frisco, Hello*, *Nob Hill*, *Oh, You Beautiful Doll*).

As is customary in Twentieth Century-Fox musicals set during other eras, the film opens with an establishing shot of a street in 1922 Greenwich Village with a guide explaining to disinterested tourists that they are in "the melting pot of genius" inhabited by "men with long hair and women with short hair." In the vicinity is a classical composer from Kansas (Don Ameche), who has come to New York to peddle his concerto. Instead, he wanders into William Bendix's speakeasy, where Carmen Miranda is inexplicably singing "I'm Just Wild About Harry" in a candy-striped costume with puffed sleeves that look as if they had been inflated and a headdress with peppermint sticks. Such was the composer's introduction to the melting pot of genius.

The speakeasy's attraction is Vivian Blaine, whose first number, "Swingin' Down the Lane," is proof that she was not like any other Twentieth Century-Fox star. Her years as a band singer made her a storyteller in song, delivering the lyrics as if she were experiencing them. She did more than personalize a number; she made it seem as if you were swingin' down the lane with her. Her true medium was the theater, which was evident when she made her Broadway debut as Miss Adelaide in *Guys and Dolls* (1950). When Vivian sang "Whispering," the movie's hit tune, it was in the style of a performer who knows that even if a song has little or no bearing on the plot, it has to be sung as if it did. "Whispering" is unusual; it figures in both "the composer and his concerto" and the "putting on a show" plots. When Bendix, who wants to move out of the speakeasy business and produce a musical revue, hears the composer play some of his concerto, he is particularly taken with a section that, if orchestrated differently, could become a popular song. The melody becomes "Whispering," and Bendix commissions the rest of the concerto for conversion into the revue's score. Tricked into believing that a famous conductor is interested in his concerto, Ameche withdraws it, expecting that it will be performed in Carnegie Hall. Discovering the truth, he is about to return to Kansas when the conductor, who has learned of the deception, agrees to conduct the orchestra on the opening night of Bendix's show, thus settling the classical vs. popular music debate. The concerto and the revue are not mutually antagonistic.

Despite its title, "Whispering" cannot be sung in a whisper or sotto voce even though "whispering" and "whisper" occur ten and four times, respectively, in a four-stanza lyric. Composed in 4/4 meter, with four beats for each measure ("Whispering while you cuddle near me / Whispering so no one can hear me"), the singer is whispering his or her love for another outside of anyone else's hearing range, trusting that the beloved will appreciate the depth of the lover's devotion. It is a love song with a lulling effect, which Vivian turns into ballad of longing, directed at Ameche whom she loves so much that even when he decides to withdraw his concerto, she bears him no ill will because she realizes he has a chance to have it played as written. What else but a reprise of "Whispering" could constitute the finale, and what better fade-out than Ameche and Vivian in a tight embrace?

Vivian's art was on display, but only twice. She proved to be a much better actress than either Betty or June, and it was not surprising that years later she did serious drama like *A Hatful of Rain* (1956), when she took over the role of a drug addict's wife from Shelley Winters. Miranda was the draw in *Greenwich Village*, particularly after *The Gang's All Here* solidified her reputation at Twentieth Century-Fox. But she could also grow tiresome, with the same hand and eye movements, undulations, and cult priestess costumes, particularly the one in "Give Me a Band and a Bandana"—a metallic ruby red outfit with a split skirt lined with pink ruffles. You were in awe of her energy, but wished for less of it, especially in a film that marked the musical debut of an artist like Vivian, who was neither a Betty Grable nor June Haver type and thus could not be kept in reserve if either defected or proved difficult. Miranda was the star with three big numbers compared to Vivian's small but beautifully expressive two. In terms of performance style, Vivian was closer to Alice Faye and could easily have become her successor if Zanuck had given her the right kind of buildup. She could bring the essence of Broadway to Hollywood—an appealing sophistication that was neither studied nor artificial, but sincerely elegant. That may have been the reason for her brief hour at the studio: she was more Broadway than Hollywood. Betty and June had generic voices, pleasant but not distinctive. Vivian's could be mellow and earthy, strong and plaintive, soft and seductive. She had a range, while the others had a scale. What Vivian could and could not do was apparent in *Three Little Girls in Blue*. In the first number, she, June Haver, and Vera-Ellen, owners of a chicken farm, romp through a haystack singing "A Farmer's Life Is a Very Merry Life." June and Vera-Ellen could pass as farmers, but not Vivian, who was not meant for chicken coops. But when she sang "Somewhere in the Night," her only solo, it was in the style of such musical theater performers as Vivienne Segal, Carol Bruce, Mary Martin, and Barbara Cook: carefully phrased and emotionally honest. When she sang "That's For Me" in *State Fair* (1945), she used a rich mezzo that rose in intensity as she described the object of her affection, which at the moment was an enthralled Dick Haymes, letting the song end naturally as if she had found what she wanted and no longer had to elaborate.

For the time being, Vivian completed the trio of Twentieth Century-Fox's musical stars, but her tenure was brief. She made only seven musicals at the studio between 1944 and 1946—two in 1944, three in 1945, and two in 1946. Then she began doing stock—*One Touch of Venus* (1948), *Bloomer Girl* (1949), and finally *Guys and Dolls* (1950), which marked her triumphant Broadway debut, followed by *A Hatful of Rain* (1956), with Steve McQueen as replacements for Shelley Winters and Ben Gazarra. The theater—Broadway, regional, and stock—then became her natural habitat, where she proved to be equally adept at drama (*The Glass Menagerie, A Streetcar Named Desire*), comedy (*Light Up the Sky, Last of the Red Hot Lovers, Don't Drink the Water*), and musicals as dissimilar as *Damn Yankees, Gypsy, Company, Follies, Hello, Dolly!*, and *Zorba*.

SOMETHING FOR THE BOYS (1944)

Cole Porter's 1943 musical *Something for the Boys* should have been a natural for Vivian in the role of Blossom Hart, originated by Ethel Merman. While Vivian lacked Merman's volcanic power, her voice had enough heft to bring a number to a clarion finish, as she showed on several occasions when she performed Merman's favorite stage role, Momma Rose, in *Gypsy*. As happens with so many Broadway shows, Porter's score was discarded except for the title song by Porter; the ones that were added were jukebox fare but not show tunes. As Blossom, Vivian had to sing a few of them, making you wonder what she would have done with Porter's words and music.

Until the 1950s, Zanuck never showed much interest in bringing Broadway musicals to the screen. Universal set the standard with a superb *Show Boat* (1936), which retained both the spirit and scope of the Jerome Kern-Oscar Hammerstein original. As for the other studios, there was Paramount, with Porter's *Anything Goes* (1936) and *Let's Face It* (1943) and Irving Berlin's *Louisiana Purchase* (1941); and Warner Bros., with Rodgers and Hart's *On Your Toes* (1940) and Berlin's *This Is the Army* (1943). But it was MGM that really excelled at adaptations of stage musicals: Porter's *Panama Hattie* (1942), and *Du Barry Was a Lady* (1943); Rodgers and Hart's *Babes in Arms* (1939) and *I Married an Angel* (1942); Vernon Duke and John Latouche's *Cabin in the Sky* (1943); Hugh Martin and Ralph Blane's *Best Foot Forward* (1943) and George Gershwin's *Girl Crazy* (1943). Not all of them were faithful recreations of the originals. The same is true of *Something for the Boys*.

The credits are misleading: "Based on the musical comedy, Book by Herbert and Dorothy Fields, Songs by Cole Porter." "Songs" should have been singular, since only the title song survived the transplant. *Something for the Boys* appealed to Zanuck because its wartime theme would complement his other World War II musical, *Pin Up Girl*, scheduled for release in April 1944, with *Something for the Boys* opening seven months later. He also wanted *Something for the Boys* to evoke *The Gang's All Here* with its "war hero torn between flighty fiancée and true love" plot, which meant using the book purely as a point of departure for another movie about a soldier in a similar situation, with Sheila Ryan again playing the fiancée, but this time spoiled, snooty, and suffocating.

The musical itself was minor Porter, even though it racked up 422 performances, largely on the strength of Merman's name. The one-joke book concerns three cousins (Vivian, Carmen Miranda, and Phil Silvers in the film) who have inherited a Texas ranch (a decrepit Southern plantation in the film) which they convert into a residence for army wives, arousing the suspicion of an army official who, convinced it is a front for a brothel, plans to close it. One of the cousins is Blossom Hart, a former welder in a defense plant, who somehow got carborundum in a tooth filling, enabling her to pick up radio signals and help a plane with engine trouble make a safe landing. The army is grateful, the wives get their house back. Blossom gets her man, and his fiancée gets the gate.

Since Carmen Miranda was top-billed as Chiquita Hart, followed by Michael O'Shea as Rocky, an army sergeant in love with Blossom (Vivian, third-billed), her role was enlarged, and plot points reassigned. Chiquita is now the welder with carborundum in her tooth (Miranda is actually seen welding), and Blossom is just a singer looking for a break. Like Alice Faye's character in *The Gang's All Here*, who learns that James Ellison is "engaged" to Sheila Ryan. Blossom discovers that Rocky is informally engaged to Melanie (Sheila Ryan again). The imperiled plane climax is scrapped in favor of a war games exercise which Rocky's side wins thanks to Chiquita's dental transmitter. The war games sequence is at least imaginative, which is more than can be said for most of the film.

The songs by Jimmy McHugh and Harold Adamson could never be mistaken even for faux Cole Porter and were pleasantly hummable at best. Vivian and O'Shea sang a lovers' question-and-answer duet, "Wouldn't It Be Nice?," which Vivian, actress that she is, sang convincingly, rhyming "paradise" with "rice" (as in weddings), as if she believed marriages were made in heaven. O'Shea sang the lyrics as written. Miranda looked less outrageous than usual: red and green in one number, green and white in another, and puffy sleeves in both. For "Samba-Boogie," she was ill advised to don a grape-encrusted hat that clashed with her two-piece outfit.

Something for the Boys marked the film debut of the popular singer and recording artist Perry Como as an army sergeant. The role only required him to sing "I Wish We Didn't Have to Say Goodnight," which Vivian reprises in an attempt to detain a lieutenant (Glenn Langan) during the war games, so that Rocky's team can win; and the more emotionally intense "In the Middle of Nowhere," which Vivian also sings in a voice that extends from a low mezzo to a lustrous soprano broken by the hint of a sob, turning the song into a lament as she muses on Rocky's presumed faithlessness.

The finale is a revue celebrating the reopening of the manor, which had been closed when the army discovered that unmarried men were frequenting it. Miranda performs "Samba-Boogie," followed by a reprise of "Wouldn't It Be Nice?" by Blossom and Rocky, who go into the obligatory embrace. In the original, the finale was a reprise of "Something for the Boys," which should have been the case in the film. At least it would have been *echt* Porter.

DOLL FACE (1945)

Vivian's getting top billing in *Doll Face* (1945) came with a price: the lead in a black-and-white film that cost $1.120 million and looked it, compared to the handsomely produced *Three Little Girls in Blue* that cost more than twice as much, making it a more typical Twentieth Century-Fox musical than *Doll Face*, which looked as if it came off the "B" movie assembly line, which indeed it did. The producer was Bryan Foy, who headed the "B" unit at Warner's and did the same at Twentieth Century-Fox from 1942 to 1945. And Vivian's billing should have made Carmen Miranda wonder where her future lay when her name came fourth. The credits reflected a new alignment of talent: Vivian, Dennis O'Keefe, Perry Como, and Carmen.

Although Dick Haymes was America's most popular recording artist in the 1940s, he was a dimensionless actor. Como was even blander, but for some reason Zanuck thought Como had the makings of a leading man. Since O'Keefe, on loan from producer Edward Small, could handle comedy, but not the musical kind, Vivian shared the finale with Como, with the final close-up suggesting that they are the film's stars as well as those of the revue in which they are appearing, the ending being another stage performance/movie musical finale.

In his *New York Times* review of *Doll Face* (March 26, 1946), Bosley Crowther wrote that Twentieth Century-Fox's "paying a tremendous amount of coin" for a play by Louise Hovick (Gypsy Rose Lee) was a "terrible deal." None of the stars came off well, particularly Vivian, whom Crowther found "unimpressive." *Doll Face* may be a mediocre musical, but it has some historical significance. According to the credits, *Doll Face* derived "from a play by Louise Hovick," which was Gypsy Rose Lee's actual name. The play is not named, nor could it be, as Production Code czar

Joseph Breen found the play's title, *The Naked Genius*, a violation of the Code, warning Zanuck against making a picture depicting "the very lowest form of public entertainment." The screenplay by Leonard Praskins and Howard Buchman bore little resemblance to Hovick's *The Naked Genius*, which starred Joan Blondell and ran for a mere thirty-six performances in fall 1943. That the producer was the flamboyant Michael Todd (whom Blondell married in 1947) and the director was the renowned George S. Kaufman suggest that both of them thought the play had the makings of a hit comedy, particularly with its autobiographical overtones. Joan Blondell played burlesque queen Honey Bee Carroll, who sets out to change her image by becoming a well-read *artiste* whom intellectuals would take seriously after reading her autobiography, *The Naked Genius*, which portrayed her an erudite ecdysiast rather than a brainless dancer. Feeling the need for guidance by a serious writer, she finds one, but the experience is so disillusioning that she returns to burlesque, having established her credentials as a self-educated dancer.

Gypsy Rose Lee's quest for respectability was parodied in the song "Zip" in Rodgers and Hart's *Pal Joey* (1940), in which a reporter recounts an interview with Gypsy in which she boasts that "it took intellect to master my art," and that, while stripping, her thoughts ranged from Arthur Schopenhauer's philosophy and William Saroyan's plays to Leopold Stokowski's conducting and the teachings of the Kabballah. Gypsy herself was an author, whose mystery novel *The G-String Murders* (1941) was filmed as *Lady of Burlesque* (1943), with Barbara Stanwyck. The novel may have been ghostwritten by Craig Rice, although the Gypsy Rose Lee Collection at the New York Public Library for the Performing Arts contains some drafts and correspondence suggesting that Gypsy wrote a considerable part of it herself with assistance from Rice and her editor, George Davis. By 1943, Gypsy had had enough experience with ghost writers, editors, and litigious collaborators to write a play about her journey through the literary labyrinth. But just as she needed an editor for her fiction, she needed a mentor for her play. It is surprising that George S. Kaufman—who, with Moss Hart, wrote three of the American theater's greatest comedies (*Once in a Lifetime* [1930], the Pulitzer Prize-winning *You Can't Take It with* You [1936], and *The Man Who Came to Dinner* [1939])—did not provide the mentoring she needed. Instead of staging *The Naked Genius*, Kaufman should have helped Gypsy revise it, leaving the direction to someone like George Abbott, who knew how to fine-tune a comedy so that there is no loss of momentum, an art that Kaufman lacked. Lewis Nichols of the *New York Times* (October 22, 1943) dismissed *The Naked Genius* as a "sad and dreary" affair, urging Michael Todd to do what burlesque patrons demanded of performers: "Take it off," which Todd did a month later.

When Zanuck bought the screen rights to *The Naked Genius*, he was convinced that he could turn it into a starring vehicle for Carole Landis. Then he must have realized that "Carole Landis" and "burlesque" are mutually exclusive and went with Vivian, believing that she could at least be convincing as a dancer, as indeed she was when she strutted across the runway to the approval of leering middle-aged men. Very little of *The Naked Genius* remained after the writers transformed it into the story of a burlesque performer, stage name Doll Face Carroll (Vivian), whose goal is to be a musical comedy star. Told by a producer that she lacks "class," she is ready to give up on Broadway until her fast-thinking manager (Dennis O'Keefe) comes up with the idea of hiring a ghost writer to pen her autobiography, *The Genius De Milo*, a clever evocation of the play's forbidden title, which will make her Broadway worthy. When a motor boat malfunction causes the writer and Doll Face to spend the night together, however innocently, the manager's suspicions are aroused, and the inevitable rift in the relationship occurs. But not for long. When the producer who was so dismissive of Doll Face encounters problems with a new show, the writer suggests a musical version of *The Genius De Milo,* now a best seller. One has to take it on faith that the show represents "class." We see one complete number, "Chico Chico," Carmen's only one, which she performed with her usual verve but less flamboyantly costumed; then the finale with reprises of "Somebody's Walking in My Dream"; "Dig You Later (A-Hubba Hubba Hubba)," which became a hit single for Perry Como; and "Here Comes Heaven Again," all sung by Vivian and Como. In typical Twentieth Century-Fox fashion, the three-part finale marks the end of both *The Genius De Milo* and *Doll Face.*

IF I'M LUCKY (1945)

If I'm Lucky (1946) marked the end of Vivian's, Perry Como's, and Carmen Miranda's tenure at the studio. Ironically, it was Como's only leading role, suggesting that Zanuck believed he could carry a picture as a singer-songwriter suckered into running for governor. *New York Times* critic Bosley Crowther (September 20, 1946) thought otherwise. In addition to finding the film "rather grim," he wrote that Como's only qualification for governor was "a mellifluous singing voice." Vivian came off as "mechanical," and Carmen as "an animated noise." That the film ran a mere seventy-eight minutes and opened in New York at the Victoria rather than at Twentieth Century-Fox's flagship theatre, the Roxy, was indicative of the studio's expectations. Compared to Vivian's other 1946 film, *Three Little Girls in Blue*, it was neither a long nor demanding shoot: mid-April through early June 1946. *Three Little Girls in Blue*, on the other hand, went into production in early November 1945, wrapped up in late February 1946, and opened at the Roxy on September 25, 1946. *If I'm Lucky* cost $1.615 million; *Three Little Girls in Blue*, $2.595 million. A delighted Bosley Crowther (September 26, 1946) found the latter "a pleasant surprise" and a "ray of sunshine."

If I'm Lucky, another Bryan Foy-Lewis Seiler production, was a remake of *Thanks a Million* (Fox, 1935), although it was not credited as such. But the plot is basically the same, with baritone Perry Como in place of tenor Dick Powell as the naif whom a group of crooked politicians endorse for governor, believing he can serve their interests but never suspecting that at the last minute he will pull a "Mr. Smith Goes to Washington" and publicly denounce each of them by name. The movie is indeed "rather grim," not only in its depiction of political corruption but also in the studio's exploitation of Vivian and Carmen, who were expected to invigorate a plot that was anemic to begin with, but more so of Como, whose charisma was in a voice that had the soothing quality of a hot chocolate on a cold day. His love scenes with Vivian are low voltage, Vivian gives the role her best, melting eyes to suggest attraction, but Como reacts mechanically, as if acting were something one does between songs.

Black-and-white cinematography showed neither Vivian nor Carmen at her best. Carmen must have realized that the days when she was the embodiment of the Good Neighbor Policy had come to an end. She was made for lush Technicolor that gave her the look of a tropical totem in colors as yet to be named. In monochrome, she looked desaturated in her white split skirt when she appeared in the only real production number, the lavishly staged "Batocudo," gyrating feverishly in an attempt to convince audiences they were watching a musical about politics, not a political melodrama with music. "Batocudo" was her only solo. She shared "Bet Your

Bottom Dollar" with Vivian, who had only one solo, the title song, which Como introduced. It then became a duet for Como and Vivian, a trumpet solo for Harry James, and a tearful reprise by Vivian when she believes Como has sold out to the political machine. But her fear is short-lived when Como exposes the miscreants, and the finale is a reprise, thankfully not of "If I'm Lucky," but of the first number, "Follow the Band," intermingled with a swinging Bridal Chorus from *Lohengrin*, anticipating Como and Vivian's marriage at the governor's ball.

It was not a happy experience for any of the principals. Vivian had to wait a few years before creating the role by which she will always be remembered, Miss Adelaide in Frank Loesser's *Guys and Dolls* (1950), which she reprised in the 1955 Samuel Goldwyn movie version. Carmen made a few more films, two of which were in color: *A Date with Judy* (MGM, 1948) and *Nancy Goes to Rio* (MGM, 1950). Retiring from the screen in 1953, she passed away two years later at forty-six. Perry Como made a cameo appearance in *Words and Music* (MGM, 1948), continued recording, and enjoyed great success as the star of his own television shows, first on CBS (1950–55) and then on NBC (1955–63). He was an Emmy Award winner and a recipient of the Kennedy Center Award for outstanding achievement in the performing arts. For Como and Vivian, there was life after Twentieth Century-Fox. For Carmen, it was a few more movies and then the grand fade-out.

Chapter 18

PIN DOWN GIRL

For Betty Grable, 1950 was the year that celebrated the old and ushered in the new. In a single year, Betty was her old self as she ran the gamut from saloon singer to Broadway star in *Wabash Avenue* (1950), a geographically altered *Coney Island* (1943), released in March 1950; seven months later, *My Blue Heaven* (1950) opened, with Betty and Dan Dailey as a husband and wife team making the transition from radio to television, which is difficult enough without the bureaucracy they encounter when trying to adopt a baby. Producer Sol C. Siegel thought that the story "Storks Do Not Bring Babies," which Twentieth Century-Fox purchased for $50,000, had the makings of a comedy-drama with Fred MacMurray, but Zanuck felt it was more suited to a musical with Betty and Dailey. Siegel was right. The plot had to honeycombed so that numbers could be periodically inserted to create the semblance of a musical, although the subject matter itself was ill-suited to the genre.

MY BLUE HEAVEN (1950)

Betty's reluctance to make the film is understandable: *My Blue Heaven* is a musical in name only. Essentially, it is the story of a popular radio couple (Betty and Dailey) whose life is upended when the wife suffers a miscarriage and is told she can never have another child. Her disappointment is briefly allayed when the couple move into television where they discover that their writers, David Wayne and Jane Wyatt, had adopted two children. Betty and Dailey plan to do likewise, only to encounter interference from the agency's director who is initially suspicious of show-business couples but relents. When the couple return to their apartment with the baby and

the director in tow, a surprise party in honor of the new parents is in progress. Shocked, the director takes the baby and departs, leaving the couple
childless, until Wayne learns that a woman, deserted by her husband, wants
to give her baby up for adoption. Betty and Dailey are at first reluctant, but
the baby wins them over.

No more plot complications, one thinks. Actually, there are five. Dailey
become attracted to a young dancer (Mitzi Gaynor in her feature film
debut), whom Betty sweetly puts in her place. Then, the deserter-husband
returns to reclaim the baby. As if that were not enough, the puritanical
director takes pity on the couple and offers them baby #2; the deserter-
husband takes off again, leaving the couple with baby #1. Finally, Betty
learns that she is pregnant with baby #3. The significance of the title, the
same as the popular song by Walter Donaldson and George Whiting that
inspired it, becomes clear: "Just Molly and me / and baby makes three /
We're happy in my blue heaven."

The musical numbers, most of which are from the couple's television
show, have nothing to do with the plot. Adoption is too serious a subject for
a musical, and the numbers are too lavish for (a) the plot and (b) a television
studio in 1950. In "I Love a New Yorker," Betty and Dailey play an affluent
couple's maid and butler who imagine themselves going out on the town
like their employer—he in a tux; she in a glittering blue gown and ermine
wrap. They breeze into a ballroom that is pure Hollywood soundstage, far
beyond the capacity of any TV studio in 1950. But that's the point: TV is
film writ small. While taking care of baby #1 at home, Betty watches Dailey
and Mitzi perform "Live Hard, Work Hard, Love Hard" live on a device that
looks like an early version of a laptop. By 1949, the year *My Blue Heaven*
went into production, a million Americans owned television sets, one of
the most popular being the Motorola with a twelve-inch circular screen.
At least Zanuck acknowledged the advent of television and may even have
envisioned a time when the TV screen would be rectangular, but more
likely he was contrasting the dimensions of the two media and assuming
that audiences would get the message.

Except for "Don't Rock the Boat, Dear," a Harold Arlen-Ralph Blane
duet that is a model of syncopation, the rest of the score is forgettable, and
one number is an insult to the great Rodgers and Hammerstein musical,
South Pacific (1949). In "Friendly Islands," which could never have been
done on television in 1950 or any year, Betty appears in brownface wearing

a two-piece sarong with a flowery vine dangling from the back of her head. Changing to a distinctly tribal costume, she and Dailey, dressed like a medicine man, proceed to do a racially offensive ritual dance. Then Dailey does an excruciatingly bad imitation of Italian basso Ezio Pinza, who costarred with Mary Martin in *South Pacific*. One can only wince so many times, but when Dailey turned the first lines of "Some Enchanted Evening (You May Meet a Stranger)" into "Some Enchanted Stranger," "Friendly Islands" sank into the swamp of witlessness.

My Blue Heaven was atypical Betty Grable, but *Wabash Avenue*, the remake of *Coney Island* (1943), was the genuine article.

WABASH AVENUE (1950)

Wabash Avenue is a case of the remake surpassing the original. In both, a performer (Betty) goes from saloon singer to Broadway star while being romanced by frenemies (now Victor Mature and Phil Harris in place of George Montgomery and Cesar Romero), who have a long history of double-crossing each other, or as Harris puts it, "twisting each other's arm." *Wabash Avenue* replicated *Coney Island*'s plot points, but the result is a bawdier and brassier version that reveals the full range of Betty's performance style: lowbrow, middlebrow, and highbrow. She shimmies, bumps, high-kicks, sings ballads, dances elegantly, and finally finds her niche in musical theater.

Wabash Avenue's establishing shot is just a sign post rather than the usual row of attractions, as Victor Mature arrives at the Loop Café in Chicago, owned by his former business partner (Phil Harris), who cheated him out of his share in a carnival. The café's leading attraction is Betty, who comes on stage demurely dressed in a blue blouse and lavender skirt, which she quickly sheds behind a screen, from which she extends a leg enticingly and then emerges in a gold fringed tights, singing "I Wish I Could Shimmy Like My Sister Kate." She is so desirable that a man jumps up and tries to embrace her. She pushes him away and continues the number, bumping (no grinds) as the fringes shake with her. It was the closest Betty ever came to doing a burlesque act, even pulling the curtain back at the end and throwing out a leg. In her second number, she performs "Honey Man" with a cool Walter B. Long as her "little, lovin' honey man," a parody of a torch song, in which she swears she would "sigh, cry, and lay me down and die" without him, while doing a send up of a mating dance in her black dress and arm-length red gloves. She mocks the torch song conventions (hand to forehead, yearning look, pleading eyes) as she leans against his back, kicking her leg in time with the music. She even gives her honey man a kick, too.

In both films, the original and the remake, Betty has to be taught to sing a ballad as written. In *Coney Island*, George Montgomery ripped the excess off her gown and handcuffed her, so that she would not bounce all over the stage while singing "Cuddle Up a Little Closer." In *Wabash Avenue*, Victor Mature just de-feathered her and conducted "Baby, Won't You Say You Love Me?" in the right tempo, leaving her no other choice but to follow his beat. "Baby" marked the end of act one: the emergence of an artist from tawdry Wabash Avenue. Next stop: Broadway. At that point, there is no return to shimmying and bumping. In her Broadway debut, she arrives on stage in a carriage, dressed in a full-length blue dress with matching hat and parasol. She is greeted by various men ("I Remember You"), none of whom is her favorite, Bill. His name provides the segue into "Billy," in which she enumerates everything she did with him, noting that "when I sleep, I always (pause) dream of Bill." The pause said it all. She knew what the audience expected to hear, but she withheld it, preferring the suggestive to the obvious.

When Betty stars in Oscar Hammerstein's fictitious operetta, her big number is "Wilhemina," who is "the cutest little girl in Copenhagen," pursued by men but to no avail. The number had great charm (it was Oscar-nominated), if limited possibilities for rhyming ("Copenhagen" with "noggin" and "toboggan"), but it also gave Betty a chance to dance energetically with a chorus of men and exhibit the innocence of an ingénue, which was remarkable for a woman of thirty-three.

The finale is the standard reprise-close-up. After Betty learns that the men's hoodwinking each other was their way of bonding, she realizes that Harris's sabotaging her marriage to Mature was pay back for an earlier deception. To prove her love for him, she arranges to replace the singer at his Bowery saloon and perform the song that brought her to Oscar Hammerstein's attention: "Baby, Won't You Say You Love Me?" which closes out the film. Unfortunately, none of her later musicals reached the level of *Wabash Avenue*, and her career went into a slow downspin.

CALL ME MISTER (1951)

Why Zanuck decided to buy the rights to the musical revue, *Call Me Mister* (1946), knowing that it could never be filmed in its original form, is hard to fathom, unless he thought that it could be refitted with a storyline for a Betty Grable and Dan Dailey musical. *Call Me Mister* was their final pairing on film; it is also the weakest of their four musicals in terms of both script and soundtrack. Harold Rome's score was winnowed down to three songs; absent was the best known one, "South America, Take It Away," which sold a million records in the Bing Crosby- Andrews Sisters version. But it really did not matter, since the movie bore no resemblance to the original, which celebrated the return of former members of the armed services to civilian life where they would be addressed as "Mister" (hence the title), not by rank. The cast wore their uniforms until the finale in which they appeared in the latest fashions singing the title song.

For the similarly titled movie (it cannot be called "movie version"), Albert E. Lewin and Burt Styler threw together a plot about a divorced couple (Betty and Dailey) who find themselves in postwar Japan—she as an entertainer; he, as an army sergeant stationed in Tokyo. Naturally, they rediscover each other, and after a series of complications, love blossoms anew. Meanwhile, one has to sit through some pedestrian numbers, the nadir being "Japanese Girl Like 'Merican Boy" ("Gee, I wish I had a G.I."), with Betty as a geisha in a kimono surrounded by a group of young Japanese women who look coy and flutter their fans. Anyone who winced during "Friendly Islands" in *My Blue Heaven* will do the same at this number, particularly since the setting is occupied Japan. It was not only insulting to a defeated nation but it also perpetuated the notion that everything American, including sex, is superior to the foreign equivalent.

Call Me Mister was also Betty's last picture with a costar who was a Twentieth Century-Fox contract player. Now, without Dan Dailey, Victor Mature, and Dick Haymes, she was set adrift with Macdonald Carey, Eddie Albert, Dale Robertson, Jack Lemmon, and Gower Champion. In her last film, *How to Be Very, Very Popular* (1955), which could hardly be called a musical, she was reunited with her *Moon Over Miami* costar, Robert Cummings; he was forty-five; she, thirty-nine. In addition, she had directors with whom she had never worked: Richard Sale (*Meet Me after the Show*), H. C. Potter (*Three for the Show*), Henry Levin (*The Farmer Takes a Wife*), and Nunnally Johnson (*How to Be Very, Very Popular*). None of these filmmakers could compare with her favorites: Walter Lang, Irving Cummings, George Seaton, and Henry Koster. Although she had some good songwriters (Jule Styne and Leo Robin in *Meet Me After the Show*; Harold Arlen and Dorothy Fields in *The Farmer Takes a Wife*), they provided her with second-rate songs. Except for *Meet Me after the Show*, her movies were musical remakes: *The Farmer Takes a Wife* (1953), from a 1935 romantic comedy of the same name with Henry Fonda and Janet Gaynor; *Three for the Show* (Columbia, 1955), of *Too Many Husbands* (Columbia, 1940); and *How to Be Very, Very Popular*, of *She Loves Me Not*, originally a novel by Edward Hope, dramatized by Howard Lindsay, and filmed as a musical (Paramount, 1934), with Bing Crosby and Kitty Carlisle. *How to Be Very, Very Popular* was the fourth iteration of *She Loves Me Not* as well as Betty's cinematic swan song.

MEET ME AFTER THE SHOW (1951)

Meet Me after the Show (1951) could at least claim to be an original screenplay, although it is basically a screwball comedy of remarriage with Betty and Macdonald Carey as a show business couple—he, a Pygmalion-type producer who boasts that he turned Betty from a nightclub performer into a Broadway star (see *Coney Island* and *Wabash Avenue*). Carey's "involvement" with another woman (see *My Blue Heaven*) leads to a divorce (see *Call Me Mister*), although Betty's so-called rival is really a backer of her husband's new show. Betty fakes amnesia and returns to her old Miami nightclub. Then Carey develops a real case of amnesia when Betty accidentally hits him on the head with an oar. She feels guilty, he recovers, and it's time for another round of wedding bells.

The musical sequences are undistinguished, although one is notable for its weird incongruousness. In "I Feel Like Dancing," Betty and Gwen Verdon, uncredited except for her name in a playbill, impersonate street kids who seem to be playing cops and robbers and/or cowboys and Indians until it's fantasy time, as Betty envisions herself in a red-tinged gown arriving at a ballroom where men in black masks carrying candelabras weave in and out of dancing couples. Jule Styne's music owes much to Ravel's "La Valse," with its swirling and restless rhythms suggesting a waltz gone out of control, as if everyone were trying desperately to keep the evening from ending by dancing feverishly until the music reaches its inevitable climax, and the dancing ends abruptly. Although "I Feel Like Dancing" is a street urchin's reverie, it represents the most sophisticated dancing Betty had ever done. She gives herself completely to her (uncredited) partner who whirls her around so gracefully that they seem to be airborne.

THE FARMER TAKES A WIFE (1953)

There was very little grace in *The Farmer Takes a Wife* (1953), despite a score by first-class songwriters, Harold Arlen and Dorothy Fields, who were ill at ease with a story set along the Erie Canal in 1850. Zanuck had been thinking of remaking *The Farmer Takes a Wife* (1935) as early as 1944, with Lon McCallister and Jeanne Crain as a follow up to *Home in Indiana* (1944), with McCallister in the Henry Fonda role of a mild-mannered farmer in love with a cook (Crain in the Janet Gaynor role), whose boyfriend is a punch-throwing boater. Crain was destined for better films (*State Fair, Margie, A Letter to Three Wives*), while McCallister left the studio after *Scudda Hoo! Scudda Hay!* (1948), made a few forgettable films, and retired from the screen in 1953. Zanuck then decided to remake *The Farmer Takes a Wife* as a musical, with Mitzi Gaynor, according to the *Hollywood Reporter* (August 16, 1951). Gaynor, then twenty-one, was the right age for the character of Molly Larkins. But when Gaynor was cast as Eva Tanguay in *The I Don't Care Girl* (1953), the part went to Betty, then in her mid-thirties and still (but not for long) a Twentieth Century-Fox contract player, whose glory days were rapidly coming to a close. The musical was planned as vintage Americana with *Oklahoma!*-style dancing and a harbor setting that recalled *Carousel*, but despite director Henry Levin's good intentions, it became a boisterous display of brawn, song, tepid romance, men beating each other up, jumping into the canal, or getting tossed into it. Even Betty had to fall into the canal so that farmer-turned-boater Dan Harrow (a burly Dale Robertson) can rescue her, signaling the beginning of their romance. The canal is so much a part of the plot that it seems more like a character than a waterway.

The period costumes with their hoopskirts did not flatter Betty's figure. One got a brief glimpse of her fabulous legs when she lifted one of them up while bathing, but what was so unique about her in the earlier films now seemed plain and ordinary. Betty had one good number, "Today I Love Everybody," which she sang while rushing down the street, excited by the annual opening of the canal. But the rest of the score was so commonplace that even Betty could not elevate it to anything higher than middling.

Any feminist hoping that the ending of the remake would be more enlightened than that of the original (in which Molly, who is initially loath to leave the canal, finally agrees to be a farmer's wife and immediately asks where the kitchen is), would have been disappointed. In the remake, Molly, who was born on her father's boat, agrees to marry Dan but refuses to live on a farm. From Betty's impassioned speech about staying on the canal, despite the threat of the transcontinental railroad, one assumes there will be some kind of compromise. However, in the next scene, a double wedding ceremony is about to begin: Molly and Dan, and a wealthy widow (Thelma Ritter) and a peddler (Eddie Foy Jr.) with the emblematic names of Lucy Cashdollar and Fortune Friendly. In the interim, Molly must have undergone an epiphany, since she is now happy to embrace farm life (although one cannot imagine her planting crops) and reprises "Today I Love Everybody," leaving audiences with a simple message: a woman's place is on a farm, not a canal.

The Farmer Takes a Wife cost $1.860 million and only brought in $1.15 million domestically. Gone were the days when *Sweet Rosie O'Grady* (1943) and *The Dolly Sisters* (1945) were Twentieth Century-Fox's top grossing films.

Betty's other 1953 film, *How to Marry a Millionaire* (1953), with Lauren Bacall and Marilyn Monroe, was not a musical. She was billed first in the credits, as she had been since 1941. But after Marilyn caused such a sensation in *Gentlemen Prefer Blondes* (1953), the order was reversed in the ads and the trailer. Marilyn's name preceded Betty's, which was followed by Lauren's. In terms of plot, Lauren's character, Schatze, was the most important; she was the only one who succeeded in marrying a millionaire—but for love, not money. Although the "three women in search-of wealthy-husbands" plot seemed like another *Three Blind Mice/Moon over Miami/Three Little Girls in Blue*, *How to Marry a Millionaire* was actually inspired by Zoë Akins's play *The Greeks Had a Word for It* (1932), with a character replacement. Producer-screenwriter Nunnally Johnson realized that while Lauren and Marilyn would be right for Schatze and Polaire, now renamed Paola, Betty would not as the unscrupulous Jean. For Jean, he substituted Loco Dempsey from the 1946 Broadway flop, *Loco*, believing the character was better suited to Betty's sunny screen image. *Loco*, which ran on Broadway for a month in fall 1946, had starred Jean Parker as a model whom a businessman brings to his lodge where she contracts measles. In the film, Betty/Loco is a model whom Fred Clark takes to his Maine lodge where *he* develops a case of measles, and she finds a forest ranger (Rory Calhoun) who is not a millionaire but quite a hunk.

Betty never had to share the screen with two women like Lauren and Marilyn, who possessed such powerful personas. If she remained at Twentieth Century-Fox, it would be more of the same: secondary roles under the guise of leads. She knew it was time to leave and parted amicably with Zanuck. When she returned to the studio to make *How to Be Very, Very Popular* (1955), she was considered freelance—not contract—talent. Betty still felt she could do musicals, if not at Twentieth Century-Fox, then elsewhere, even at Harry Cohn's Columbia Pictures. Cohn was pleased with the way Columbia's classic screwball comedy *The Awful Truth* (1937) was remade as the musical *Let's Do It Again* (1953), with the divorcing couple (Jane Wyman and Ray Milland) as a former Broadway star and her producer-husband.

It may have been Columbia's music supervisor and voice coach, Fred Karger, who persuaded Cohn to do something similar with *Too Many Husbands* (1940), in which Jean Arthur, believing her husband (Fred Mac-Murray) has drowned, remarries (Melvyn Douglas), only to discover that he is alive. Since Karger had guided the then unknown Marilyn Monroe through her two numbers in *Ladies of the Chorus* (1949) and did the same for Jane Wyman in *Let's Do It Again*, one could well imagine Karger's convincing Cohn that *Too Many Husbands* could also profit from a musical makeover called *Three for the Show* (Columbia, 1955), with a similar show-business theme: a musical comedy star (Betty), who, after learning that her songwriter-husband (Jack Lemmon) was killed in action in Korea, marries his partner (Gower Champion). Inevitably, the husband shows up at the last performance of her show. She faints, and after much dickering over who will break the news to husband #1, the two men are reduced to sharing a bedroom while Betty makes up her mind, even envisioning herself as the only woman in an all-male harem dancing with abandon to the music of Borodin's *Polovetsian Dances*. Compared to the eighty-one-minute *Too Many Husbands*, *Three for the Show* goes on for another eleven minutes on the principle that if the plot cannot move along at its own speed, accelerate with song.

One also suspects that the hybrid score was Karger's idea, probably in conjunction with music arranger George Dunning: Gershwin standards ("I've Got a Crush on You" and "Someone to Watch Over Me," the latter danced sublimely by Marge and Gower Champion); familiar classics ("Polovetsian Dances," the "William Tell" overture); unhummable new songs ("Down Boy," "Which One"); a 1924 oldie ("How Come You Do Me Like You Do"); and a repeat ("I've Been Kissed Before," which Rita Hayworth introduced in *Affair in Trinidad* [Columbia, 1952]).

When Betty performed—or, rather, vamped her way through—"I've Been Kissed Before" and "How Come You Do Me Like You Do," she didn't so much sing the lyrics as purr them. It was obvious she was imitating, but not parodying, Marilyn. She sings "I've Been Kissed Before" when she is auditioning for a job in a Greenwich Village club. She performs "How Come You Do Me Like You Do" at a dress rehearsal to show husband #1 that he is her true love. She slinks down off the stage on to the top of the piano he is playing, addressing him personally and elongating all the "o's" as if she were cooing. If Marilyn performed the song, it would have been with her usual feral sensuousness. Betty is just eerily sexy, but it is feigned sexiness from a woman in her mid-thirties who never had to work so hard to convince a man that she was in love with him. Perhaps with age comes effort, which is the main problem with *Three for the Show*. The effort shows, as does the strain. Someone—perhaps director H. C. Potter—was familiar enough with the Twentieth Century-Fox finale to have the four principals (Betty, Jack Lemmon, Gower Champion, Marge Champion) exit the stage door reprising "I've Got a Crush on You." The finale may have been in the Twentieth Century-Fox tradition, but *Three for the Show* was a Columbia anomaly. Of the stars, only Jack Lemmon, who had a multi-picture contract with Columbia, could claim any association with the studio. Betty was, and always will be, a Twentieth Century-Fox star; the Champions were chiefly MGM. H. C. Potter, who was primarily a stage director, had never worked at Columbia. *Three for the Show* was just a mediocre musical that happened to bear the Columbia Pictures trademark.

Very few movie careers end in a blaze of glory, and Betty Grable's is no exception. Some of the old Betty hovers over *Three for the Show*, but it's too spectral to be anything other than a ghost of musicals past.

HOW TO BE VERY, VERY POPULAR (1955)

Three for the Show was minor Betty. *How to Be Very, Very Popular* (1955) was an embarrassment. *Three for the Show* was in production from mid-February to mid-May 1954 and released in February 1955; *How to Be Very, Very Popular*, from February 21 to April 14, 1955, and released that July. Betty probably had no idea that one of the *Three for the Show* writers was Edward Hope, who wrote the novel *She Loves Me Not*, which Howard Lindsay dramatized under the same title. The play, in which a nightclub performer who has witnessed a murder, takes refuge in a Princeton dormitory at a time when Princeton was a men's college, enjoyed a run of 360 performances during the 1933–34 season. Paramount immediately bought the rights and filmed it under the same title with Miriam Hopkins as the murder witness, Bing Crosby as a Princeton undergrad, and Kitty Carlisle as the Dean's daughter. With America's entry into World War II, Paramount thought it was time for a remake: *True to the Army* (1943), with an army base in lieu of a university, and a tightrope walker (Judy Canova) instead of a dancer. This time, the victim is a circus owner, and the sole witness (Canova) hides out at Fort Bray disguised as an army private. In both films, men (students, army personnel) conceal a woman's identity by dressing her up as a man.

In 1954, Nunnally Johnson had been given a new writer-producer-director contract at Twentieth Century-Fox, where he had been since 1934, except for a brief period in the 1940s when he worked at other studios. But his best screenplays were for Zanuck: *The Grapes of Wrath, The Moon Is Down, The Keys of the Kingdom, The Gunfighter, Three Came Home, How to Marry a Millionaire*, etc. On December 4, 1954, Zanuck congratulated Johnson on his contract "not only because you earned it and deserve it, but because you have . . . relieved me of a lot of headaches and extra work." One of Johnson's first duties as writer-producer-director was to find a project that would reunite Marilyn Monroe and Jane Russell, the stars of *Gentlemen Prefer Blondes*, Twentieth Century-Fox's third highest-grossing film of 1953 ($5.1 million). Johnson thought that such a combination would work with another makeover of *She Loves Me Not* in CinemaScope and color with not one but two murder witnesses: "exotic dancers" befriended by members of a college fraternity. Since the college is now coed, there is no need for drag, which would have looked ludicrous on them. Marilyn balked at the notion of making another movie with Russell, who had starred in the *Gentlemen*

Prefer Blondes clone, *The French Line* (RKO, 1954), with Mary McCarty as her sidekick. Marilyn probably suspected that Russell's was the flashier part and bowed out, leaving Johnson no other choice but to recast the film with Betty in the part originally intended for Marilyn and Sheree North, Zanuck's latest blonde starlet, in the secondary role of Curly Flagg, the lead in the 1934 version when there was only one murder witness. As it turned out, North walked off with the movie after doing "Shake, Rattle and Roll"; at a college commencement, tearing off the graduation gown she wore over her tights (neither she nor Betty had time to change after the murder), bumping, grinding, and shaking while holding onto the podium. Johnson had seen North do a similar dance in the Broadway musical *Hazel Flagg* (1953), based on the screwball comedy *Nothing Sacred* (1937), with Helen Gallagher in the Carole Lombard role. The number was called "Salome," and although it did not require the shedding of any veils, it would have more than satisfied an ogling Herod. Johnson added a storyline in which Curly is accidentally hypnotized and starts stripping whenever she hears the word "Salome" or a soundalike. At the graduation, the commencement speaker alludes to the battle of Salamis, causing Curly, disguised as a graduating senior, to doff her gown and go into her "interpretative dance," causing the other coeds to do the same.

Any academic who saw the film must have wondered on what planet Bristol College was located. To wangle an endowment from a millionaire whose son (Orson Bean) had been expelled, the Dean (Charles Coburn) goes so far as to issue him a diploma. But the college gets the endowment after the father discovers that his son had staged a successful panty raid, proving that he is a real man and not a bookworm.

Betty, cast as the uneducated Stormy Tornado, is prone to malapropisms, which make her sound like an airhead. Although she's an exotic dancer, we only see her dancing in long shot at the beginning of the film as she, North, and two others perform the title song, which was Johnson's way of saying that *How to Be Very, Very Popular* is not a musical but an intricately plotted farce involving deception, misunderstanding, impersonation, mistaken identity, and characters getting bopped on the head when they open the wrong door.

To paraphrase T. S. Eliot, a career can end with a bang or a whimper. Betty Grable's film career ended with a bang, but the sound came from Sheree North, who never had the career at Twentieth Century-Fox that

Zanuck envisioned for her. After 1958, she was no longer a contract player. She had the "little girl lost" look that Marilyn could flash but not the mysterious allure that was also part of Marilyn's persona. A far better dancer than Marilyn, Sheree North could play secondary roles in Broadway musicals, but stardom eluded her despite her talent. Still, she is the only reason *How to Be Very, Very Popular* is worth viewing.

Chapter 19

"I HATED MARILYN MONROE!"

—Zanuck to Mel Gussow

Although Marilyn Monroe (1926–62) is often remembered as the star of movie musicals, she only made four of them (one at Columbia, three at Twentieth Century-Fox) in a career that spanned almost two decades and twenty-eight films—twenty-nine, if *Scudda Hoo! Scudda Hay!* (1948) is included, in which "her brief scene in a rowboat was cut." Twentieth Century-Fox's casting director, Ben Lyon was responsible for bringing Marilyn, then Norma Jeane Baker, to Zanuck's attention. When Zanuck saw the screen test that she made on July 19, 1946, he was unimpressed but felt there was no harm in offering her a seventy-five-dollars-a-week contract for six months with the option of renewal. Since she lacked acting experience, her contract was not renewed, but thanks to Lyon, she at least had a name with all the liquid consonants: l, m, n, r. Marilyn Monroe spelled star; Norma Jeane Baker spelled nothing.

Marilyn began taking acting seriously—or at least seriously enough for her drama coach, Natasha Lytess, to persuade Max Arnow, Columbia Pictures' casting director, to consider her for the role of a burlesque queen's daughter who follows in her mother's footsteps in *Ladies of the Chorus* (Columbia, 1949). Marilyn displayed a voluptuousness that was as natural as it was performative. She was capable of bringing a feline sleekness to a number, rather like a Persian cat that knows it's being admired and preens in acknowledgement. No one at Twentieth Century-Fox appears to have seen *Ladies of the Chorus*; otherwise, Marilyn would have been welcomed back and groomed as Betty Grable's successor, which is eventually what happened, but not until 1952.

Marilyn was fortunate in her early career to have an agent like Johnny Hyde who could get her small but impressive roles in *The Asphalt Jungle* (MGM, 1949) and *All about Eve* (TCF, 1950). In March 1951, she finally received a new contract at Twentieth Century-Fox, which became her home studio for the next seven years. At first there were only secondary, not even supporting, roles (*As Young as You Feel*, *Love Nest*, *Let's Make It Legal*, all 1951), until she was cast in *Don't Bother to Knock* (1952) as the emotionally disturbed (and frighteningly unstable) niece of a hotel elevator operator who recommends her to a couple seeking a babysitter for the evening. As Nell Forbes, Marilyn made paranoia seem normal. When she puts on the mother's black negligee and gazes at her image in a mirror, she is not the dowdy poor relation any longer but a seductively glamorous woman like the one young Norma Jeane must have seen when she imagined herself as the love goddess she eventually became. If Marilyn could play Nell Forbes, the suicidal babysitter in *Don't Bother to Knock*, she could play Rose Loomis, the adulterous wife conspiring with her lover to kill her husband in *Niagara* (1953). And if she was scary as Nell Forbes, she was lethal as Rose Loomis in a symbolically red dress that needed no decoding.

GENTLEMEN PREFER BLONDES (1953)

When Zanuck decided to film the 1949 Broadway musical *Gentlemen Prefer Blondes* (1953), it had already been a 1925 novella by Anita Loos that she and her husband turned into a stage play in 1926, which Paramount purchased and filmed as a silent two years later. Zanuck felt the role of Lorelei Lee would be perfect for Betty Grable, who could humanize the character and keep her from becoming viewed as a gold digger. Then he realized that he would have to pay Betty $150,000, the same amount he paid for the rights to the musical. Marilyn, however, came cheap. When *Gentlemen Prefer Blondes* went before the cameras on November 17, 1952, Marilyn was in the second year of her 1951 contract, which guaranteed her $500 a week for the first year and, if renewed, as it was, $750 a week for the second. Marilyn only made $18,000 for the film, which wrapped up in late January 1953; her costar, Jane Russell, loaned out by RKO's Howard Hughes, not only received top billing but also $200,000. While Russell was a good choice for Dorothy Shaw, Lorelei's bosom buddy, *Gentleman Prefer Blondes* was Marilyn's movie; Jane's was *The Outlaw* (1943).

As with many film adaptations of Broadway musicals, the book was substantially rewritten and the score severely reduced. The stage version was considerably more sophisticated. It begins with Gus Esmond, a button manufacturer and Lorelei's "sugar daddy," seeing Lorelei and Dorothy off as they board the *Isle de France* for Paris. Gus assumes that Dorothy will be the impressionable Lorelei's chaperone, but Dorothy has other plans, as she admits in "It's High Time (That We All Got Stinking)," in which she looks forward to booze and male companionship. Gus is conflicted about leaving Lorelei and sings the plaintive "Bye, Bye, Baby," asking her to promise that "though on the loose, you are still on the square." Lorelei, however, is uncertain about their relationship because of a past incident: she shot a man in self-defense. In the delightfully risqué "A Little Girl from Little Rock," she describes herself as a girl from the wrong side of the tracks until she met a man who taught her wrong from right. On board, Lorelei attracts the attention of two men, Joseph Gage, a zipper manufacturer (she at least stays within the garment trade), and Sir Francis Beekman, whose wife has a diamond tiara that she is eager to sell for $5,000 and that Lorelei is eager to buy—with a loan from Sir Francis. In the meantime, Dorothy has grown fond of Henry Spofford, a wealthy Philadelphian, but realizes she would never be accepted by his family. Love eventually conquers class, but not until Gus arrives in Paris and is shocked to see Lorelei with the zipper king. At a club, Lorelei performs "Diamonds Are a Girl's Best Friend," in which she explains her preference for diamonds instead of cash for services rendered. Like "A Little Girl from Little Rock," "Diamonds Are a Girl's Best Friend" is suggestive in a strangely innocent way, as if sex was wholesale; and its benefits, retail. Gus relents and expresses his love for Lorelei, who wins over his father when he sees her in a dress covered with his buttons.

Gentlemen Prefer Blondes never received any Tony Awards, yet it managed to run for 749 performances, largely because of Carol Channing, whose Lorelei was not the original Material Girl but a life-loving flapper who discovered early in life that there are men so eager for female companionship and its concomitants that they would set up a bank account for her in return for her favors, which she would dispense as if every night were the first time for her, if not for them. Channing's face registered a perpetual look of surprise and wonderment, and her eyes bespoke an innocence that may have been compromised but not sullied. Taken together, "A Little Girl from Little Rock" and "Diamonds Are a Girl's Best Friend" are Lorelei's bio and credo.

Since the film is "Howard Hawks' *Gentlemen Prefer Blondes*," as the main title attests, Zanuck's involvement was minimal. He insisted, however, that Hawks and screenwriter Charles Lederer never lose sight of two vital plot points: Dorothy's love for Ernie Malone (formerly Henry Spofford and now a private detective) and her "real affection" for Lorelei, whom she imper- sonates when Lorelei is accused of stealing Lady Beekman's tiara. There was no problem with the Dorothy-Malone relationship. Dorothy is only interested in finding the right man, not necessarily a millionaire, and Jane Russell played her that way. And since male bonding is a recurring theme in Hawks's films, he did not need Zanuck to tell him that bonding could work just as well with two females. The Lorelei-Dorothy relationship was one that Hawks understood. Russell's Dorothy is a wisecracking buddy to the irresponsible Lorelei, whose eyes glaze over whenever she hears "diamonds." When Lorelei meets Lord Beekman, who tells her about his diamond mine in South Africa, she sees his head in the form of a sparkling diamond.

Only two songs and a radically revised third survived the winnowing of the original score which consisted of fifteen musical numbers: "Bye, Bye, Baby" and "Diamonds Are a Girl's Best Friend" were retained. "A Little Girl from Little Rock" became "Two Little Girls from Little Rock," which Marilyn and Russell, dressed in identical red slit skirt gowns and matching hats with a spray of feathers, began singing in the pre-credits sequence and finish in the first scene, indicating that it was part of their nightclub routine and not just an eye-catching opening. Dorothy's "I Love What I'm Doing" in the original became "Anyone Here for Love?," which she sings in the ship's gym while moving among members of the Olympics team looking as if they had stepped out of a Grecian urn. They exercise and flex their muscles, indifferent to Dorothy in her black bodysuit except to let her feel a bulging bicep. The milieu is a strange combination of the homoerotic and the heterosexual. Hawks left the musical numbers to choreographer Jack Cole, who was gay, and took advantage of the presence of athletes on board to stage a number juxtaposing their sculpted poses with Dorothy's frustration at being an ignored earth mother.

"Anyone Here for Love?" was more imaginatively staged than "Diamonds Are a Girl's Best Friend," which begins with couples waltzing gracefully as if they were trying to demonstrate the art of dancing to music in three-quarter time. Marilyn is seated, back to camera, oblivious to the swirling that is going on around her. When she turns around, she is wearing a strapless pink gown with braceleted arm-length gloves and sporting an ornate necklace that looks as if it came from a G-string. Men offer her baubles, but she repeats "no" in a high soprano as if she were in an operetta. (The high notes were Marni Nixon's.) Never much of a dancer, but adept at letting her body speak for itself by giving every undulation a meaning of its own, she vamped her way through the number, shaking her hips and endorsing her favorite jewelers by calling out, "Tiffany's! Cartier! Talk to me, Harry Winston. Tell me about it." This was a far cry from Carol Channing, who stood alone on stage and sang the song the way it was written.

Gentlemen Prefer Blondes presented a Marilyn Monroe to the public that conformed to its expectations: a mentally vacant and shamelessly conniving voluptuary whose chief asset was her body. That was her public image, the Hollywood creation. There was the other Marilyn: the serious actress equally at home in drama (*Don't Bother to Knock, Niagara, Bus Stop, The Misfits*) and romantic comedy (*The Seven Year Itch, The Prince and the Showgirl, Some Like It Hot*)—the latter two proving she could hold her own with Sir Laurence Olivier, Jack Lemmon, and Tony Curtis.

If there is an air of vulgarity about Marilyn's Lorelei Lee, Hawks is partly responsible for it. He found her "colossally dumb and profoundly vulgar," which is also the way he perceived the character. Zanuck may have thought so, too, but the characterization suited the script which depicted Lorelei as a diamond struck blonde, more calculating than dumb. In an attempt to explain the film's portrayal of Lorelei as a gold digger, writer Charles Lederer has her say, "I can be smart when I want. But most men don't like it." That confession, however, is at odds with her behavior. Before boarding the *Isle de France*, she asks if it is going to "Europe, France." Lorelei is smart only in the ways of the world.

Zanuck was always ambivalent about Marilyn. When she wanted to bring Natasha Lytess on the set of *Don't Bother to Knock* as a "special dialogue director," Zanuck informed her in writing that she is to "place [herself] in the hands of the director—or else ask to be released from the role." Marilyn remained in the film and continued to rely on Lytess until she discovered the Actors Studio and a new coach, Lee Strasberg's wife, Paula. And yet, when Zanuck saw Marilyn's *Don't Bother to Knock* screen test, he sent her "a glowing note." On the other hand, Zanuck told his biographer that he "hated" Marilyn and "wouldn't have slept with her if she paid me." Zanuck could claim credit for launching her career, but not for creating her persona. Marilyn did that herself.

THERE'S NO BUSINESS LIKE SHOW BUSINESS (1954)

Marilyn was second-billed in *Gentlemen Prefer Blondes*. In *There's No Business Like Show Business* (1954), she was third-billed after Ethel Merman and Donald O'Connor, followed by Dan Dailey, Johnnie Ray, and Mitzi Gaynor. With five well-known stars and one pop singer (Ray), no one could rightly be called "the lead." *There's No Business Like Show Business* was the second film in Merman's two-picture deal with Twentieth Century-Fox. The first was *Call Me Madam* (1953), released as *Irving Berlin's Call Me Madam*, in which Merman was clearly the star, reprising the role she created on Broadway where she played Sally Adams, an ambassador to a mythical European country. The movie version replicated the original for the most part. "They Like Ike" was cut because it was too political. When the film was released, Harry Truman was still president and figured as an unseen character. Even if the song were retained, the final line, "The hell with Harry / They like Ike," would have to go. In "The Hostess with the Mostes' on the Ball," Sally admits she has no problem entertaining an ambassador and his new affair, "but she mustn't leave her panties in the hall." The song remained in the film; the reference to the ambassador and his lover's underwear was cut.

Although Merman knew she was not the star of *There's No Business Like Show Business*, she had her attorneys insist on top billing, partly because she was concerned about her image but mostly out of fear of being eclipsed by Marilyn, which is ironic since initially Marilyn's character not did not exist in Lamar Trotti's original story about a show business couple and their two children—a son who falls in love with a "Mitzi Gaynor" type; and a daughter who finds romance with a famous dancer. When Trotti died in 1952, Phoebe and Henry Ephron inherited the project. Marilyn, who went on suspension for refusing to do the film version of *The Girl in Pink Tights*, Sigmund Romberg's posthumously produced operetta, was offered a role in the film which she agreed to do if her next would be *The Seven Year Itch* (1955), as it was. When Marilyn came on board, the "Mitzi Gaynor

type" became Katy Donahue (Mitzi Gaynor), who, along with her brother
Tim (Donald O'Connor), is part of a vaudeville team, the Five Donahues,
headed by their parents, Molly and Terry Donahue (Ethel Merman and
Dan Dailey). The fifth is Steve (Johnnie Ray), who is more of a vocalist
than a performer and more committed to becoming a priest than staying
a Donahue—but not before he sings "If You Believe" at his send-off, which
Ray delivers with the fervor of an evangelist.

This was Zanuck's type of musical, "a combination of comedy and
pathos," although there was little comedy and a great many of Irving Berlin's
songs, with the pathos reserved for the ending. The role of Vicky Hoffman
(Marilyn), a hatcheck girl who becomes stage performer Vicky Parker,
was added to the script as the love interest for Tim, who, when she shows
more interest in her career than in him, turns to drink and later joins the
navy—but arrives in time for the grand (and it is indeed) finale. Zanuck had
not made such an emotionally charged musical since *Alexander's Ragtime
Band* in 1938. *There's No Business Like Show Business* would not follow the
storylines of most Twentieth Century-Fox musicals in which a vaude-
villian/saloon singer goes from a dive in San Francisco's Barbary Coast/
New York's Coney Island/Chicago's Wabash Avenue to Broadway. It would
be about a family of five entertainers, whose parents survived the Great
Depression by doing radio commercials and working at carnivals. One of
their sons turns to liquor out of what he thinks is unrequited love; another
joins the priesthood. At a benefit performance on the closing night of the
Hippodrome, it seems that the Five Donahues will only be represented by
Molly and Katy. Terry has not returned from searching for Tim, but Steve,
now an army chaplain and ready to join them, has arrived. Finally, Terry
appears with the prodigal son, who had enlisted in the navy. This was
every bit Zanuck's movie, as the main title proclaims: "Darryl F. Zanuck
Presents / A CinemaScope Production / Irving Berlin's *There's No Business
Like Show Business.*" Since the legendary Hippodrome closed in August
1939, the regulation attire of Donald O'Connor and Johnnie Ray was out
of place, unless we are to assume that they anticipated the war that was to
break out in Europe the following month and were eager to do their part
before America entered it.

There's No Business Like Show Business might have been a better film with
Mitzi Gaynor as Donald O'Connor's romantic partner and June Haver as
his sister. Zanuck felt, however, that it needed some sex, first with Sheree

North if Marilyn was still balking about appearing in what was clearly a supporting role, despite the billing. When Marilyn finally joined the cast, not even she could get the $4.430 million production to gross more than $4.5 million in domestic rentals. Any musical with Marilyn required the numbers to be tailored to her Lorelei Lee image, which is the only one that the public had of her as a musical performer. "The age demanded" the Marilyn who could wiggle and undulate, lounge around indolently as if she were perpetually unemployed, and stir up sex with a shimmy and a shake.

When Vicky Hoffman becomes Vicky Parker, the nightclub entertainer, she slinks onto the floor in a form-fitting, split-down-the-side white gown with a sheer bodice and a hat with an array of white feathers. Not much of a singer and even less of a dancer, Marilyn relied on her body to parse the lyrics of "After You Get What Want (You Don't Want It)," moving among the tables, flirting with the male patrons, and even sliding onto a table and extending a leg. "After You Get What You Want" was discreet compared to "Heat Wave," in which Marilyn arrives on stage reclining in a cart, wearing a hat festooned with curlicues of cord and a two-piece outfit with a skimpy top and a low-slung skirt designed to separate into two ruffle-lined sections, so that Marilyn could shake them while enticing a chorus of bare-chested males. Ed Sullivan found "Heat Wave" "one of the most flagrant violations of good taste" he had ever seen. It was just supremely vulgar, but that was the way choreographer Robert Alton staged it. He gave the public the Marilyn they expected: sultry-voiced and defiantly uninhibited.

Alton staged "Lazy" with Gaynor and O'Connor as a Greek chorus commenting on the sight of Marilyn in high heels and a black unitard with an aquamarine sash, lolling around on a chaise longue and ignoring phone calls because inertia had gotten the best of her. Instead of working the room, Marilyn worked the chaise, sliding down the back and stretching out, as if she expected it to respond to her blandishments. Languor did not affect O'Connor and Gaynor, who are entrusted with the real dancing, which they continued doing even when Marilyn joined them, behaving as if she was too world weary to do much of anything. If she did, it would have put her at a disadvantage. Gaynor and O'Connor were accomplished dancers. Marilyn was an accomplished poseur.

The finale of *There's No Business Like Show Business* was in the grand tradition of closure à la Twentieth Century-Fox, in which a stage production with reprises ends the film, so that the performance we are seeing and the movie we are watching end simultaneously. Merman, spotlighted on a staircase, walks down to the stage in a white gown with a winged bodice designed to create an hour-glass figure. It was a thrill to hear her sing, as only she can, "There's No Business Like Show Business," which she introduced on stage in Irving Berlin's *Annie Get Your Gun* (1946). When Merman gets to the line "There's no people like show people," she shouts out "people" with such intensity that there was no doubt that she knew the territory after having spent, at that time, nearly a quarter of a century in the theater. Twice, director Walter Lang cuts to the wings, first to show Steve and Katy watching their mother perform; and then, when Merman gets to the line "Let's go, on with the show," Tim appears in his navy uniform. As Merman moves closer to stage left, she sees her family in the wings, and her voice breaks in joy. The Donahues are reunited and, along with Vicky, now reconciled with Tim, begin the reprises, starting with "Alexander's Ragtime Band," which had been heard twice before. An elaborate rendition of the title song follows with the six stars, arm in arm, walking down a staircase bathed in blue with a star-sprinkled background, while dancers wave colorful banners in a wide shot suggesting the actual Hippodrome Theatre's enormous 100' x 200' stage.

There's No Business Like Show Business should have been Marilyn's last venture into musicals, but one more remained: *Let's Make Love* (1960). After *Show Business*, Marilyn embarked upon the most fulfilling period of her career in a series of films that showcased her versatility: romantic comedies (*The Seven Year Itch, Some Like It Hot, The Prince and the Show-girl*) and dramas (*Bus Stop, The Misfits*). In 1955, Marilyn signed a contract with Twentieth Century-Fox that called for four films over a seven-year period. As of 1959, she had only made one, *Bus Stop* (1956). *Let's Make Love* (1960) was planned as the second, from an original screenplay by Norman Krasna, conceived as the companion piece to *The Prince and the Showgirl*, in which Marilyn played an American musical comedy performer who becomes involved with a prince (Laurence Olivier).

LET'S MAKE LOVE (1960)

In *Let's Make Love*, Marilyn is the star of a musical revue who becomes involved with a billionaire. Since there can be no future for a commoner and a royal, the prince and the showgirl can only enjoy an evening together, after which they part. Billionaires, however, are not peers, so *Let's Make Love* can end happily but only after a round of deceptions that begins when a French business tycoon (Yves Montand) learns he is being satirized in an off-Broadway revue and drops in on a rehearsal, where he is mistaken for an actor. What he sees is Marilyn in a baggy sweater and black tights sliding down a pole and teasing the double entendres out of Cole Porter's "My Heart Belongs to Daddy." Jack Cole was again the choreographer, and again we are treated to Lorelei Lee in her latest incarnation. Mary Martin introduced "My Heart Belongs to Daddy" in Porter's *Leave It To Me* (1938), in which she did a genteel strip while looking virginally innocent and singing what *New York Times* critic Brooks Atkinson called "the bawdy ballad of the season." Martin personified the far side of innocence; Marilyn, the underside of experience. Marilyn may have been rehearsing the number, but she is pitching it to an audience, the camera, whose gaze is the only one that matters. She shakes anything that can move and the camera captures it all. She begins the number by sliding down a pole and declaring with a look of mock innocence: "My name is Lolita [pause] and I'm not supposed [pause] to play [pause] with boys." Thereupon she not only plays with them but they play with her, and she plays with the pole, treating it as more of a fetish than a prop. At the end, she pulls off the sweater, shaking it back and forth the way a dancer does with her last item of apparel, and flings it at Montand.

Marilyn had some excellent directors during her career: Howard Hawks (*Monkey Business, Gentlemen Prefer Blondes*); John Huston (*The Asphalt Jungle, The Misfits*); Joseph L. Mankiewicz (*All About Eve*); Fritz Lang (*Clash by Night*); Henry Hathaway (*Niagara*); Jean Negulesco (*How to Marry a Millionaire*); Otto Preminger (*River of No Return*); Joshua Logan (*Bus Stop*); Billy Wilder (*The Seven Year Itch, Some Like It Hot*). For *Let's Make Love*, she had George Cukor, who concentrated on the script rather than the production numbers and managed to get Marilyn to seem natural for a change as she tries to help Montand, whom she believes is an unemployed actor, adapt to the performance style of a musical revue. This is the kind of narrative made up of layers of deception at which Billy Wilder excelled. Cukor, on the other hand, preferred comedies of wit and sophistication, including *Dinner at Eight, Adam's Rib*, and *Born Yesterday.*

When a host of actors, including Yul Brynner, turned down the role of the billionaire in *Let's Make Love*, Gregory Peck signed on, but "bowed out when he learned that [Marilyn] had demanded script changes" that would have diminished the size of his part. If Wilder were directing, he probably would have sought out Tony Curtis, who did a spot-on imitation of Cary Grant in *Some Like It Hot* and could sound like Charles Boyer if the character remained French. With Montand in the role, the character had to be French, but Montand's limited command of English made his line readings sound leaden. One gimmick, however, worked beautifully. Milton Berle, Gene Kelly, and Bing Crosby are hired to teach Montand, respectively, the techniques of comedy, dance, and song. As Bosley Crowther wrote in his *New York Times* review (September 9, 1960), "In a matter of five minutes, Uncle Milty takes things in hand, knocks off some solid, lowdown humor, and gets the show on the road," thereby stealing the movie. Wilder could have made something out of this "meet cute" (his specialty), in which boy meets girl when she throws her sweater in his face. Cukor could not.

Yet Cukor was assigned to Marilyn's next film, *Something's Got To Give*, a remake of Leo McCarey's *My Favorite Wife* (RKO, 1940), in which Nick Arden (Cary Grant), whose wife Ellen (Irene Dunne) has been declared legally dead, has just married Bianca (Gail Patrick) when Ellen arrives, having been shipwrecked for five years on an island with Stephen Burkett (Randolph Scott), who played Adam to her Eve. The remake was to have starred Marilyn as Ellen, Dean Martin as Nick, and Cyd Charisse as Bianca. With that lineup, *Something's Got To Give* could easily have been a musical and perhaps at some stage was planned as one. It was never completed; in fact, very little of it was shot. The extant footage and outtakes can be viewed on YouTube. Part of the main title had already been designed, with the credits coming on to the sound of Dean Martin's singing Johnny Mercer's "Something's Gotta Give."

It is interesting to see Marilyn's reaction when Cukor calls, "Camera!" Previously, she had been silently speaking her first line, but when she hears "Camera," she immediately goes into character, rarely letter-perfect but always convincing. When Martin confronts her with the Adam and Eve story that has made the newspapers, she had just finished taking a swim and is combing her hair, insisting that her island companion was "a dear old man who wouldn't hurt a fly." In the subsequent takes, she kept alternating between "wouldn't touch a fly" and "wouldn't harm a fly." Even Martin got so rattled that he exclaimed, "For Christ's sake!" What is especially touching is the scene in which Ellen is reunited with her two children, who share memories of their mother, not knowing they are speaking to her. The affection Marilyn showed the children and even the family dog suggested a new Marilyn without the artifice and the beckoning look, a reborn Norma Jeane Baker, nurturing and empathetic, but traces of the old Marilyn remained: the Marilyn who was late to the set, unaccountably absent, and never in full command of her lines. This was unfortunate since the little that was shot indicated that she could handle the role if she had a director like Billy Wilder, who knew that, despite her unpredictable and erratic behavior, in time he would get a good performance from her.

Marilyn knew how to play a scene; the problem was that she did not always deliver the lines as written but rather a version which, in its own way, made sense. She also knew that in playing scenes with Dean Martin, she would use her natural voice, not the kittenish purr. But when she had to be seductive, she morphed into Lorelei Lee. In *My Favorite Wife*, Ellen, not wishing Nick to know that she spent five years on an island with a man who could pass for a bodybuilder, goes into a shoe store and asks a meek salesman to pose as her marooned companion. In *Something's Got To Give*, Marilyn does the same and asks the shy Wally Cox for a particular shoe. Cox replies by describing the kind of alligator from which it was made. Marilyn, affecting a look of seductiveness born out of desperation, asks him to have lunch with her. "I bring my lunch to the store," Cox explains. Marilyn then coos, "Can you take it out?"

When Cukor realized that all he had from Marilyn was "about five days' work," he knew the film could never be made. Marilyn was fired, and production was terminated on June 12, 1962. Marilyn died on August 5, 1962, from "acute barbiturate poisoning—ingestion of overdose."

Marilyn's successor was to have been Sheree North (1932–2005), who would have replaced her in *There's No Business Like Show Business* if she refused the role. Sheree made only seven films at Twentieth Century-Fox between 1955 and 1958, two of which were musicals, and one, a faux musical, *How to Be Very, Very Popular* (1955) in which her "Shake, Rattle and Roll" was the film's highlight. The two musicals were *The Best Things in Life Are Free* (1956), in which she lip-synced the title song to Eileen Wilson's vocal and danced "Black Bottom" and "Birth of the Blues" with Jacques d'Amboise; and *Mardi Gras* (1958), fourth-billed in a supporting role with the personable Pat Boone in the lead. If she had been at MGM, a producer like Arthur Freed or Joe Pasternack might have been able to showcase her talent. Her singing voice always had to be dubbed, but as a dancer she would have been a more than worthy partner for Gene Kelly.

It was evident as early as 1956 that Zanuck was losing interest in Sheree North. She could never be the new Marilyn because she could only be sensuous, not sexual. Marilyn could be both and, in fact, made them synonymous.

WILL SUCCESS SPOIL ROCK HUNTER? (1955)

On October 13, 1955, George Axelrod's comedy, *Will Success Spoil Rock Hunter?* opened at New York's Belasco Theater for a run of 444 performances. Axelrod, inspired by Christopher Marlowe's *The Tragical History of Doctor Faustus*, recast the "man-who-sells-his-soul-to-the-devil" tale as a satire of 1950s Hollywood, in which an inexperienced journalist, George MacCauley (Orson Bean), manages to snag an interview with sex symbol Rita Marlowe (Jayne Mansfield)—the surname being Axelrod's homage to his source. When a Hollywood agent, "Sneaky" LaSalle (Martin Gabel), a stand-in for Mephistopheles, fails to persuade a successful playwright, Michael Freeman (Walter Matthau), to sign with his agency, LaSalle turns his attention to the unsuspecting MacCauley, who agrees to representation, not knowing that he has engaged in a Faustian pact. Immediately his wishes are granted, including sleeping with Rita Marlowe and winning an Oscar for his first script.

Axelrod saw the Hollywood agent, aka "flesh peddler" and "ten-percenter," as an avatar of Mephistopheles, so powerful that he can demand 100 percent of a client, essentially gaining control of his or her soul. But at the end, LaSalle is thwarted when MacCauley gives up Rita, and Freeman, who had pledged 90 percent to LaSalle, withholds the other ten, thus escaping from his thrall.

THE GIRL CAN'T HELP IT (1956)

In his *New York Times* review (October 13, 1955), Brooks Atkinson, while not enamored of the comedy, remarked that Jayne Mansfield played "the platinum-plated movie siren with the wavy contours of Marilyn Monroe . . .

with commendable abandon." Zanuck thought so, too, and Jayne Mansfield (1934–67) was signed to a six-year contract on May 3, 1956, while *Will Success Spoil Rock Hunter?* was still running, although she left before the show closed on November 3, 1956. She was rushed into Frank Tashlin's *The Girl Can't Help It* (1956), a quasi-musical in CinemaScope about the dark side of show business, with cameo appearances by rock 'n' rollers of the period (Little Richard, Fats Domino, Eddie Cochran, Eddie Fontaine), vocalists (Abbey Lincoln and Julie London, the latter of whom is integral to the plot), groups (the Jokers, the Trenlers, the Chuckles), and Ray Anthony and His Orchestra. The film opens with an introduction by Tom Ewell as an agent with a drinking problem, addressing the audience within a black-and-white rectangular frame in the once traditional 1.33:1 aspect ratio, in which the screen is approximately one- and one-third times wider than it is high. He then has the frame expand to the 2.5:1 aspect ratio of CinemaScope, in which the screen is two- and one-half times wider than it is high. Color is added, and the audience is now in the widescreen era. Why Tashlin, who also wrote the screenplay, felt that moviegoers needed an introduction in 1956 to the already established CinemaScope process, is hard to fathom; CinemaScope had been around for three years, beginning with *The Robe* (1953).

The plot of *The Girl Can't Help It* was the underside of the "star is born" template, in which a slot machine racketeer (Edmond O'Brien) pays a clientless agent (Tom Ewell) to make his inamorata (Jayne Mansfield) into a pop star and recording artist. Ewell is both an alcoholic and a torch carrier, never having gotten over losing his biggest star, Julie London, who appears in his drunken fantasies singing (what else?) "Cry Me a River."

The blank-faced Ewell was the right costar for Marilyn in *The Seven Year Itch*; if there was anyone who could reawaken the libido of a middle-aged husband whose wife and son were on vacation, it was she. Since the casting of Ewell and a voluptuous blonde worked so well in *The Seven Year Itch*, Zanuck tried it again in Frank Tashlin's *The Lieutenant Wore Skirts* (1956), with Ewell and Sheree North, which brought in $2.240 million in rentals. *The Girl Can't Help It*, with Ewell and Jayne Mansfield, did even better: $2.8 million. Unlike Marilyn, Jayne was a platinum blonde who only played the sex kitten when she was with Edmond O'Brien; when she realized how ruthless he was, she stopped purring and denounced him in her natural voice, the kind she used when she was with Ewell. Jayne was quite believable as a competent singer who pretends to have no ear for music and can only emit odd sounds because she would rather be a wife and mother than a performer. The best she can do is supply a siren shriek in a song that O'Brien had written in prison, "Rock Around the Rock Pile." At the end, the charade is over when Jayne sings "Ev'rytime" splendidly, courtesy of Eileen Wilson, her voice double, who performed the same service for many stars, including Ava Gardner in *One Touch of Venus*. (Universal-International, 1948). Ewell and Jayne shared the acting honors, with Ewell giving his best screen performance as a manipulative agent who discovers his conscience and grows too fond of Jayne to allow her to be bullied by a sleazebag like O'Brien. For anyone who wondered if agent and client lived happily ever after, Ewell and Jayne appear in the epilogue with their four children, and O'Brien sings "Rock Around the Rock Pile" on TV—Tashlin's subtle way of contrasting the expansiveness of widescreen and the limitations of the (then) standard twenty-one-inch television set.

WILL SUCCESS SPOIL ROCK HUNTER? (1957)

Tashlin was set to adapt and direct *Will Success Spoil Rock Hunter?*, with Jayne reprising her Rita Marlowe characterization when he realized that George Axelrod's play could not be transferred to the screen or even given a makeover. There were too many inside references, and powerful Hollywood agents like Irving "Swifty" Lazar, the inspiration for "Sneaky" LaSalle, and MCA's Lew Wasserman did not take parody lightly—especially Wasserman, whose clients were Hollywood royalty (e.g., Doris Day, Charlton Heston, Warren Beatty, Jane Wyman, Kirk Douglas, Paul Newman, Gregory Peck, Dean Martin, Fred Astaire). Although the original was really a morality play in which good trumps evil, MacCauley never repents of having sex with Rita Marlowe or winning an Oscar he did not deserve. Tashlin was not taken with the idea of a last-minute atonement, which might have satisfied the Production Code Administration and the National Legion of Decency, but would have violated the integrity of the play in which Mac-Cauley, having enjoyed Rita Marlowe's favors, is willing to give them up for an agent-free life.

If Hollywood is a sacred cow, television is the sacrificial lamb. All that remained of Axelrod's play is the title. Rita Marlowe, and the LaSalle Agency, minus its head. The title character, who never appears in the play, becomes

Rockwell Hunter (Tony Randall), who works at LaSalle in the TV division. To keep the agency from losing the Stay Put lipstick account, he must persuade movie star Rita Marlowe to endorse the product for a commercial. Hunter eventually becomes head of the agency, not through satanic intervention but rather through luck and perseverance. Success neither spoils him nor brings him happiness. He gives up the LaSalle presidency to raise chickens with his wife (Betsy Drake), while Rita is reunited with the strongman actor played by Mickey Hargitay, who actually married Jayne on January 13, 1958.

Tashlin turned Jayne into a caricature with a giggly squeal, whereas Axelrod's Rita was a shrewd business woman with her own production company. Anyone who saw Jayne in the original, as did the author, knew that she was an actor playing Rita Marlowe, sex symbol, who was playing a similar role herself: the love goddess who could walk with a wiggle, squeal "divoon" for "divine," and be every male's fantasy lover—and knew it.

Jayne's next film for Zanuck was *The Wayward Bus* (1957), a *Grand Hotel* on wheels based on John Steinbeck's 1947 novel about a diverse group of passengers, including Jayne as a dancer, on a bus trip through rugged California terrain. Joan Collins was first-billed as the alcoholic wife of the driver, although no one was really the star. Jayne's character, Camille, was very much like Marilyn's Cherie in *Bus Stop*, a waif whose sense of self-worth is restored by a compassionate salesman (Dan Dailey). The film cost $1.465 million but only grossed $1.75 million. Still, Jayne managed to win a Golden Globe for New Star of the Year. By 1958, the star's light was flickering. Jayne was just another Twentieth Century-Fox contract player. She was cast as Kate, a hotel owner in a frontier town in Raoul Walsh's *The Sheriff of Fractured Jaw* (1958), a British production that Twentieth Century-Fox distributed, which starred Kenneth More, a master of high comedy, as a sheriff, who, with the aid of some Native Americans, restores law and order and marries Kate. Jayne, second-billed, had three songs, with Connie Francis as voice double. Although Walsh reportedly wanted only Jayne for Kate, he mentions neither the film nor her in his autobiography, *Each Man in His Time* (1974).

By 1962, Jayne was no longer bankable, and her contract was terminated. She continued to be active on television and in nightclubs until June 28, 1967, when she died tragically in a horrific car accident in Louisiana at the age of thirty-four.

Neither Sheree North nor Jayne Mansfield could have been the next Marilyn. Each had some of her features: the ability to play to the camera (less so with Sheree), affect a "little girl lost" look, and walk, as Jack Lemmon described Marilyn in *Some Like It Hot*, "like Jell-O on springs." They were not given her range of roles or scripts tailored to their talents. If, somehow, *Will Success Spoil Rock Hunter?* had been made with some concessions to the Production Code that left the Faustian storyline intact, it could have been a career-defining role for Jayne. In the transmogrification, Tony Randall became the star; and Jayne, a fluttery sex object.

There was, however, a young woman at Twentieth Century-Fox who was a real triple threat: actor, singer, and dancer who could perform on pointe, if necessary.

Chapter 20

THE BLONDE EXCEPTION
Mitzi Gaynor

The daughter of a dancer mother and musician father, Mitzi Gaynor (born 1931) began taking ballet lessons as a child and, by thirteen, was performing with the Los Angeles Civic Light Opera Company. Offered the choice of appearing in a featured stage role in the Cole Porter musical, *Out of This World* (1951), and a seven-year contract at Twentieth Century-Fox, she opted for the latter, making her film debut in *My Blue Heaven* (1950) as Betty Grable's rival for Dan Dailey. Fifth-billed, she appeared in two sequences, a cosmetics commercial, in which she spoofed the product she was promoting with deadpan glee; and a torrid dance routine with Dailey ("Live Hard, Work Hard, Love Hard"). Her debut performance impressed Zanuck enough to star her in *Golden Girl* (1951), a biopic about entertainer Lotta Crabtree.

GOLDEN GIRL (1951)

When it came to the musical biopic, Zanuck knew he would have to find subjects other than composers and songwriting teams on whom MGM had a monopoly: Johan Strauss II (*The Great Waltz*), Jerome Kern (*Till the Clouds Roll By*), Richard Rodgers and Larry Hart (*Words and Music*), Bert Kalmar and Harry Ruby (*Three Little Words*). Ever since *The Jazz Singer* and *My Man* made Zanuck aware of the great appeal of performers like Al Jolson and Fanny Brice, he realized that he must go a different route. Stephen Foster and Paul Dresser may have been too lowbrow for MGM, but not for Twentieth Century-Fox, which celebrated their lives in *Swanee*

River and *My Gal Sal*, respectively. If MGM could enshrine Anna Held in *The Great Ziegfeld* and refurbish the life of Enrico Caruso in *The Great Caruso*, Twentieth Century-Fox could do the same with entertainers who appealed to less sophisticated audiences.

Zanuck may have heard of Lotta Crabtree (1847–1924) from his grand-father, Henry Torpin, who could have seen her in person when she toured the country in the 1870s and 1880s. Lotta's early life (1863–65) became the basis of a disjointed but tuneful biopic, *Golden Girl* (1951), which, like most specimens of the genre, is one-quarter fact and three-quarters fancy. The film opens with the Crabtrees in a northern California mining town where Lotta's mother, Mary Ann, runs a boarding house and her father, John, gambles away their money when he should have been prospecting for gold. The historical John Crabtree was a New York book seller who hoped to make a fortune in gold country. As portrayed by James Barton, who sings in a relaxed baritone and does an effortless soft-shoe, he is a loveable dreamer who finally redeems himself by winning big in a poker game and buying the Bella Union, a variety theater on Kearny Street in San Francisco, for Lotta, who actually appeared there in the early 1860s. The Bella Union dates back to 1849, and John Crabtree has no connection to it.

Although the historical Lotta began performing for miners at the age of eight, the film's Lotta (Mitzi Gaynor) is sixteen when she embarks upon her career after seeing the dancer Lola Montez. The film does not even allude to the real-life relationship between Lotta and Montez, even though Montez saw potential in Lotta, gave her dancing lessons, and offered her a role in her company that was about to tour Australia. Emulating Montez, Lotta rigged up a wagon emblazoned with her name, and with a makeshift band and a dulcet-voiced tenor (Dennis Day), began touring the mining camps. As happens in film, where time is malleable, Lotta becomes an established star in record time and is so well known that a Union officer pays her a backstage visit with a strange request, resulting in a subplot that seems to have been intended for another film but wound up in *Golden Girl* instead.

The officer asks her to transport $10,000 in gold to the army paymaster at Fort Yucca for the Union cause. Lotta Crabtree was a natural actress, and Mitzi played her as one, intrigued by the idea of taking on the role of a Union courier. She makes the mistake of telling Tom Richmond (Dale Robertson), supposedly an Alabama gambler but really a Confederate Army officer pos-ing as a Spanish bandit who intercepts Union-bound shipments. Although she unmasks the "bandit," she is so enamored of Richmond that she allows him to make off with the gold, even misdirecting the Union officers, after he tells her that he has been ordered to raid gold shipments to aid the beleaguered Confederacy. The political implications are manifold, particularly when one realizes that the Crabtrees were Northerners who came West because of the Gold Rush. That Lotta aided a Confederate officer would seem a serious breach of allegiance, except that Mitzi's Lotta is an apolitical romantic who vows that someday she will sing "Dixie" for Richmond.

In hindsight, the pro-South sentiments of *Golden Girl* seem pitifully unenlightened, but in 1951, well before the civil rights era, they were in line with plantation sagas like *Gone with the Wind*, *Jezebel*, *Tap Roots*, and *The Foxes of Harrow*. The gold shipment subplot is totally fictitious. In 1864, Lotta Crabtree was performing in San Francisco and soon left to tour the East Coast in dramatizations of *Uncle Tom's Cabin* and *The Old Curiosity Shop*.

Although Mitzi deserved a better script for her first starring vehicle, she revealed a range that would have served her well a decade earlier, but not in the 1950s, when the musical was slowly going into sleep mode. Zanuck would continue to make musicals, but the most memorable ones of the 1950s came from Broadway, which did not involve Twentieth Century-Fox contract talent in leading roles.

Mitzi Gaynor was a unique artist. Alice Faye and Betty Grable performed with a burnished professionalism that left you awestruck at such perfection. But they never exhibited the exhilaration that comes from the inner joy of performing, a joy that radiates outward to the audience and back to the performer so that both enjoy the same experience. With Marilyn Monroe, it was all artifice with an overlay of decadence. Mitzi reveled in performing and beamed her delight to the camera, which captured it for moviegoers. That two-way exchange of joy experienced simultaneously by performer and spectator comes through in "Sunday Morning," in which Mitzi conveyed Lotta's fascination with Lola Montez, who would kneel down and shake her hair from side to side, causing men to throw gold pieces at her. Mitzi begins "Sunday Morning" demurely and then rips off her skirt and gets down on her knees, tossing her hair like Montez. Her mother was mortified, but the barrage of gold mitigated the shock. Dressed in a red-striped white dress with a ruffled hem, Mitzi displayed the same ebullience when she sang and danced "Kiss Me Quick and Go," kicking with abandon and relishing every moment. "When Johnny Comes Marching Home" is a real tour de force, with Mitzi switching to ballet slippers in the middle of the song and dancing on pointe to "Oh, Dem Golden Slippers," which had been woven into the orchestration. The most affecting number is "California Moon," which Mitzi performs with James Barton. It was a true father and daughter number with both of them tapping while sitting on chairs, which Mitzi arranges in the form of a carriage to push Barton off stage.

Earlier, Lotta told Richmond that she would sing "Dixie" for him. The Civil War had just ended, and as Lotta is about to go on stage, she learns that Richmond has been seriously wounded and may not be returning. (Spoiler alert: he's alive.) She informs the audience, "On this occasion I want to sing 'Dixie.'" Wearing a white gown with floral decorations in her hair, she begins singing it as a dirge. The audience, obviously anti-South, voices its displeasure, prompting Mart Taylor (Dennis Day) to remind them that "the men of the South were fighting for what they believed in" and that "we're all united. We're all Americans." Mitzi continues uninterrupted, and gradually the entire audience joins in, resulting in a rousing finale and a victory for Jim Crow. Taylor did not add that the men of the South were fighting for the preservation of the "peculiar institution" known as slavery. If you can get past the politics, *Golden Girl* has myriad pleasures: James Barton's showmanship, Dennis Day's crystalline tenor, and Mitzi Gaynor's impressive performance, the culmination of years of ballet training and four seasons singing and dancing with the Los Angeles Civic Opera. By eighteen, Mitzi Gaynor was ready for the movies.

Zanuck was displeased by *Golden Girl*'s mediocre performance at the box office ($1.5 million), realizing it would not play well internationally. The subject matter may have been too American for European tastes, and the absence of big-name stars also limited its appeal abroad. Still, Zanuck went ahead with a trio of musicals for Mitzi, first-billed in each: *The Blood-hounds of Broadway*, *The I Don't Care Girl*, and *Down Among the Sheltering Palms*, released, respectively, in November 1952, January 1953, and March 1953. (*Down Among the Sheltering Palms* was filmed in 1951 but not released until 1953.)

THE I DON'T CARE GIRL (1953)

The I Don't Care Girl was the most elaborate of the three, costing $1.860 million but grossing a disappointing $1.25 million. It was even more of a pseudo-biopic than *Golden Girl*, this time of Eva Tanguay (1878–1947), the "Queen of Vaudeville." The film reunited Mitzi and *Golden Girl* director Lloyd Bacon, producer George Jessel, and writer Walter Bullock, whose screenplay derived from Jessel's original story. The historical Eva "delivered frenzied performances that at once sated audiences and left them thirsting for more." That aspect of her art came through in Jack Cole's eroticized choreography, but not in the bland story that unfolded in seventy-eight (eighty-one in some prints) minutes, suggesting that the studio did not have much faith in the picture, which seems to have been substantially altered en route to release. At the premiere, the audience saw a pre-credits sequence in which Eva seems to be ailing during a *Ziegfeld Follies* performance. The curtain comes down, and the sequence ends, leading one to expect an epilogue that never materializes. Since the historical Eva Tanguay developed cataracts that left her vision-impaired, the sequence may have been intended as a kind of flash forward to something that should have been, but was not, dramatized—at least not in the release print. Next comes a prologue in which George Jessel as himself, a Twentieth Century-Fox producer, is having trouble finding a suitable script for an Eva Tanguay biopic. He instructs the writers to seek out Eddie McCoy (David Wayne), who supposedly discovered her, resulting in a *Citizen Kane*-like interview film, in which a pianist (Oscar Levant) discounts McCoy's version, adding that he does not know what happened when Eva's true love, the singer-songwriter Larry Woods (Bob Graham), went off to World War I. Woods arrives at the end of the film, which he resolves by explaining to Jessel that Eva waited for him and that they enjoyed successful careers.

Fact check: there was no Eddie McCoy or Larry Woods. Eva Tanguay was married twice, once to a dancer, and then to her accompanist. Eva stopped performing in her mid-fifties because of vision problems and died at sixty-eight in 1947. Actually, Eva's real life would have made better copy than Bullock's version.

Mitzi had to alternate between playing an ingénue in love with a married man and a fiery entertainer who sheds her inhibitions in performance. Jack Cole's choreography, anachronistic as it was, at least suggested the kind of sensation that Eva created on stage. "I Don't Care" is danced to a jungle beat, with Mitzi first seen with two kittens and then emerging against a yellow background, dancing into the frame, with men lurking about as if they were ready for action. Mitzi looked like an exotic bird in black tights with a white mesh top and a headpiece of black feathers that matched the ones jutting from her hips. She poses defiantly and even dives into a pool, all the while declaring her indifference to convention. As can only happen in film, she changes from black to red in the (literally) fiery finale, where, amid artificial flames, she ends her declaration of independence. That sequence, more than any other in the movie, distilled the essence of Eva Tanguay in a number that she could never have performed in real life, but that Mitzi Gaynor could in a display of unapologetic sex. No one, not even Betty Grable or Sheree North, could have expressed contempt for convention with such naked defiance.

DOWN AMONG THE SHELTERING PALMS (1953)

Down Among the Sheltering Palms (1953) was another financial disappointment, costing $1.400 million and grossing $1 million. The film was typical of Hollywood's treatment of race at the time. In the final days of World War II, an army captain (William Lundigan) is trying to keep his men from fraternizing with the native woman on one of the Gilbert Islands in the South Pacific. Mitzi played a native who falls in love with the captain. With two leads as attractive as Mitzi and Lundigan, one would think that they would pair off at the fade-out. But the problem is race. Mitzi's character, Rozouila, is Micronesian. The Production Code took a dim view of mixed-race unions, particularly between whites and Blacks: "Miscegenation (sex relationships between the black-and-white races) is forbidden." Rozouila may not be Black, but she is also not white, resulting in the captain's ending up with a minister's niece (Jane Greer); his lieutenant (David Wayne) with a novelist (Gloria DeHaven); and Rozouila with another islander—each with one of his or her own, racially speaking.

Gloria DeHaven had the better numbers: the title song, "All of Me," and "When You're In Love." Mitzi did an energetic tribal dance and sang "What Make De Diff'rence," Harold Arlen and Ralph Blame's idea of Islandspeak. In his *New York Times* review (June 13, 1953), Bosley Crowther had mixed feelings about the film, but not about Mitzi, who had a way of "stopping the show cold, or hot, as usual." But she was not enough to entice moviegoers into spending some time among the sheltering palms.

BLOODHOUNDS OF BROADWAY (1952)

Of the three musicals, only *Bloodhounds of Broadway* (1952), an $875,000 production, made a decent profit: $2.0 million. Another George Jessel production directed by Lloyd Bacon, it was advertised as *Damon Runyon's Bloodhounds of Broadway,* "The Screen's Big Broadway [*sic*] Musical with all the fabulous Damon Runyon Guys and Dolls," to capitalize on the success of *Guys and Dolls* (1950), which was still running on Broadway when the film opened. It is true that the characters had such Runyonesque names as Dave the Dude, Liver Lips Louie, and Pittsburgh Philo, but the "big Broadway musical" had virtually no connection with Damon Runyon's short story of the same name except for the bloodhounds, Nip and Tuck, who belonged to the illiterate John Wrangle from rural Georgia, whom a promoter brings to New York with the idea of renting the dogs for crime movies. Instead, the dogs are employed to sniff out a murderer, who confesses to the crime, and Wrangle and the bloodhounds go back in glory to Georgia.

The plot was updated from Prohibition-era New York to around 1950, the year the Kefauver Committee was formed to investigate organized and municipal crime. The story was totally rewritten as a vehicle for Mitzi as Emily Ann Stackerlee, who, like Wrangle, comes from Georgia farm country and has two bloodhounds. Robert "Numbers" Foster (Scott Brady), a bookie, and his sidekick, Harry "Poorly" Sammis (Wally Vernon), are en route to New York from Florida, where they were hiding out to avoid being subpoenaed by a crime commission. They run out of gas somewhere in Georgia and stumble upon Emily Ann singing "In the Sweet Bye and Bye" at her grandfather's funeral. The scene not only serves to introduce the two main characters, but also to show that Emily Ann can sing and, in a later scene when she performs a combination tap dance-hoedown with the sensational six-year-old Sharon Baird, that she can dance as well, which explains (somewhat) the fact that she can work at a New York nightclub.

"Numbers" finds himself attracted to Emily Ann and, after a jealous suitor threatens violence, offers to take her to New York and help her find a job. Mitzi plays Emily Ann with a beguiling Southern accent and projects the right kind of ingenuousness that one would expect of a twenty-year-old who had never set foot out of her county. But here is where Mitzi is required to play another role, a well-trained dancer with a voice to match, who, when the script requires Emily Ann to become the accomplished artist that Mitzi Gaynor is, makes the transition so naturally that it seems that Mitzi Gaynor was always within Emily Ann. When Emily Ann auditions for "Curtaintime" Charlie at Dave the Dude's, he asks her to repeat the time steps that he and Tessie (Mitzi Green) do. She does—perfectly. Zanuck was right. If the number is believable, the audience will accept what it sees. Mitzi must alternate between Emily Ann and the accomplished performer she becomes. What makes "Numbers'" conversion believable is Emily Ann's determination to keep him from avoiding another session of the crime commission. She and the bloodhounds track him and "Poorly" to a pier where they are preparing to flee New York. After a minor mishap, he agrees to testify, pay his back taxes in cash, serve a year's sentence, and finally return to Dave the Dude's, where Emily Ann is the main attraction.

The musical numbers revealed the full range of Mitzi's talents. She could invest a dreamy ballad like "I Wish I Knew" with a sincerity that stops short of heartbreak. She can go from parodying her Georgia cracker image in "Bye Low" to a sultry "Jack o' Diamonds" in orange and black tights and a pale blue feather boa. But Zanuck could not find a real star-defining vehicle for her. It certainly was not *There's No Business Like Show Business* (1954), in which Marilyn usurped the spotlight whenever she could.

After *There's No Business Like Show Business*, Mitzi moved over to Paramount for three films (*Anything Goes*, *The Birds and the Bees*, and *The Joker Is Wild*), followed by *Les Girls* (MGM, 1957), in which she danced with Gene Kelly in a movie that was stolen by Kay Kendall. Then came her most popular film, *South Pacific* (1958), in which she played nurse Nellie Forbush, a role created by Mary Martin. Although *South Pacific* was released under the Twentieth Century-Fox trademark, Zanuck had nothing to do with the film, which was a South Pacific Enterprises production, a company that was formed shortly after the show opened to market memorabilia such as "*South Pacific* scarves, dolls, perfume, underwear, sheets, and pillowcases" and was later expanded into a partnership between the creators of the musical, Richard Rodgers and Oscar Hammerstein; its producer, Leland Hayward; director, Joshua Logan; and the Magna Theatre Corporation, the owner of Todd-AO, the 70 mm format in which *South Pacific* was filmed. Magna handled the two-a-day roadshow engagement, while Twentieth Century-Fox distributed the film in CinemaScope for general release in theaters unequipped for Todd-AO. Twentieth Century-Fox did not do badly by *South Pacific*, contributing $2.0 million toward production costs that totaled $5.610 million, in exchange for ten percent of the profits and world-wide distribution rights. *South Pacific* grossed $15 million domestically.

Originally, the film version was to have starred Mary Martin and Ezio Pinza, who created the roles of Nellie Forbush from Little Rock, Arkansas, and Emile de Becque, the French planter with whom she falls in love during the Pacific campaign. Although Mary Martin seemed ageless and managed to look boyish at forty when she starred in the title role of *Peter Pan* (1954) on Broadway, she would have been forty-four when filming began. Stage makeup can work wonders, but the camera eye is all-seeing. When Pinza died suddenly in May 1957, Joshua Logan, who was set to direct the film, sought out Elizabeth Taylor, whose audition proved disastrous. Doris Day was also considered; at least she came close to radiating the winsome charisma that was Martin's signature. Mitzi wanted the role, and after auditioning twice for Rodgers, finally got it. Actually, Mitzi's performance style was uncannily close to Martin's, and unlike the other actors in key roles, she did not require a voice double. Her costar, Rossano Brazzi, did; his was the Metropolitan Opera basso, Giorgio Tozzi, who played Emile opposite Martin when *South Pacific* went on tour. In fact, of the principals, only Mitzi and Ray Walston (Luther Billis) did their own singing.

Martin was not happy with Logan's decision to cast Mitzi in *her* role, snubbing Mitzi and her husband, producer Jack Bean, when they went backstage after a performance of *South Pacific* in Los Angeles. But Martin soon got over her disappointment when Rodgers and Hammerstein came up with another show for her, which turned out to be their last collaboration: *The Sound of Music* (1959).

For the film version of *South Pacific*, Logan aimed for a color-immersion experience, with filters used to alter the visual texture of the scenes. Nellie's credo, "A Cockeyed Optimist," begins, "When the sky is a bright canary yellow," which is exactly the kind of sky audiences see. When Bloody Mary sings "Bali Ha'i," the effect is similar to looking through a kaleidoscope. The color effusions gave the film a garish look, which was at odds with the naturalistic performances, especially Mitzi's. As a singing actor, she knew she had a character arc to trace, as Nellie struggles with the knowledge that Emile, whom she loves, has two biracial children from his marriage to a Polynesian woman. She must gradually shed the racial prejudices of a typical 1940s Southerner and accept racial equality after being exposed to a culture when skin color is no barrier to love. In *Bloodhounds of Broadway*, Mitzi had to toggle between a Georgia hillbilly and a nightclub entertainer; in *South Pacific*, she had to undergo a transformation from an optimist to a realist, showing great empathy for Bloody Mary's daughter, Liat (France Nuyen), when Liat insists that she will not marry anyone but Lieutenant Cable (John Kerr), not knowing that he has been killed while on a secret mission.

Mitzi's movie career ended three pictures later: *Happy Anniversary* (United Artists, 1959), *Surprise Package* (Columbia, 1960), *For Love or Money* (Universal, 1963). But during the years she spent at Twentieth Century-Fox, there was no one else at the studio who could act, sing, and dance in any style. Her musicals afford a glimpse of what we might have seen if she had arrived in Hollywood when the studio system was still in its heyday. Television audiences were more fortunate; they witnessed the panoply of her art on her specials (1967–78), a few of which (e.g., *Mitzi: Roarin' in the Twenties, Mitzi: What's Hot, What's Not,* and the documentary *Mitzi Gaynor: The Razzle Dazzle Years*) can be viewed at the Paley Center for Media in both New York and Beverly Hills.

Chapter 21

FOUR FROM RODGERS AND HAMMERSTEIN

State Fair, Carousel, The King and I, and
The Sound of Music

When Rodgers and Hammerstein's *Oklahoma!* opened at New York City's St. James Theatre on March 31, 1943, musical comedy became musical theater where the numbers complemented, embellished, or deepened the narrative as opposed simply to interrupting it for the inclusion of a song, a dance, or a chorus. The curtain rose on a woman, later identified as Aunt Eller, churning butter as off stage a baritone, later identified as the cowboy Curly, begins singing "Oh, What a Beautiful Mornin'" as he enters. The song is the equivalent of a soliloquy, in which Curly expresses his joy at the dawning of a day that seems to hold great promise. The characters conveyed their feelings and inner thoughts in song and dance, achieving the same effect as dialogue would in a non-musical. As musical theater historian Ethan Mordden put it, with his usual succinctness: "The songs pop out of the script so naturally that the singing is like dialogue, only more so."

STATE FAIR (1945)

Zanuck knew that Richard Rodgers and Oscar Hammerstein had revolutionized the Broadway musical and wanted Twentieth Century-Fox to be the first studio to hire them. Zanuck offered to pay each $50,000 to provide the music and lyrics for a remake of *State Fair* (1933), a Fox Film Corporation production which the studio now owned as a result of the 1935 merger. Both agreed, with the understanding that Rodgers would compose the music at his Fairfield, Connecticut, estate, while Hammerstein would write the lyrics and the screenplay on his farm in Doylestown, Pennsylvania. Zanuck consented but was still determined to exercise his authority as studio head. When the screenplay and score were completed, he brought the two of them and their wives to Los Angeles for a week. On their last day, Zanuck met with Rodgers and Hammerstein, saying nothing about the score but only reminiscing about his experiences in North Africa during World War II. Then he dismissed them. As Rodgers reflected in his autobiography, "[Zanuck] paid us a lot of money and acceded to our working conditions, but he wanted the satisfaction of making us do as he wished."

Hammerstein's screenplay adhered to the basic plot points of the original, a bittersweet and occasionally folksy comedy-drama about an Iowa family—father (Will Rogers), mother (Louise Dresser) and children (Janet Gaynor and Norman Foster)—who attend a state fair at which the father's boar, Blue Boy, wins first prize, as does the mother's pickles and mince pie. The children find romance: the son with an aerialist (Sally Eilers), who seduces him and then makes it clear that theirs was a casual affair; the daughter, with a reporter (Lew Ayres) who is at first reluctant to give up his roving ways but finally concedes. *State Fair* was made a year before the enforcement of the Production Code in 1934. Since the beloved Will ("I never met a man I didn't like") Rogers was playing the father, the bedroom scene between the son and the aerialist offended many moviegoers, who expected their idol to star in a more edifying picture. In 1935, the bedroom scene was deleted in circulating prints to satisfy the Production Code Administration. Still, the plot points were there, and with a few changes (the aerialist became a singer), Rodgers and Hammerstein had the perfect vehicle for their first and only original movie musical.

Rodgers and Hammerstein's second collaboration, *Carousel*, had been playing on Broadway for four months when *State Fair* premiered on August 29, 1945. The score was inferior to *Carousel*'s, which is arguably Rodgers's best. Actually, for a movie musical, there is a paucity of songs—six in all, with three reprises. Except for one name change, the characters are the same as those in the 1933 film. The parents are still Abel and Melissa Frake (Charles Winninger and Fay Bainter); their children, Margy and Wayne (Jeanne Crain and Dick Haymes); and the reporter Pat Gilbert (Dana Andrews). The aerialist, Emily Joyce, became band singer Emily Edwards (Vivian Blaine).

Rodgers and Hammerstein were still in their *Oklahoma!* mode when they began working on *State Fair*, opening it as they did their first musical: with no preliminary spoken dialogue. Percy Killbride begins singing "Our State Fair" in his pickup truck, followed by Charles Winninger outside with the boar, Blue Boy, and Fay Bainter in the kitchen. The difference, however, is that "Oh, What a Beautiful Mornin'" is Curly's soliloquy, while "Our State Fair" is simply the title set to music.

The songs do not so much "pop out" of the action, as they did in *Oklahoma!*, as accompany it. The second number, "It Might as Well be Spring," is Margy's expression of her emotional state as the family is about to leave for the fair. What she experiences is spring fever, "but I know it isn't spring." It's August, but her restlessness is typical of an adolescent yearning for something to enliven her uneventful life. It is the best number in the movie and won an Oscar for Best Original Song. It is partially reprised twice. While Dana Andrews and Jeanne Crain had voice doubles (Ben Gage for Andrews for a bit of "It's a Grand Night for Singing," and Louanne Hogan for Crain in "It Might as Well Be Spring" and her part in "It's a Grand Night for Singing"), Dick Haymes and Vivian Blaine needed no dubbing. When Emily sings "That's for Me," Wayne seems to think she's singing it to him, beaming with joy like a love-struck kid. But Blaine was playing a band singer who had to pitch the song to the entire room, so that every man would think she meant him. That song is later reprised by the siblings (Crain dubbed again by Hogan), with each singing about his and her new romance. Haynes and Blaine perform a sweetly innocent duet, "Isn't It Kind of Fun?," which is not reprised, nor could it be once Wayne learns that Emily is married. "It's A Grand Night for Singing," on the other hand, is reprised. It begins in the dance pavilion and spills out on to the midway, with couples, including the principals, singing joyously on the fair's amusement rides.

Rodgers and Hammerstein must have known that Twentieth Century-Fox musicals usually end with a reprise, this time with Haymes singing some of "It's a Grand Night for Singing" at the fade-out as he is driving with his old girlfriend, now his new love (Jane Nigh). The problem is that it's afternoon, not evening. Since the setting is Iowa, Rodgers and Hammerstein wrote their idea of a state tribute, the country-western "All I Owe Ioway," which Vivian and William Marshall sing as if they were professional corn huskers. But the rationale was simple: Vivian and Marshall play performers, and when in Iowa, celebrate the Hawkeye State in song. *State*

Fair was the studio's second highest-grossing film of 1945 ($4.0 million). It also came out at the right time: two weeks after V-J Day. The public was in a mood for soft-hearted Americana with no heroes or villains, but only good country people.

Zanuck was not finished with Rodgers and Hammerstein. He set his sights on *Carousel*, which opened in April 1945 and played for 890 performances at the Majestic Theatre on West Forty-Fourth Street., diagonally across from the St. James, where *Oklahoma!* was still going strong. By the fall of 1945, the team could boast of two Broadway shows on the same block and a movie musical in wide release.

CAROUSEL (1956)

John Raitt and Jan Clayton were *Carousel*'s original Billy Bigelow and Julie Jordan, neither of whom was familiar to moviegoers. Although Rodgers was ambivalent about the movie version of *Oklahoma!* (1955), he was pleased with the performances of Gordon MacRae and Shirley Jones as Curly and Laurey while questioning some of the other casting. For Billy Bigelow, the carousel barker, Zanuck envisioned Frank Sinatra, who "was born to play this role." So Zanuck believed—or came to believe—after Sinatra kept "hounding" him about it. July Garland's agent was also after Zanuck to cast her as Julie Jordan. For a time, Zanuck was actually thinking of Sinatra and Garland as the leads; and if not Garland, then possibly Doris Day, asking for "Oscar and Dick's opinion on the combination of Frank Sinatra and Judy Garland or Frank Sinatra and Doris Day or any other suggestions they have." Zanuck was not always spot on when it came to casting. Part of his interest in Sinatra was his emergence as a serious actor in *From Here to Eternity* (Columbia, 1953). He also felt that an "offbeat love story," which is how he viewed *Carousel*, would work with Garland and Sinatra, whose screen personas were totally at odds with each other and would have resulted in a bipolar production of "an offbeat love story."

Zanuck was also considering Jean Simmons for Julie Jordan, whom Billy courts, marries, and leaves pregnant after committing suicide. Simmons had been cast against type as Salvation Army Sergeant Sarah Brown in *Guys and Dolls* (Goldwyn, 1955), in which she did her own singing. He was initially opposed to the idea of reteaming the stars of *Oklahoma!*, Gordon MacRae and Shirley Jones, in *Carousel*, insisting it "would be a terrible mistake." The "ideal cast" would be Sinatra and Simmons.

After Jean Simmons bowed out, "convinced that she must now play only sexy and vivacious girls," Zanuck agreed with Rodgers and Hammerstein that Shirley Jones would be Julie Jordan: "[Jones] was the first choice of Oscar and Dick." He cabled producer Buddy Adler, directing him to "tie her up." "Not interested in Garland." Zanuck may have sensed trouble with Judy, whose mood swings were known to hold up production. Zanuck could deal with temperament; neurosis was another matter.

It was evident that Zanuck did not understand *Carousel*, with its wife-beating antihero and all-suffering heroine, nor did he realize that Billy requires a lyric baritone like John Raitt or Howard Keel (who, as Harold Keel, played Billy for three weeks while Raitt was on vacation), not a crooner. But Zanuck was primarily interested in Sinatra's marquee value.

Carousel would be filmed in a new widescreen process, CinemaScope 55, with an aspect ratio of 2.55:1 as distinct from the more common 2:35:1, resulting in a projected image that was a little more than two and a half times wider than high. Those who saw *Carousel* during its first run in any theater equipped for CinemaScope 55 saw it the way it had been filmed: in 55 mm with a six-track synchronized stereo soundtrack; elsewhere, it was released in 35 mm with a four-track stereo soundtrack. CinemaScope 55 was short-lived, since in the mid-1950s exhibitors were not inclined to incur further expenses in equipping their theatres with a new system when so many theatres had closed, becoming chain stores after television replaced movies as America's favorite mass medium. *The King and I* was also filmed in CinemaScope 55, but release prints were reduced to 35 mm.

Zanuck was taking no chances. As enthralled as he was by CinemaScope 55, even refusing to admit at first that the studio was preparing an alternate 35 mm version of *Carousel*, he began to have doubts about the longevity of the process. When Sinatra learned that director Henry King would be shooting "half of the usual number of takes (three to ten per scene) with the CinemaScope camera and the other half with the new 55 mm camera," he balked, claiming that he would be working in two films but only getting paid for one, although Shirley Jones suspected that he left the production because he was suspicious of his wife, Ava Gardner, whose eye roved as widely as his.

Zanuck had a new format and a Julie Jordan. He needed a Billy Bigelow—and quickly. In late April 1955, Richard Rodgers recommended Gordon

MacRae for the part, noting that "MacRae will become a star after the release of OKLAHOMA!" But Zanuck was still holding out for Sinatra. On June 15, 1955, Zanuck received a telegram from MacRae, who boldly informed him that "you can win an award with CAROUSEL . . . provided you use me in the part of Bigelow. I admire and respect Mr. Frank Sinatra's talents but think just as I thought I was Curly in OKLAHOMA I'm Billy Bigelow in CAROUSEL." He ended by reminding Zanuck that he would be playing Billy in Dallas from July 18 through July 31. "Please don't sign anybody until you come see me in the role." Zanuck replied the next day: "The role of Billy Bigelow has already been cast, however I would certainly like to use you in another picture should the opportunity present itself."

Two months later, Zanuck was desperate, wiring "Frankie" that he "sponsored [Sinatra] in the role because I thought you would be great in it," adding that Rodgers and Hammerstein were initially skeptical but finally came around. As for Sinatra's balking at the idea of filming in both 55 and 35 mm, Zanuck reminded him that *Oklahoma!* was also filmed two ways: in Todd-AO 70 mm and 35 mm CinemaScope. As it happened, cinematographer Charles C. Clarke later found a way of transferring scenes in *Carousel* from 55 mm to 35 mm, thus eliminating the need for two cameras. But even if Sinatra had known that, he still would have been bothered by Ava's threat to begin an affair with Rossano Brazzi, who would be appearing with her in *The Barefoot Contessa*, if he did not accompany her on location to Italy. One would like to think that Sinatra might have sensed that he was wrong for the part. The musical makes it clear that Mrs. Mullin hired Billy as a barker for her carousel because he had a raw virility that attracted young women and kept them coming back. Frank Sinatra was a great artist, but he was no Billy Bigelow. By September, Gordon MacRae had the part.

Zanuck's problems were just beginning. The stage version began with the brilliant "Carousel Waltz," whose swirling rhythms replicated the up and down movements of the wooden horses. Then Julie and her friend Carrie leave the mill where they work and head for the carousel, which offers temporary relief from their drab existence. If staged properly, Julie and Billy's eyes must meet fatalistically when they see each other. Theirs is a fatal attraction of a different kind: they marry, but Billy, realizing he needs money once he learns he will be a father, joins his friend Jigger in an attempted robbery that is foiled by the arrival of the police. Rather than face prison, Billy stabs himself and dies.

Zanuck knew that the National Legion of Decency would slap a "B" ("Morally Objectionable in Part for All") rating on the film for the customary reason: "Suicide in plot solution." Instead, Billy falls on his knife, like Jud Fry in *Oklahoma!* The change from suicide to accidental death was also necessary to make the film palatable to a mass audience that would have found a musical in which the lead kills himself at odds with the conventions of the genre, in which characters die (the King in *The King and I*) or are killed (Lt. Cable in *South Pacific*) but do not take their own lives. The change reduced the starkness of the work, but its effect was minimal compared to the changes that screenwriters Henry and Phoebe Ephron made to the musical's beginning and end, of which Zanuck heartily approved.

In the second act of the stage musical, Billy is seen "up there" in a starry purgatory presided over by the Starkeeper, who informs him that he is unworthy of heaven, but might qualify if, by returning to earth for one day, he can prevent his rebellious daughter from becoming a version of himself. Billy redeems himself and even lets Julie know that, despite his rough ways, he always loved her. Then he returns "up there," this time to heaven.

Zanuck believed that instead of showing Billy in purgatory *after* his death, as was the case in the play, he should be seen "up there" at the beginning, thus making most of the movie a flashback, except for Billy's return to earth on the day of his daughter's high school graduation. Zanuck came up with the idea of a heavenly prologue in the form of a pre-credits sequence. with Billy "up there" polishing stars. Finding a damaged star, he throws it away. Falling through space, the star explodes into the main title. Zanuck loved the pre-credits sequence, calling it "the most magnificent photographic scene I have ever seen." Then the film begins, fifteen years *before* Billy's death and quasi-transfiguration. And if Billy is seen "up there" at the beginning, he should return at the end, making *Carousel* an audience-friendly movie instead of a wrenching musical drama.

Zanuck was wrong about *Carousel* from the beginning. He may have identified with Billy, and in some ways was as crass, insensitive, and aggressive. That Zanuck envisioned Sinatra in the lead suggests that he conceived of Billy as a lowlife and a punk, rather than a self-destructive, deeply conflicted man who is more an example of tragic waste than a tragic figure. Anyone who saw Joshua Henry as Billy in the magnificent 2018 Broadway revival with Jessie Mueller as Julie and Renée Fleming as Cousin Nettie saw the character that Oscar Hammerstein had delineated: a man so defiant in his selfhood that he kills himself rather than see it diminished, if not destroyed, by incarceration. MacRae could play Billy the braggart and chauvinist and perform a moving "Soliloquy" in which he imagined himself as a dad, but the character's darker side eluded him. Shirley Jones sang beautifully, as she always did, but they were just Curly and Laurey in Maine instead of Oklahoma, costarring in an operetta with a death and an upbeat ending.

Zanuck had great hopes for *Carousel,* of which he was the uncredited executive producer, supervising every aspect of the production, including creating a rough cut: "I have already completed the editing of the film," he informed music supervisor Alfred Newman. He wanted ambient sound for outdoor scenes, especially in "June Is Bustin' Out All Over," which Rod Alexander choreographed, making it an exuberant Broadway number performed out of doors. Zanuck wanted a long shot of the carousel in the opening scene and another after Billy flirts with Julie while she is riding on it; and a long shot of the clambake and "an arbitrary direct cut" to Julie's singing "What's the Use of Wond'rin.'" The movie may have been "Rodgers and Hammerstein's *Carousel,*" but it was a Darryl F. Zanuck production, which, unfortunately, was not a box-office triumph. *Carousel* cost $3.380 million, but only grossed $3.75 million. Even the stage musical never enjoyed the popularity of *Oklahoma!, South Pacific,* and *The King and I.* It was musical theater of an unusual kind: a blend of realism and fantasy. The 1945 original and the 2018 revival integrated what would ordinarily have been warring plot elements; by moving the fantasy that followed Billy's death in the second act to the beginning of the film, the writers made it into a prologue, and the ending into an epilogue with the main action a flashback supplying whatever realism the movie has. Richard Rodgers does not mention the movie version in his autobiography, *Musical Stages,* nor does Zanuck in Mel Gussow's biography.

THE KING AND I (1956)

Although the first title reads "Darryl F. Zanuck Presents Rodgers and Hammerstein's *The King and I,*" Zanuck had little involvement in that film. He devoted most of his attention to *Carousel,* particularly the editing. *Carousel* began filming in early August 1955, ended three and a half months later, and premiered in February 1956. *The King and I* began production in early December 1955, ending in late January 1956 with a June 1956 release date. Unlike *Carousel*, some of which was shot on location in Maine and Malibu, *The King and I* was a soundstage shoot (stages 6 and 20). Ernest Lehman's screenplay followed Oscar Hammerstein's book closely, and the score was mostly intact except for "My Lord and Master," "Shall I Tell You What I Think of You?," and "I Have Dreamed," all of which had been recorded but had to be cut because Zanuck did not want the film to exceed 140 minutes (it runs 133). The stage musical's running time was about three hours with an intermission. "Western People Funny," sung by the King's wives at the opening of the second act, was not even considered for the film, although it would have provided a non-Western view of English dress.

Zanuck had read Margaret Landon's novel, *Anna and the King of Siam* (1944), suggested by the memoirs of Anna Leonowens, *The Governess at the Siamese Court* (1870) and *Siamese Harem Life* (1873). He immediately optioned the novel, believing it would be "a wonderful film" if the story is kept "intimate" with a minimum of "spectacle." Talbot Jennings and Sally Benson adapted the novel, which was filmed under the same title, with Irene Dunne as Anna and Rex Harrison as King Mongkut, whose children she has been hired to educate. Released in June 1946. it was Twentieth Century-Fox's fourth highest-grossing movie of the year ($3.5 million). In 1950, Rodgers and Hammerstein turned *Anna and the King of Siam* into a musical, *The King and I* (1951), as a vehicle for Gertrude Lawrence, with the relatively unknown Yul Brynner as the King.

If one can speak of realism in a film set in Bangkok and shot mostly on soundstage 2 on the Twentieth Century-Fox lot, *Anna and the King of Siam* is a more accurate portrayal of culture shock from the points of view of both Anna and the King than *The King and I*. When Anna arrives in Bangkok, she is greeted by the bare-chested prime minister (Lee J. Cob), who treats her indifferently, as does the King when she is finally allowed to see him. It is not that Anna is a woman and thus an inferior; she is also a Western woman. What starts as a battle of the sexes evolves into a relationship based on respect once Anna realizes that the King, as intelligent as he is, also needs to become less insular in his thinking so he can impress English and European diplomats who view his country as a potential colony.

But in some respects, the King cannot change. When his latest wife, Tuptim (Linda Darnell), flees the harem to join her former fiancé, a Buddhist monk, she is captured and sentenced to be burned at the stake along with the monk. Appalled by the verdict, Anna calls the King a "barbarian." It is here that the film becomes culturally murky. As monarch, he could have spared Tuptim, but it would have been perceived as a display of weakness and acquiescence to a Western woman. But no one seems to object to this barbaric form of death (which is probably spurious), including the King's first wife, Lady Thiang (Gale Sondergaard). The burning of Tuptim and the monk is graphically shown, taking place under Anna's window, which is darkened by the smoke. Hammerstein omitted the immolation, leaving Tuptim's fate unresolved. In the stage version, Tuptim has her moments: a solo ("My Lord and Master") and two glorious duets ("We Kiss in a Shadow," "I Have Dreamed"). She also narrates her version of Harriet Beecher Stowe's *Uncle Tom's Cabin*, "The Small House of Uncle Thomas." But the title of the musical, *The King and I*, speaks for itself: this is the story of Anna and the King. To keep the focus on them, Hammerstein omitted the death of Anna's son, Louis, in a horse riding accident, which is shown in the film. He also changed Tuptim's fiancé from a monk to just her lover.

What Hammerstein wanted to achieve through his book and lyrics, and Rodgers through his music, is operetta with nothing more serious than the onstage death of the King, surrounded by his wives and children, with Anna at his bedside and Lady Thiang singing a reprise of "Something Wonderful." Almost ten years elapse in *Anna and the King of Siam*, while in *The King and I* the action takes place over several months.

There is a moment of sheer magic in both the stage and screen versions of *The King and I* when it becomes apparent that the King is attracted to Anna, who behaves similarly toward him. She describes her first dance and sings "Shall We Dance?" in its entirety. Then she wistfully dances by herself as if she were reliving the experience. The King studies her movements as he slowly approaches her, asking her to teach him to dance: "Teach, teach," he demands. She teaches him the polka, the form in which "Shall We Dance?" was composed. He fumbles a bit but quickly masters the rhythm. Then he remarks, "Something is not right," referring to the way Anna danced at the reception with Sir Edward Ramsey, the visiting representative of the British government. He slowly puts his arm around her waist and asks, "Like this?" She answers, "Yes," in such a way that her response is both an invitation to the dance that, under ordinary circumstances, would have been the prelude to romance. It is as if an electrical discharge had passed between them when he drew her to himself and she responded to the clasp of his arm around her waist. Then they launch into the polka, whirling around the room in one unbroken shot, the dancers inseparable from the dance. At the end, Anna is exhausted, but the King is not: "Come. We do it again." This time, however, they are interrupted by the guards who have found Tuptim after she disappeared following the performance of "The Small House of Uncle Thomas." Enraged, the King is about to lash her, but cannot in Anna's presence and rushes off. The love dance is over, and Anna's affection for the King remains dormant until the end, when she places her hand on his as he dies. Their hands touched at the moment of their unstated declaration of love, and again at the moment of the King's death.

The King and I was Twentieth Century-Fox's top grossing film of 1956, netting $8.5 million domestically, and making up for *Carousel*'s poor box-office performance. Deborah Kerr looked ravishing and played Anna as a determined but exceedingly feminine woman with a sensuous side as she revealed in her choice of a bare-shoulder gown for the banquet scene. Marni Nixon was Kerr's vocal double, but Kerr's lip-syncing was impeccable, and Nixon's tone and timbre were perfect for the schoolteacher who was as much a woman as she was a lady. Although Rita Moreno (Tuptim) later became a successful cabaret performer, her voice was dubbed by Leona Gordon. Brynner did his own singing, as did Terry Saunders as Lady Thiang. On Broadway, the ballet "The Small House of Uncle Thomas" had been choreographed by Jerome Robbins, who incorporated elements of Southeast Asian court dance into it. Robbins also choreographed the ballet for the film, although it had to be shortened in compliance with Zanuck's directive to ensure a reasonable running time. Still, it remains an exquisitely staged dance piece that avoids the usual clichés of Orientalism through the use of authentic costumes, masks, and stylized hand movements.

The King and I turned out to be Twentieth Century-Fox's last musical on Zanuck's watch. Three months before the June 1956 release, Zanuck suddenly announced that, at age fifty-three, he would be leaving Hollywood and setting up shop in Paris, making pictures under his own banner, DFZ Productions, with Twentieth Century-Fox as distributor. His behavior had become erratic, causing the press to wonder if Darryl F. Zanuck was becoming a caricature of himself: a womanizing producer past his prime. In February 1954, Zanuck staged a party at Ciro's for his daughter Susan and actress Terry Moore. A trapeze had been left on the stage by one of the performers.

Seeing it, Zanuck stripped off his shirt and attempted to do chin-ups, succeeding three out of four times. A few years earlier, while Zanuck and his wife Virginia were vacationing on the French Riviera, they met Bella Wegier, soon to be known as the actress Bella Darvi, resulting in a bizarre *ménage à trois* with Bella becoming Virginia Zanuck's constant companion and, at the time unknown to Virginia, her husband's lover. Virginia was so desperate to keep Bella with her that their relationship struck some as lesbianic. (Bella's surname was a composite of the first three letters of Darryl, "Dar,": and the first two of Virginia, "Vi.") Virginia got Darvi movie work at the studio, but her acting, especially in *Hell and High Water* and *The Egyptian* (both 1954), failed to impress critics. When Virginia discovered that Bella had become her husband's latest bed companion, she severed their relationship. Meanwhile, Zanuck was in Paris; Virginia stayed in Los Angeles.

When gossip columnist Hedda Hopper asked Zanuck why he was leaving Hollywood for Europe, he was brutally frank, railing that "actors have taken over Hollywood with their agents [wanting] approval of everything—scripts, stars, still pictures" and that, as a result, "the producer hasn't got a chance to exercise any authority." Except for *The Longest Day* (1962) and, arguably, *The Sun Also Rises* (1957), the other DFZ productions—*Island in the Sun* (1957), *The Roots of Heaven* (1958), *Crack in the Mirror* (1960), and *The Big Gamble* (1961)—were minor Zanuck. The screenplay for *Crack in the Mirror* is attributed to "Mark Canfield," one of Zanuck's early pseudonyms. The plot with its interlocking themes of jealousy, infidelity, and murder would have appealed to Zanuck, whose early fiction tended toward the lurid and melodramatic.

Buddy Adler (1906–1960) replaced Zanuck as production head in 1956, and for almost a decade, the Twentieth Century-Fox musical seemed moribund. The few that were released were mediocre, at best: *Mardi Gras* (1958), with Pat Boone; the third remake of *State Fair* (1962), with Boone again and Alice Faye in the comeback role of his mother, which was unworthy of her; and Marilyn Monroe's last musical, *Let's Make Love* (1960), with its "cliché-clogged" script, which, as Bosley Crowther complained in his *New York Times* review (September 9, 1960), suppressed the "old Monroe dynamism."

In early fall 1962, Zanuck's epic, *The Longest Day*, was set to open first as a roadshow engagement on a reserved-seat basis with two performances daily, followed by nationwide release—a distribution platform on which Zanuck insisted. He was now in a position to dictate terms. First, it was his film, a DFZ production. But equally important, Zanuck had been wooed back to Twentieth Century-Fox in July 1962 after president Spyros Skouras (1893–1971) was removed when the studio began hemorrhaging financially because of the mounting costs of *Cleopatra* (1963), a spectacle that ended up costing $42 million but, despite being the studio's biggest 1963 money-maker, only brought in $26 million in domestic rentals. Although *Cleopatra* was more historically accurate than anything Cecil B. DeMille ever made, it was known at the time as the film whose stars, Elizabeth Taylor and Richard Burton, engaged in a widely publicized adulterous affair while on location in Italy.

Zanuck was now president of Twentieth Century-Fox, a position quite different from vice president, production. In need of a production head, he asked his son Richard for suggestions. Richard replied that he was the best choice. His father concurred, and the studio became a father/son operation. Zanuck immediately shut down production until the returns from *The Longest Day* came in. And once the film was deemed a success, eventually grossing $30 million worldwide, production resumed.

THE SOUND OF MUSIC (1959)

On November 16, 1959, Rodgers and Hammerstein's musical about the Trapp Family Singers, *The Sound of Music*, opened on Broadway at the Lunt-Fontanne Theatre. In the audience was the then Twentieth Century-Fox president Spyros Skouras seated next to Irving "Swifty" Lazar, the legend-ary agent who represented the composer and lyricist as well as the book writers, Howard Lindsay and Russel Crouse. Lazar knew about Twentieth Century-Fox's history with Rodgers and Hammerstein and was hoping for Skouras's reaction to a sentimental musical (really an operetta) about the Trapp Family Singers, in which a postulant (Mary Martin), learning that she is not meant for the religious life, marries a widower (Theodore Bikel) with seven children, teaches them to sing so that they can eventu-ally perform before an audience, and then flees with husband and children when the Nazis annex Austria in 1938. The musical had everything: nuns chanting in Latin, hummable tunes ("Do-Re-Mi," "Climb Ev'ry Mountain," "My Favorite Things," and the title song), and a thrilling finale with the Trapp family crossing the Alps into Switzerland while the nuns reprise

"Climb Every Mountain." Lazar did not have to pressure Skouras, who wept unabashedly during the performance. On June 13, 1960, *Daily Variety* reported that Twentieth Century-Fox paid over $1 million (actually $1.25 million) for the rights. The movie version, however, could not be released until the show had closed, which it did on June 15, 1963, after 1,443 performances. As production head, Richard Zanuck decided it was time to begin preparations for the movie version.

The Sound of Music received generally favorable, if not ecstatic reviews, with *New Yorker* critic Kenneth Tynan dismissing it as "a show for children of all ages, from six to about eleven and a half." What no theater critic noticed was how subtly Lindsay and Crouse worked the rise of Nazism into the plot. Georg von Trapp is a navy submarine captain who considers himself Austrian, not German. The musical does not become political until midway in the first act when Rolf, who has been courting the oldest von Trapp child, Liesl, arrives in search of her and greets everyone with "Heil."

The second act is more political. The baroness, to whom the Captain had been betrothed, and his producer-friend, who wants to promote the von Trapps as a singing family, shrug off Anschluss in "No Way to Stop It" ("Be wise, compromise")—their acceptance of appeasement in marked contrast to the Captain's refusal of a commission in the German Navy. Maria and the Captain know they must leave Salzburg, but they have agreed to perform at a folk festival, which they do and then leave the stage one by one so that, by the end when the von Trapps are announced as the winners, they are on their way to freedom.

THE SOUND OF MUSIC (1965)

The Sound of Music was the most profoundly spiritual work that Rodgers and Hammerstein had created for the stage. The nuns are not merely members of the community that Maria leaves. They appear in both acts and are especially important in the second when they furnish the family with a temporary refuge before they make their way across the Alps. Rodgers wrote some exquisite music for them. They are heard chanting "Dixit dominus," his setting of Psalm 110, as soon as the curtain goes up. In the second act, they sing "Gaudeamus Domino" and "Confitemini Domino." In the film, the nuns sing the "Dixit Dominus," but not the other two Latin chants.

"No Way to Stop It" was also eliminated in the film. While one can assume that the baroness and the producer would have no problem adjusting to a Nazified Austria, the song characterized them as shallow and apolitical, although Max, the producer, does give the von Trapps time to leave the theater so that the Captain does not have to be accompanied by a Nazi escort to his new post. Ernest Lehman's faithful screenplay is just as anti-Nazi as the play. In fact, when the Captain returns to his villa and finds a Nazi banner there, he tears it down. In the play, Rolf knows where the family is hiding but does not betray them. In the film, he does, but by then they are driving away in the nuns' car. Lehman adds his own denouement by foiling the Nazis' attempt to follow them because the nuns have removed some parts from their cars.

The opening credits read: "Twentieth Century-Fox Presents Rodgers and Hammerstein's *The Sound of Music* A ROBERT WISE Production." Wise, the producer-director, supervised every aspect of the production. He proved he could handle widescreen in *West Side Story* (1962), and the results were even more impressive in *The Sound of Music*, which was filmed in 70 mm. The opening shot is one of the most admired in film. The movie version does not begin with the "Preludium" ("Dixit Dominus"), as it did on stage, but with an aerial view of a mountain-dominated landscape and a vast field across which a figure (Julie Andrews as Maria) runs, comes into view, twirls around, and begins singing the title song. When Maria describes her heart wanting "to beat / Like the birds that rise / from the lake to the trees," she stands between two trees, clasping each of them and then pressing her hands against her breast. When she describes her heart laughing like a brook and tripping over stones, she carefully balances herself on the stones in a pond. Wise conceived the opening sequence as a visualization of the lyrics, so that Maria appears to feel an almost mystical union with nature. One thinks of William Cullen Bryant's "Thanatopsis," which begins: "To him who in the love of Nature holds / Communion with her visible forms, she speaks / A various language." Maria heard Nature speak, or rather, sing in the most spiritual lyrics Oscar Hammerstein had ever written.

The Sound of Music cost $8.020 million and made $83.9 domestically. By the fall of 1966, it had become the highest-grossing film up to that time. There would be no further Rodgers and Hammerstein musicals. On August 22, 1960, when Oscar Hammerstein died of stomach cancer, the stage version of *The Sound of Music* was still selling out at each performance.

Chapter 22

RICHARD ZANUCK'S FOLLIES

Doctor Dolittle, Star!, and *Hello, Dolly!*

The phenomenal success of *The Sound of Music*—which the American Film Institute (AFI) ranked fourth among the greatest movie musicals—led Richard Zanuck (1934–2012) to believe in 1966 that the genre was far from moribund and put *Doctor Dolittle* (1967) into production, to be followed by *Star!* (1968) and *Hello, Dolly!* (1969), all of which fared dismally at the box office.

DOCTOR DOLITTLE (1967)

Despite the thirteen numbers and one reprise, *Doctor Dolittle* remains a piece of gooey whimsy, buoyed up by music that it really didn't need, even though "Talk to the Animals" had an offbeat charm and won an Oscar for Best Song. When Twentieth Century-Fox commissioned a first draft screenplay in 1962 based on Hugh Lofting's Doctor Dolittle books about the Victorian eccentric who could talk to animals, the studio was thinking in terms of a feature film, not a musical. The project was put on hold until producer Arthur Jacobs inherited it in 1964, envisioning it as a musical that would reunite the *My Fair Lady* team with Rex Harrison as the title character, and a score by Alan Jay Lerner and Frederick Loewe. Since Loewe had retired, Jacobs sought out André Previn, who was unavailable. And when Lerner seemed indifferent, Jacobs brought in Leslie Bricusse, best known at the time for the stage hit *Stop the World—I Want to Get Off* (1962), to write the screenplay and compose the score.

The film, budgeted at $6.0 million, ended up costing almost three times as much ($17 million), but only made $6.2 million domestically. The production was plagued by mishaps, tension between Rex Harrison and Anthony Newley, inclement weather, angry locals, animals in need of quarantine, and a lawsuit brought by a producer involved in an earlier screenplay draft that was settled out of court.

Doctor Dolittle is a musical in the sense that it is a movie in which people *sing*. Most of the songs do not so much move the plot forward as stop it periodically. It was similar to *Aaron Slick from Punkin Crick* (Paramount, 1952), another critical and box-office failure, even though the cast included Metropolitan Opera baritone Robert Merrill, popular vocalist Dinah Shore, and a score by the team of Jay Livingston and Ray Evans ("Buttons and Bows," "Golden Earrings," "Dear Heart," "To Each His Own," "Que sera, sera") that consisted of eleven numbers, which were just filler providing a distraction from a mediocre movie. At least none of the principals in *Aaron Slick from Punkin Crick* had to communicate with a two-headed llama, sing to a seal, or fly away on a giant moth as Rex Harrison did in *Doctor Dolittle*.

STAR! (1968)

Star! (1968), a $14 million production, was another disaster, although, if planned less extravagantly and with greater fidelity to its subject's life, it might have broken even, instead of generating only $4.2 million in domestic rentals. When Julie Andrews signed on for *The Sound of Music*, it was the first of a two-film arrangement, the second of which was to be the life of Gertrude Lawrence, which Andrews was at first reluctant to do because of Lawrence's celebrity. Gertrude Lawrence (1898–1952) was so revered that on the day of her funeral, the *New York Times* (September 10, 1952) reported that 5,000 spectators gathered outside the historic Fifth Avenue Presbyterian Church at 7 West Fifty-Fifth Street while, 1,800 others attended the service, which included a eulogy by Oscar Hammerstein. The press made much of the fact that she was buried in the gown she wore in *The King and I* when she danced the polka with Yul Brynner, who was one of the mourners.

However, when Andrews learned that *Sound of Music* director Robert Wise would be back on board for *Star!*, she signed on. For some reason, the screenwriter, the British-born William Fairchild, decided to dramatize (and sometimes mythologize) twenty-five years of Lawrence's life, from 1915 to 1940, ending with her second marriage to Richard Aldrich in 1940, instead of, perhaps, the opening night of *The King and I* in March 1951, especially since Twentieth Century-Fox had produced the movie version. The opening would have been a natural ending, even if Fairchild wanted to ignore the fact that during the run, Lawrence became progressively ill, missing performances and in poor voice when she was able to go on. Finally, on August 16, 1952, she collapsed backstage and had to be admitted to New York Presbyterian Hospital, where she died of advanced liver and abdominal cancer on September 6.

If Fairchild brought Lawrence's life up to 1951, he could have included an episode that would have made for exciting cinema. In 1944, she and other British performers traveled to Normandy after D-Day as part of the Entertainments National Service Association, which was created shortly after World War II broke out in Europe in 1939. She had never endured such privation: sleeping in unheated attics and eating whatever food was available. She proved to be a real trouper and later went to the South Pacific to entertain the troops. Also little known, if at all, is that in September 1951 she was invited to teach an advanced course in scene study at Columbia University's School of Dramatic Arts. Gertrude Lawrence as performer, wartime entertainer, and college professor. Fairchild concentrated solely on the performer with occasional forays into her love life.

Like most biopics, *Star!* is an amalgam of fact and fancy. As for the facts, Fairchild has Gertrude Lawrence achieving fame in revues; enjoying a lifelong relationship with Noel Coward, who remained her closest friend and confidant, despite her frequent displays of temper; marrying a dancer with whom she had a daughter, Pamela, and whom she later divorced; living beyond her means and encountering numerous financial problems; rejecting a marriage proposal from a peer who would have wanted her to accompany him to India; becoming the toast of New York after making her Broadway debut in 1924; meeting and marrying her second husband, Richard Aldrich, who operated the Cape May Playhouse, in Cape Dennis, Massachusetts, where she appeared in *Skylark* prior to its 1939 Broadway premiere; and scoring a personal triumph in Kurt Weill's *Lady in the Dark*.

Names and dates have been changed and details altered. Lawrence's first husband, Francis Gordon-Howley, is renamed "Jack Roper"; the peer, Captain Philip Astley, "Sir Anthony Spencer"; Beatrice Lillie, for whom

Lawrence went on in a revue, "Billie Carleton." It was Lawrence's idea to have *Skylark* try out at the Cape May Playhouse because she believed it was not quite ready for Broadway. (The actual front of the Cape May Playhouse is shown in the film.) Perhaps to build up the role of Aldrich to justify second billing for Richard Crenna, Fairchild added two earlier meetings between Lawrence and Aldrich, one in London; the other in New York, although there is no record of them. To have the film end in 1940, the year she married Aldrich, Fairchild transferred the opening of *Lady in the Dark* from 1941 to 1940, leading audiences to believe that her triumphant return to the musical stage preceded her marriage, as if there was some connection.

Richard Zanuck had high hopes for *Star!* since Julie Andrews had become a household name after *Mary Poppins* (1964), *The Sound of Music* (1965), and *Thoroughly Modern Millie* (1967). *Star!* was marketed as a roadshow engagement in 70 mm Todd-AO and in 35 mm for wide release. When it premiered at New York's Rivoli Theatre on October 22, 1968, it ran almost three hours. The first image suggested a stage musical: a wide shot of a blue theatre curtain with a view of the orchestra pit and the first front rows. The curtain opens, revealing a backdrop inscribed with the names of Lawrence's shows. The overture begins, a medley of songs associated with her such as "Someone to Watch Over Me," "Limehouse Blues," and "The Saga of Jenny." There is no main title, just the Twentieth Century-Fox logo followed by "*Star!*" with the voice of Julie Andrews singing the title song, which Jimmy Van Heusen and Sammy Cahn had written especially for the film.

Any expectation of a stage musical on film is dispelled by the next image: London at the turn of the twentieth century, part of a newsreel-style documentary that might be entitled "The Life and Times of Gertrude Lawrence." The time is 1940, and Lawrence is viewing a documentary of her life, or rather her life intercut with authentic and staged incidents from it within the wider context of the years 1915–40. *Star!* is a biopic within a documentary, parts of which appear at various intervals within the film proper. It is evident that the documentary is being screened for Lawrence; when the narrator is about to describe the "poignant" reconciliation between Lawrence and her improvident father, she corrects him. Her father, a music hall performer whose stage name was Arthur Lawrence, was such a heavy drinker that his wife, who does not appear in the film, left him shortly after Gertrude was born. In 1915, Lawrence left home to locate her father, who was performing in Brixton, hoping that he could find her work in music halls. There was nothing "poignant" about their meeting. Arthur Lawrence took one look at her and said to his mistress, Rose, "Now we can be a trio. Go out and get a bottle of Scotch." Lawrence's reunion with her father was short-lived. He had accepted a gig in South Africa, leaving her and Rose to fend for themselves.

Star! finally becomes a musical when Lawrence goes on for the star (historically, Beatrice Lillie) in a 1921 revue. The song was to have been "Limehouse Blues," which Lawrence also sang in the *André Charlot Revue of 1924*, both in West End and on Broadway. In *Star!*, when Lawrence goes on for the ailing Beatrice Lillie character, she sings "Berlington Bertie from Bow," which Andrews performs superbly—dressed in a tuxedo, smoking a cigar, using an umbrella as a walking stick, and affecting the nonchalance of an dandy ("I'm Berlington Bertie / I rise at ten-thirty"). By 1922, Gertrude Lawrence was a star, appearing with Noël Coward in his revue *London Calling!* Dressed as a harlequin, she sang Coward's exquisite "Parisian Pierrot" in a mime's costume, affecting a mime's posture and movements.

Two years later, Lawrence was on Broadway in the *André Charlot Revue of 1924*. The "Limehouse Blues" number, as choreographed by Michael Kidd, bears no resemblance to what audiences would have seen in 1924. It was designed for 1968 moviegoers who knew nothing about seedy Limehouse in London's Chinatown. Andrews, looking vaguely Asian, works in a Limehouse dance hall that doubles as a brothel. She uses a bluesy voice when she recalls the "Limehouse kid / Going the way that the rest of them did." Her melancholy abates with the arrival of a patron who looks like a dock worker. They don't so much dance as ignite, suggesting that she has found her soul mate. But when the brothel owner bars her from leaving, she stabs him. Her potential soul mate, unwilling to become involved, flees, leaving the Limehouse kid to face the consequences.

One is grateful whenever a musical sequence arrives in *Star!*, even if it is not staged authentically. But authenticity is not the question; rather, the question is, "Can you generate interest in a Gertrude Lawrence biopic for an audience, most of whom have no idea who she was, by having her portrayed by Julie Andrews, whose name everybody knows?" Since Andrews was not part of the golden age of the movie musical, Kidd modernized the numbers, so that they would seem contemporary, not as they would have been when originally staged, keeping the context but updating the choreography. In *Lady in the Dark* (1941), "The Saga of Jenny" is part of a dream sequence with a circus setting in which Liza Elliott, a magazine editor, is on trial for not being able to make up her mind. Kidd retained the circus motif but staged the number with Andrews as a circus performer in a glittering black gown, the lower part of which is detachable. When Andrews pulls it off, she is in a stunning unitard. She slides down a pole, breaks through a paper façade, climbs a ladder, and exits ascending on angel wings. On the opening night of *Lady in the Dark*, Lawrence realized that the number preceding "The Saga of Jenny" was "Tchaikovsky," a tongue-twister in which Danny Kaye tossed off the names of fifty Russian composers that was bound to stop the show. It did—somewhat—but Lawrence topped it by adding bumps and grinds to "The Saga of Jenny," which created a sensation. Her gyrations were so explicit that the Pentagon forbade her to perform the number when she joined a USO tour of the South Pacific in 1945.

The final scene has Lawrence telling the narrator of the documentary, "Leave it just the way it is. Just the way it was." And it was pretty much "The Life and Times of Gertrude Lawrence" in the biopic tradition.

Andrews was a revelation as a career-driven actor, a narcissistic drunk, and a self-dramatizing diva. She and Daniel Massey as Noël Coward were splendid together recreating the opening scene of Coward's *Private Lives* (1930), in which Lawrence and the playwright costarred in both West End and New York as a divorced couple, each of whom has remarried and on their respective honeymoons in the same hotel, occupying rooms with adjoining terraces. Within ten minutes, they move from small talk to a realization they are still in love. Massey, who was nominated for an Oscar, had mastered Coward's clipped delivery and did not so much speak, as sculpt, his lines. Andrews was aloof at first, and then meltingly real as the conversation continued. You wish you could see the two of them in a revival, but that was not destined to happen.

Star! is a film of shining moments, but there were not enough of them to hold an audience in thrall for 174 minutes.

HELLO, DOLLY! (1969)

Hello, Dolly! (1969) was another musical in Todd A-O, which opened first as a roadshow attraction with matinee and evening performances at New York's Rivoli Theatre on December 17, 1969. Although there is some dispute about how much *Hello, Dolly!* grossed, it cost $25.335 million to make, but within the first year of its release, only brought in $15.2 million. According to Nash Information Services, theatrical rentals eventually reached $26 million. Even if that were the case, the film still could not be considered a financial success.

The 1964 Broadway production was a triumph for Carol Channing as Dolly, a widow-turned matchmaker, who has set her sights on a Yonkers merchant, Horace Vandergelder (David Burns). The musical won rave notices for the cast, Jerry Herman's melody-rich score, and Gower Champion's staging, and received twelve Tony awards including Best Musical and Best Actress in a Musical.

When *Hello, Dolly!* was trying out in Detroit, the critics were unimpressed. Champion knew the show needed a rousing number to bring down the curtain on the first act. Working all day and into the early morning, Herman came up with one and summoned Channing and Champion to hear "Before the Parade Passes By," Dolly's passionate determination to "get some life back into my life." Channing began reflectively, gaining in intensity until she reached the coda, threatening "to raise the roof" and "carry on." Herman had found the "spine" of the show in Dolly's time-defying credo.

Champion added another touch that could not be replicated on screen because it was a pure *coup de théâtre.* When Dolly returns to the Harmonia Gardens after an absence of several years, she walks down a carpeted staircase, resplendent in a red gown and white arm-length gloves, and begins singing the title song to the waiters, addressing some by name ("Hello, Harry. Well, hello, Louie"). It seems to be just a song-and-dance number with Dolly and the waiters at one point doing a soft-shoe, swinging their arms up and down, seesaw style. As the number is about to end, the waiters raise their voices in a soaring climax. Then Dolly steps off the stage and onto a semicircular runway wrapped around the orchestra pit as she parades in front of the audience. And at the curtain call, whoever is playing Dolly—and besides Channing, there were, among others, Ginger Rogers, Pearl Bailey, Phyllis Diller, Martha Raye, Betty Grable, and Ethel Merman, who had originally turned down the part—struts across the runway, often to a standing ovation.

The 1969 film version was a generally faithful transcription of the original. Herman replaced Dolly's opening number, "I Put My Hand In," in which she describes her matchmaking skills, with the less boastful "Just Leave

Everything to Me." Since Barbra Streisand was playing Dolly, Herman felt that the character had to be seen as helpful yet cunning in a way that would endear her to audiences, so they would not think of her as a meddler in other people's lives. Streisand was not Channing, who embodied Broadway glitter and grit and had done eight shows in New York before *Hello, Dolly!* as compared to Streisand's three, one of which was an off-Broadway flop that lasted for one performance. Channing was also in her early forties when *Hello, Dolly!* premiered, while Streisand was twenty-six when production began, making her a rather youngish widow. Instead of playing Dolly as a wily survivor, as Channing had, Streisand made her into a crafty charmer and an endearingly manipulative matchmaker.

Twentieth Century-Fox was impressed that Streisand's first film, the movie version of her Broadway triumph *Funny Girl* (Columbia, 1968), which was budgeted at $14 million, grossed almost twice that amount. Since *Hello, Dolly!* was even a bigger stage hit than *Funny Girl*, the studio expected similar results, hoping to make up for the disappointing revenues of *Doctor Dolittle* and *Star!* Unfortunately, that was not the case.

The problem was the director, Gene Kelly, and Streisand's costar, Walter Matthau. It was a tension-ridden set: "Everyone, it appears, hates everyone." Choreographer Michael Kidd and costume designer Irene Sharaff clashed over Streisand's gold gown in the Harmonia Gardens sequence. The dancers were stepping on its flowing train, and Streisand was tripping on it. Sharaff told Kidd to restage the number, leaving them no longer on speaking terms. Eventually, the gown was trainless.

Unlike Carol Channing and David Burns in the original, Barbra Streisand and Walter Matthau were a mismatched pair in the film. Matthau called her "a pip squeak who didn't have the talent of a butterfly's fart." She retorted that he was just jealous, apparently unable to come up with an equally colorful rejoinder. Matthau's best costar was his buddy, Jack Lemmon, who, unlike Matthau, was not a grumpy middle-aged man in 1969 and would have been a perfect Horace Vandergelder, a guileless quarry for Dolly to trap. While Streisand played Dolly like a younger version of Mae West, Matthau played Vandergelder as if his character had been born with a perpetual scowl, so that at the end, when Vandergelder is waiting in front of the church for Dolly on their wedding day, you feel sorry for both of them.

As one critic observed, "*Dolly* is a case of 'too much' . . . and 'more is more.'" The "Before the Parade Passes By" number "involved 4,000 extras and cost $200,000 a day for four days shooting." The wide shot of the parade was impressive, but the number of participants was excessive. Four thousand extras for a local event like the Fourteenth Street Association Parade? On stage, Dolly takes a banner, waves it, and brings "Before the Parade Passes By" to a stirring conclusion.

The film's highlight, as it was on stage, is the Harmonia Gardens sequence. It was here that Streisand ceased playing Dolly Levi and became the iconic Barbra Streisand by way of Mae West. Instead of walking down the staircase with grace and elegance, she slinked down it, hips swaying, as if she were about to go onto a burlesque runway, even though the film is set in 1890. That it had become an 1890 update was obvious when Louis Armstrong appeared as the band leader in what might be called a contemporary anachronism: a modernized Gay Nineties milieu. In 1964, Armstrong recorded the song "Hello, Dolly!," which became so popular that it led to a similarly titled album *Hello, Dolly! Louis Armstrong* (Kapp Records, 1964) that included the title song, as well as such standards as "It's Been a Long, Long Time," "Moon River," and "I Still Get Jealous." There was some interplay between Armstrong and Streisand, who called him "Louis," not "Louie." Streisand even did some skat singing, which was totally out of character, but then so was she. This was the film's center piece, chronologically askew but revelatory of Streisand's art as a performer, if not as an actor. To see her as both, watch *Funny Girl*, which won her a Best Actress Oscar.

Gene Kelly, arguably the greatest dancer in movie musicals, had both directed and choreographed *On the Town* (1949) and *Singin' in the Rain* (1952) with Stanley Donen. When he directed Rodgers and Hammerstein's *Flower Drum Song* (1958) on Broadway, the choreographer was Carol Haney, a superb dancer and his assistant on *Singin' in the Rain* and *Invitation to the Dance* (1956). Since they had worked together before, there was no friction. It was different with *Hello, Dolly!* Kelly was the director; Michael Kidd, the choreographer: two choreographers, each a master of his craft, working in the same movie. Inevitably, Kelly and Kidd would clash. In fact, the Harmonia Gardens sequence was largely Kidd's creation. Accustomed to the rectangular screen, Kelly had difficulty adjusting to Todd-AO, nor could he harmonize the totally dissimilar acting styles of Streisand and Matthau, who were at odds with each other as well as with their characters. Like *Star!*, *Hello, Dolly!* has its moments, but they are few.

Chapter 23

FADE-OUT

Richard Zanuck's tenure at Twentieth Century-Fox was coming to an end. In 1969, Darryl left the presidency and became chairman of the board. Richard briefly replaced his father as president. It was not the most auspicious of times. By 1970, the studio's deficit had reached $77.4 million. There had been some hits (*Butch Cassidy and the Sundance Kid*, *M*A*S*H*, *Patton*), but too many expensive flops, including the three roadshow musicals; the universally derided *Myra Breckinridge* and *Hello-Goodbye* (both 1970), the latter starring Darryl's latest inamorata, Genevieve Gilles; and his attempt to tell the true story of December 7, 1941, in the ambitious failure, *Tora! Tora! Tora!*, which cost $25.485 million but only took in $14.5 million. In 1970, it became the reverse of "like father, like son." First, Richard was, for all practical purposes, "fired." And the one who fired him was his own father, heeding the mandate of the board. To make it seem less of an act of father throwing son under the bus, Richard simply "resigned" on December 29, 1970; then, a year later on April 19, 1971, the board removed Darryl as chairman, leaving him with the honorific, Chairman Emeritus. The Zanuck era was over. Richard, at least, had a second act. He teamed up with David Brown, who had been executive vice president of creative operations at Twentieth Century-Fox (and also resigned on December 29), to form Zanuck-Brown Productions, releasing through Universal. Within a few years, they came out with *The Sting* (1974) and *Jaws* (1975), the latter becoming, up to that time, the highest-grossing movie in Hollywood history: $130 million domestically, over $200 million internationally.

Darryl, meanwhile, was failing. Years of smoking cigars caused cancer of the jaw, for which he underwent surgery in 1972. Then his memory began to fail. In the fall of 1979, he was hospitalized for pneumonia and died two months later, on December 22. His wife, Virginia, arranged for a funeral service at the Methodist Church of Westwood. Orson Welles delivered the eulogy, which was surprisingly accurate. Darryl was "tough" but not "cruel or vindictive." One statement in his eulogy echoed what others had said about him over the years: "Darryl's commitment was always to the story. For Darryl, that is what it was to make a film, to tell a story." Similar sentiments were expressed a few years later on February 22, 1981, at the University of Southern California when the Friends of the USC Libraries hosted an evening celebrating the Zanuck legacy. That evening, writer-producer-director Philip Dunne spoke eloquently about Zanuck: he had "a mind so quick that you had only to express an idea and he would grasp hold of it. . . . There was his innate ability to handle people. He knew which writer best responded to iron discipline and which to sweet persuasion. He could be as tender as St. Francis or as terrible as Attila the Hun."

To Zanuck, the distinction between the integrated and non-integrated musical was purely academic, like classic and romantic, modern and post-modern, and in twenty-first century America, liberal and conservative. Rarely does a movie musical evidence the seamless integration of script and score in the sense that the musical sequences are the equivalent of dialogue, moving the action forward instead of stopping it for a song or dance. Even in films that are considered "integrated," such as MGM's *Meet Me in St. Louis* (1944) and *Singin' in the Rain* (1952), there are numbers that put the action on hold. In the former, "The Trolley Song" is almost like an insert. Judy Garland recounts an experience in which she boarded a trolley in a "high-starched collar" and "hair piled high upon my head," except that she never wears shirts with high-starched collars and her hair flows down her back. And who is this young man who sat down beside her and held her hand to the end of the line? She only has one boyfriend, Tom Drake, who boards the trolley after she finishes the song. Is the song a tall tale in which Judy is trying to convince the other passengers, mostly women, that she had a romantic encounter on a trolley? More likely, director Vincente Minnelli felt that the movie, which is basically a piece of Americana, needed a production number, which the songwriters, Ralph Blane and Hugh Martin, provided. In the latter, Gene Kelly comes up with an idea for the finale of a studio's first sound (or rather sound-on-disk) musical: a dance sequence called "Broadway Melody." *Singin' in the Rain*, however, is set in 1927, and the number could never have been staged as elaborately as it appears on the screen. When the producer says, "I can't quite visualize it," he was right.

It was just another opportunity for Kelly to display his awesome talent. If story and score mesh so perfectly in *Gigi* (MGM, 1958), it is because the creators, Alan Jay Lerner and Frederick Loewe, came from Broadway and had written such shows as *Brigadoon*, *Paint Your Wagon*, and particularly *My Fair Lady*, which were models not of just the synthesis of book and score but also of their symbiosis.

Zanuck's philosophy was simple: if you have a story that needs shoring up, "load it with music," as he remarked at a November 9, 1941, story conference about the Sonja Henie movie, *Iceland* (1942). Henie may have been a renowned figure skater, but audiences wanted more than just Henie on silver skates. They got Sammy Kaye and His Orchestra, with vocals by Joan Merrill. When Zanuck was planning to make *Alexander's Ragtime Band* (1938), using the songs of Irving Berlin, he looked for ways of "dropping in fifteen or twenty of his famous songs and working our story so that these songs could come in." Note the language: "dropping in," as if the songs were objects for periodic insertion. The only difference between a musical and a non-musical was that in the former, the script is treated "musically," as he noted at a December 11, 1940, story conference about *Moon Over Miami* (1941): "We don't want to make any effort to explain the music or prepare for it." The numbers come on so naturally that no one stops to ask, "Why are they now singing instead of speaking?" If anything, one should ask, "Why are they speaking when they should be singing?" Zanuck's musicals had the right blend of story and music. It was the old formula of operetta: Story stops, singing starts, story resumes—a pattern that continues to the end.

More than those of any other studio, Darryl F. Zanuck's musicals illustrate the great range of American popular entertainment and the variety of venues available to the public, sometimes several of them within the same film. He made show business seem like a democratic enterprise, with something for everyone (and within everyone's range) by featuring a vast array of talent from saloon singers to Broadway stars. Zanuck maintained that variety at each of the studios where he functioned as producer: Warner Bros., Twentieth Century, and particularly Twentieth Century-Fox, the one with which he is most associated:

WARNER BROS./FIRST NATIONAL
Saloons
The Jazz Singer (1927)

Radio
Say it with Songs (1929)

Minstrel Shows
Mammy (1930)

Dance Contests
Dancing Beauties (1930)

Nightclubs
She Couldn't Say No (1930)

Circus
Sunny (1930)

Broadway
The Jazz Singer (1927)
The Singing Fool (1928)
My Man (1928)
Gold Diggers of Broadway (1929)
Footlights and Fools (1929)
Showgirl in Hollywood (1930)
Manhattan Parade (1931)
42nd Street (1933)

TWENTIETH CENTURY
Radio
Broadway Thru a Keyhole (1933)
Thanks a Million (1935)

Broadway
Broadway Thru a Keyhole (1933)
Moulin Rouge (1934)

Music Hall
Folies Bergère (1934)
Lottery Lover (1934)

Variety Show
Thanks a Million (1935)

TWENTIETH CENTURY-FOX
Saloons
In Old Chicago (1938)
Coney Island (1943)
Nob Hill (1945)
The Beautiful Blonde from Bashful Bend (1949)
Wabash Avenue (1950)

Beer Gardens
Sweet Rosie O'Grady (1943)

Fairs
State Fair (1945)

Radio
Poor Little Rich Girl (1936)
Sing, Baby, Sing (1936)
Rebecca of Sunnybrook Farm (1938)
The Great American Broadcast (1941)
If I'm Lucky (1947)

Nightclubs
Sing, Baby, Sing (1936)
Alexander's Ragtime Band (1938)
Tin Pan Alley (1940)
That Night in Rio (1941)
Week-End in Havana (1941)
Springtime in the Rockies (1942)
The Gang's All Here (1943)
Pin Up Girl (1944)
Billy Rose's Diamond Horseshoe (1945)
Bloodhounds of Broadway (1952)
Gentlemen Prefer Blondes (1953)
There's No Business Like Show Business (1954)

Broadway

On the Avenue (1937)
Alexander's Ragtime Band (1938)
Rose of Washington Square (1939)
Lillian Russell (1940)
Springtime in the Rockies (1942)
Coney Island (1943)
Irish Eyes Are Smiling (1944)
Greenwich Village (1944)
The Dolly Sisters (1945)
Wabash Avenue (1950)
Meet Me after the Show (1953)

Vaudeville

Rose of Washington Square (1939)
Hello, Frisco, Hello (1943)
Mother Wore Tights (1947)
I Wonder Who's Kissing Her Now (1947)
The I Don't Care Girl (1953)
There's No Business Like Show Business (1954)

Variety Shows

Just Around the Corner (1938)
Footlight Serenade (1942)
Something for the Boys (1944)
Call Me Mister (1951)
Golden Girl (1951)

Burlesque

King of Burlesque (1936)
Doll Face (1946)
When My Baby Smiles at Me (1948)

London Stage

Tin Pan Alley (1940)
Hello, Frisco, Hello (1943)
The Dolly Sisters (1945)

Minstrel Shows
Dimples (1936)
Swanee River (1940)

Concert Halls
Alexander's Ragtime Band (Carnegie Hall) (1938)
Oh, You Beautiful Doll (1949)

Opera House
Hello, Frisco, Hello (1943)

Television
My Blue Heaven (1950)

Zanuck's musicals were unlike those of any other studio. They no more aspired to high art than Zanuck did when he began his career as a writer of fiction, combining the overripe style of the pulps with O. Henry's tapered narrative with a plot twist. Zanuck reveled in the florid; O. Henry in the selectively colorful. Zanuck learned economy first by writing ads, which demanded sharp and catchy phrasing; and then gags, which required one-liners and zingers. Then he was ready for scenarios, first as a writer of two-reel series, or serials as they were often called, like *Leather Pushers*, in which a self-contained story must unfold in fifteen minutes; and then as a writer of screen stories and occasional screenplays. A screen story requires the plot to be reduced to a vivid narrative which the screenwriter expands through dialogue; the screenplay requires characterization to be conveyed through dialogue, with the action limited to a few descriptive details that directors can bring to life in their visualization.

If Zanuck's musicals have a distinctive linearity, it is because he was enamored of symmetry: triads (hero/heroine/sidekick, two men in love with the same woman and vice versa); quartets (couples pairing off); a double-cross replay, with one character deceiving, misinterpreting, mis-representing, or impersonating another. Zanuck sought to recreate the Broadway stage, as perceived by the popular imagination, in show-business musicals, which could never have been staged in any theater but only on a soundstage. Still, you had the feeling you were watching a stage show with reprises in the finale, capped by a fade-out curtain call. Even the dressing rooms in the dingiest vaudeville houses looked roomier than the cubicles in many Broadway houses. But there was nothing comparable to Betty Grable's dressing room in *The Dolly Sisters*, which could accommodate the baskets of flowers arriving on opening night. Not only did it have a poof, a chaise longue, and a lacquered screen for changing, there was also a gleaming makeup table with a mirror that never needed Windex. In his musicals, Zanuck, the lover of spectacle, and Zanuck, the lover of symmetry, become one.

In 1954, Zanuck was considering a movie about the Queen of Sheba, possibly starring Marilyn Monroe. But as he stressed to producer Sam Engel (April 14, 1954), "Like everything else, it depends on the story we create and the showmanship we employ." Story and showmanship. Darryl F. Zanuck was a master of both.

NOTES

CHAPTER 1

7   "His father was a heavy drinker": Mel Gussow, *Don't Say Yes Until I Finish Talking: A Biography of Darryl F. Zanuck* (Garden City, NY: Doubleday, 1971), 8–9.

7   "families in stress": Ibid., 95.

9   "spent six months in New York": George F. Custen, *Twentieth Century's Fox: Darryl F. Zanuck and the Culture of Hollywood* (New York: Basic Books, 1997), 35.

10 "Foster's business went under": Susan Orlean, "The Dog Star Rin-Tin-Tin and the Making of Warner Bros.," *New Yorker*, August 29, 2011, www.newyorker.com/magazine/2011/08/29/the-dog-star.

10 "step by step": Darryl Francis Zanuck, *Habit and Other Stories* (Los Angeles: Times-Mirror, 1923), 129.

12 "the most beautiful flowers blossom" Ibid., 230.

12 "but publication was not until 1923": Gussow, *Don't Say Yes*, 21.

13 "Editor's Viewpoint": *Physical Culture*, July 1908, 1.

CHAPTER 2

14 "he claims to have seen": Gussow, *Don't Say Yes*, 23.

15 "rough scenario": id.

15 "Another version": Marlys J. Harris, *The Zanucks of Hollywood: The Dark Legacy of an American Dynasty* (New York: Crown, 1989), 22.

15 "averaged $20,000": Richard Koszarski, *An Evening's Entertainment: The Age of the Silent Feature Picture, 1915–1928* (Los Angeles: University of California Press, 1990), 108.

15 "twenty-four episodes": Gussow, *Don't Say Yes*, 29.

15 "a blue silk bathrobe": H. C. Witwer, *The Leather Pushers* (New York: Putnam's, 1921), 76.

16 "A-B-C": Rudy Behlmer, ed., *Memo from Darryl F. Zanuck: The Golden Years of Twentieth Century-Fox* (New York: Grove Press, 1993), 92.

17 "if the background": Ibid., 59.

18 "charm": Ibid., 92.

18 "had confined his extraordinary talents," "strong, healthy, and normal," "in the back room": Behlmer, *Memo*, 4–5.

18 "twenty-one produced feature scenarios": Ibid., 4.

19 "Because he imagined": Custen, *Twentieth Century's Fox*, 75.

19 "greatest gift": Ibid., 53.

19 "ten times faster": Ibid., 50.

22 "general manager in charge of production": Bernard F. Dick, *City of Dreams: The Making and Remaking of Universal Pictures* (Lexington: University Press of Kentucky, 1987), 72.

22 "pretty good cutter": Behlmer, *Memo*, 242.

22 "oral history interview": Custen, *Twentieth Century's Fox*, 17.

23 "any line or speech," "tempo": Behlmer, *Memo*, 222.

23 "pick up the tempo": Ibid., 23.

23 "Tempo is the cure": Ibid.

24 "firmly worded memo": Behlmer, *Memo*, 104.

24 "He deleted": Robert Lyons, ed., *My Darling Clementine* (New Brunswick, NJ: Rutgers University Press, 1984), 129.

25 "Characterization must be true to life": Gerald Else, *Aristotle's Poetics: The Argument* (Cambridge: Harvard University Press, 1963), 458–59.

25 "true to life": Behlmer, *Memo*, 120.

CHAPTER 3

26 "When I took over": Gussow, *Don't Say Yes*, 55.

27 "has revolutionized": Mason Wiley and Damien Bona, ed. Gail MacColl, *Inside Oscar: An Unofficial History of the Academy Awards* (New York: Ballantine Books, n.d.), 682.

28 "Jessel was expected to star": "You Ain't Heard Nothing Yet," *Classic Images*, February 2018, 320.

28 "offering him $75,000": Clive Hirschhorn, *The Warner Bros. Story* (New York: Crown, 1979), 14.

28 "the hybrid soundtrack": Robert L. Carringer, ed., *The Jazz Singer* (Madison: University of Wisconsin Press, 1979), 182–83.

28 "I was on the set": Gussow, *Don't Say Yes*, 44.

29 "sounding natural but indistinct": Alexander Walker, *The Shattered Silents: How the Talkies Came to Stay* (New York: Morrow, 1979), 38.

29 "A Plantation Act": www.Vitaphone 0359, 1926, Al Jolson, A Plantation Act, 10 min.

30 "Zanuck's shorthand notes": Custen, *Twentieth Century's Fox*, 99–102.

33 "associate producer credit": Ibid., 123–26.

35 "alleged to have lost their lives": Alan K. Rode, *Michael Curtiz: A Life in Film* (Lexington: University of Kentucky Press, 2017), 98–99.

CHAPTER 4

42 "merely a trade name": Hirschhorn, *The Warner Bros. Story*, 66.

42 "shortened it," "miserable previews": Richard Barrios, *A Song in the Dark: The Birth of the Musical Film* (New York: Oxford University Press, 2010), 290.

49 "Warner Bros. suffered a net loss": Hirschhorn, *The Warner Bros. Story*, 100.

CHAPTER 5

51 "clothes were impeccable": Bradford Ropes, *42nd St.* (New York: Grosset & Dunlap, 1932), 27.

52 "cheap," "Who the hell": Ibid., 151, 345.

53 ""thirty-eight-page treatment" *42nd St.*, edited with an introduction by Rocco Fumento (Madison: University of Wisconsin Press, 1980), 14–21.

54 "letter to Jack Warner": MPA Production Code Administration Records, Margaret Herrick Library, Fairbanks Center for Motion Picture Study.

57 "as a matter of principle": Gussow, *Don't Say Yes*, 57.

58 "I'm leaving Warners": Hal Wallis, with Charles Higham, *Starmaker: The Autobiography of Hal Wallis* (New York: Macmillan, 1980), 28.

58 "the self-appointed conscience": Neal Gabler, *An Empire of Their Own: How the Jews Invented Hollywood* (New York: Crown, 1988), 195.

CHAPTER 6

59 "The brothers Schenck": Ibid., 112–13.

59 "returned the studio to financial stability": Tino Balio, *United Artists: The Company Built by the Stars* (Madison: University of Wisconsin Press, 1976), 72.

59 "Twentieth Century Pictures": Aubrey Solomon, *Twentieth Century-Fox: A Corporate and Financial History* (Lanham, MD: Scarecrow Press, 2002), 20–21.

62 "tired and formulaic": Kevin Lally, *Wilder Times: The Life of Billy Wilder* (New York: Henry Holt, 1996), 66.

CHAPTER 7

66 "Carl Laemmle . . . is credited": Dick, *City of Dreams*, 25–31.

66 "Fox's Greater New York Film Exchange": Eileen Bowser, *The Transformation of Cinema, 1902–1915* (Berkeley: University of California Press, 1994), 82.

66 "Fox didn't get his $750,000": Norman Zierold, *The Moguls* (New York: Avon Books, 1969), 216.

67 "Fort Lee": Richard Koszarski, *Fort Lee: The Film Town* (Bloomington: Indiana University Press, 2004), 8–21.

67 "Fox set up his company": Ibid., 198.

67 "bought twelve and a half acres": Glendon Alvine, *The Greatest Fox of Them All* (New York: Lyle Stuart, 1969), 47.

67 "colored-glass windows": Zierold, *The Moguls*, 223.

68 "Theodore W. Case": Vanda Krefft, *The Man Who Made the Movies: The Meteoric Rise and Tragic Fall of William Fox* (New York: HarperCollins, 2017), 390–92,

68 "it was indeed a city": Ibid., 442.

69 "a mere figurehead": Ibid., 626.

69 "I insisted": Gussow, *Don't Say Yes*, 93.

69 "Building 88": Michael Troyan, Stephen X. Sylvester, and Jeffrey Thompson, *Twentieth Century Fox: A Century of Entertainment* (Lanham, MD: Lyons Press, 2017), 523–24.

CHAPTER 8

77 "You can bet your last dollar": Memo from Zanuck to director John Cromwell and producer Kenneth Macgowan, July 3, 1936, Behlmer, *Memo*, 5–6.

CHAPTER 9

78 "Alice Faye": On her life, see Jane Lenz Elder, *Alice Faye: A Life Beyond the Screen* (Jackson: University Press of Mississippi, 2003).

93 "Mikall Sinnott": Kalton C. Lahue and Terry Brewer, *Kops and Custards, The Legend of Keystone Films* (Norman: University of Oklahoma Press, 1968), 7.

93 "suspicion of Sennett's fidelity," Ibid., 108.

93 "which show the use of illegal drugs": Robert Stanley, *The Celluloid Empire: A History of the Motion Picture Industry* (New York: Hastings House, 1978), 177.

94 "*The Bangville Police*": Lahue and Brewer, *Kops and Custard*, 47.

CHAPTER 10

101 "KDKA in Pittsburgh," When the tent blew down": Christopher H. Sterling and John M. Kittross, *Stay Tuned: A Concise History of American Broadcasting*, 2nd ed. (Belmont, CA: Wadsworth, 1978), 60.

101 "The Dempsey-Charpentier fight": Ibid., 61.

102 "Charles 'Doc' Herrold": Ibid., 40.

105 "unacceptable," "If there is the slightest suggestion": Memo to Jason S. Joy, July 7, 1950, *On the Riviera*, MPA Production Code Records, Margaret Herrick Library, Fairbanks Center for Motion Picture Study.

107 "the inference of an illicit sex relationship": American Film Institute (AFI) Catalog of Feature Films, *Weekend in Havana*, History.

108 "Zanuck's formula films": Gussow, *Don't Say Yes*, 99.

110 "promoted to full colonel": Custen, *Twentieth Century's Fox*, 257.

110 "had contributed financially": Scott Eyman, *Lion of Hollywood: The Life and Legend of Louis B. Mayer* (New York: Simon & Schuster, 2005), 100.

110 "Goetz couldn't recognize a good script": Ibid., 181.

CHAPTER 11

116 "in the woman's film": Molly Haskell, *From Reverence to Rape: The Treatment of Women in the Movies*, 2nd ed. (Chicago: University of Chicago Press, 1987), 155.

122 "no effort to explain the music": Behlmer, *Memo*, 46.

122 "joined the Sisters of Charity": *Morning Democrat*, October 15, 1955, 96.

123 "the highest salaried woman": *Reading Eagle*, July 1, 1973, 1.

CHAPTER 12

124 "musicalized film": Ethan Mordden, *When Broadway Went to Hollywood* (New York: Oxford University Press, 2016), 35.

126 "taps had to be synchronized": Shirley Temple Black, *Child Star: An Autobiography* (New York: McGraw-Hill, 1988), 129–30.

126 "Be sure": Behlmer, *Memo*, 7.

130 "$100,000 for ten songs": American Film Institute Catalog of Feature Films, *Centennial Summer*, History.

131 "Arthur Freed halted production": Hugh Fordin, *MGM's Greatest Musicals: The Arthur Freed Unit* (New York: DaCapo, 1996), 180.

132 "neither the story nor the characters": Gerald Pratley, *The Cinema of Otto Preminger* (New York: A. S. Barnes, 1991), 76.

CHAPTER 13

136 "Zanuck was put off": Behlmer, *Memo*, 38–39.

136 "We don't want to make any effort": Ibid., 46.

137 "Zanuck sent a crew to New York": *Herald Journal*, November 7, 1940, 11.

CHAPTER 14

146 "four varsity shows": James A. Pegolotti, *Deems Taylor: A Biography* (Boston: North-eastern University Press, 2003), 26.

CHAPTER 15

158 "sold the rights," "no mention is made": American Film Institute Catalog of Feature Films, *The Dolly Sisters*, History.

161 "The Maas-Sager story": Frederica Sager Mass, *The Shocking Miss Pilgrim: A Writer in Early Hollywood* (Lexington: University Press of Kentucky, 1991), 232–33.

161 "various attempts": American Film Institute Catalog of Feature Films, *The Shocking Miss Pilgrim*, History.

163 "a million letters of protest": Behlmer, *Memo*, 61.

166 "follow his own lead": Gussow, *Don't Say Yes*, 144.

167 "a non-musical with Gene Tierney": TCM, *That Lady in Ermine*, Notes, www.tcm.com.

167 "ruined everything": James Bowden and Ron Miller, *Conversations with Classic Film Stars: Interviews from Hollywood's Golden Age* (Lexington: University Press of Kentucky, 2016), 103.

170 "a splendid actress": *Preston Sturges by Preston Sturges*, adapted and edited by Sandy Sturges (New York: Simon & Schuster, 1990), 308.

171 "The Lady from Laredo": Bernard F. Dick, *Radical Innocence: A Critical Study of the Hollywood Ten* (Lexington: University Press of Kentucky, 1989), 200–201.

171 "The Greeks Had a Word for It": American Film Institute Catalog of Feature Films, *How to Marry a Millionaire*, History.

CHAPTER 16

172 "because of her height": James Robert Parrish, *The Fox Girls* (New York: Arlington House, 1972), 529.

173 "had performed with some orchestras": Ibid., 530.

174 "joined a contingent": "Damon Runyon," *Three Wise Guys* Playbill, Beckett Theatre, May 2018.

177 "work her into the plot": TCM, *I Wonder Who's Kissing Her Now*, Notes, www.tcm.com.

182 "Zanuck purchased the rights": TCM, *Wake Up and Dream*, Notes, www.tcm.com.

184 "she's teaching": "Memo on June," *Modern Screen*, July 1945, 41.

CHAPTER 17

193 "warning Zanuck": American Film Institute Catalog of Feature Films, *Doll Face*, History.

193 "some drafts and correspondence": Alan J. Hubin, *Crime Fiction: 1749–1960: A Comprehensive Bibliography* (New York: Garland, 1984), 243.

CHAPTER 18

197 "a comedy-drama with Fred MacMurray": TCM, *My Blue Heaven*, Notes, www.tcm.com.

198 "a million Americans": Charles Higham, *Hollywood at Sunset: The Decline and Fall of the Most Colorful Empire Since Rome* (New York: Saturday Review Press, 1972), 67.

201 "The cast wore their uniforms": Ethan Mordden, *Beautiful Mornin': The Broadway Musical in the 1940s* (New York: Oxford University Press, 1999), 182.

207 "Zanuck congratulated Johnson": Behlmer, *Memo*, 251.

CHAPTER 19

210 "her brief scene": Carl Rollyson, *Marilyn Monroe: A Life of the Actress* (New York: DaCapo, 1993), 216.

210 ""seventy-five-dollars-a-month contract": Donald Spoto, *Marilyn Monroe: The Biography* (New York: Harper Paperbacks, 1994), 137.

211 "she finally received a new contract": Ibid., 224.

211 "he would have to pay Betty": Todd McCarthy, *Howard Hawks: The Grey Fox of Hollywood* (New York: Grove Press, 1997), 503.

211 "1951 contract": Spoto, *Marilyn Monroe*, 224.

214 "colossally dumb": McCarthy, *Howard Hawks*, 507.

214 "Zanuck informed her": Behlmer, *Memo*, 201–202.

215 "a glowing note": Spoto, *Marilyn Monroe*, 241.

215 "wouldn't have slept with her": Gussow, *Don't Say Yes*, 173.

215 "attorneys insist": Caryl Flinn, *Brass Diva: The Life and Legends of Ethel Merman* (Berkeley: University of California Press, 2007), 255.

215 "Mitzi Gaynor type": Ibid., 258.

216 "combination of comedy and pathos": id.

217 "flagrant violations of good taste": Lee Harding, *They Knew Marilyn: Famous Persons in the Life of the Hollywood Icon* (Jefferson, NC: McFarland, 2012), 146.

219 "the bawdy ballad of the season": Ronald L. Davis, *Mary Martin: Broadway Legend* (Norman: University of Oklahoma Press, 2000), 42.

218 "bowed out": Patrick McGilligan, *George Cukor: A Double Life* (New York: St. Martin's, 1991), 258.

221 "about five days work": McGilligan, *George Cukor*, 272.

221 "production was terminated": Spoto, *Marilyn Monroe*, 823.

221 "acute barbiturate poisoning": Ibid., 713.

CHAPTER 20

231 "delivered frenzied performances": Andrew L. Erdman, *Queen of Vaudeville: The Story of Eva Tanguay* (Ithaca: Cornell University Press, 2012), 12.

232 "Miscegenation": Leonard J. Leff and Jerold L. Simmons, *The Dame in the Kimono: Hollywood Censorship and the Production Code from the 1920s to the 1940s* (New York: Grove Weidenfeld, 1990), 285.

234 "*South Pacific* scarves": Davis, *Mary Martin*, 109.

235 "Twenty Century-Fox did not do badly": TCM, *South Pacific*, Notes, www.tcm.com.

235 "sought out Elizabeth Taylor": Todd S. Purdum, *Something Wonderful: Rodgers and Hammerstein's Broadway Revolution* (New York: Henry Holt, 2018), 237.

235 "snubbing Mitzi": Ibid., 258.

CHAPTER 21

237 "The songs pop out": Mordden, *Beautiful Mornin'*, 72.

238 "paid us a lot of money": Richard Rodgers, *Musical Stages: An Autobiography*, 2nd ed. (New York: DaCapo, 2002), 237.

240 "born to play this role": Purdum, *Something Wonderful*, 244.

240 "Oscar and Dick's opinion": telegram from Zanuck to TCF vice president Joe Moskowitz, June 14, 1955, Darryl F. Zanuck Papers/*Carousel*, Margaret Herrick Library, Fairbanks Center for Motion Picture Study; hereafter abbreviated as DFZP-MHL.

241 "terrible mistake": Ibid., Zanuck to Hammerstein, May 20, 1955.

241 "convinced that she must now play": Ibid., Zanuck to Moskowitz, June 14, 1955.

241 "not interested in Garland": Ibid., cablegram to Buddy Adler, June 29, 1955.

241 "when Sinatra learned": Ibid., Zanuck to Harry Brand. August 24, 1955.

241 "Shirley Jones suspected": Purdum, *Something Wonderful*, 243.

242 "MacRae will become a star": DFZP-MHL, Rodgers to Zanuck, April 28, 1955.

242 "I would certainly like to use you": Ibid., Zanuck to MacRae, June 16, 1955.

242 "wiring Frankie": Ibid., telegram from Zanuck to Sinatra, August 22, 1955.

243 "the most magnificent photograph scene": Ibid., Zanuck to Moskowitz, December 16, 1955.

244 "I have already completed": Ibid., Zanuck to Newman, November 25, 1955.

245 "intimate," "spectacle": Behlmer, *Memo*, 88.

248 "Zanuck stripped off his shirt": Harris, *The Zanucks of Hollywood*, 83–84.

248 "her husband's lover": Ibid., 80–81.

248 "actors have taken over": Behlmer, *Memo*, 259.

249   "His father concurred": Harris, *The Zanucks of Hollywood*, 112.

250 "wept unabashedly": Julia Antopol Hirsch, *The Sound of Music: The Making of America's Favorite Musical*, rev. ed. (Chicago: Chicago Review Press, 2017), 6.

250 "a show for children": Purdum, *Something Wonderful*, 287.

CHAPTER 22

252 "a feature film, not a musical": American Film Institute Catalog of Feature Films, *Dr. Dolittle*, History.

254 "She had never endured such privation": Richard Aldrich, *Gertrude Lawrence as Mrs. A* (New York: Greystone Press, 1954), 199.

254 "teach an advanced course": Sheridan Morley, *Gertrude Lawrence* (New York: McGraw-Hill, 1984), 195.

255 "Lawrence left home": Ibid., 16.

257 "Her gyrations": Bruce D. McClung, booklet notes, *Lady in the Dark* CD, Jay Masterworks edition of the Royal National Theater's 1997 production.

259 "Everyone, it appears, hates everyone": Matthew Kennedy, *Roadshow! The Fall of Film Musicals in the 1960s* (New York: Oxford University Press, 2014), 137.

259 "a pip squeak": Ibid., 136.

259 "*Dolly* is a case": Tom Santopietro, *The Importance of Being Barbra Streisand: The Brilliant, Tumultuous Career of Barbra Streisand* (New York: St. Martin's, 2007), 67.

259 "4,000 extras": Kennedy, *Roadshow!*, 138.

CHAPTER 23

261 "$77.4 million": Solomon, *Twentieth Century-Fox*, 65.

261 "fired," "the board removed Darryl": Custen, *Twentieth Century's Fox*, 368–69.

262 "a funeral service," "Darryl's commitment": Harris, *The Zanucks of Hollywood*, 232.

262 "a mind so quick": *Zanuck*, Friends of the USC Libraries, 12, USC-Cinematic Arts Library.

263 "load it with music": Behlmer, *Memo*, 56–57.

263 "dropping in": Ibid., 14.

263 "We don't want": Ibid., 46.

268   "Like everything else": Ibid., 248.

FILMOGRAPHY

C = Columbia
FFC = Fox Film Corporation
TC = Twentieth Century
TCF = Twentieth Century-Fox
WB =Warner Bros.
U = Universal

NON-MUSICALS

Film	Director
Barricade (TCF, 1939)	Gregory Ratoff
Don't Bother to Knock (TCF, 1952)	Roy Baker
The Farmer Takes a Wife (FFC, 1935)	Victor Fleming
Find Your Man (WB, 1924)	Malcolm St. Clair
Home in Indiana (TCF, 1944)	Henry Hathaway
How to Marry a Millionaire (TCF, 1953)	Jean Negulesco
Jaws of Steel (WB, 1927)	Malcolm St. Clair
The Lighthouse by the Sea (WB, 1924)	Malcolm St. Clair
The Millionaire Cowboy (WB, 1924)	Harry Garson
My Darling Clementine (TCF, 1946)	John Ford
Noah's Ark (WB, 1928)	Michael Curtiz
The Robe (TCF, 1953)	Henry Koster
The Storm (U, 1923)	Reginald Barker
Tailspin (TCF, 1939)	Roy Del Ruth
Will Success Spoil Rock Hunter? (TCF, 1957)	Frank Tashlin
Young Mr. Lincoln (TCF, 1940)	John Ford

MUSICALS

Film	Director
Adorable (FFC, 1933)	William Dieterle
Alexander's Ragtime Band (TCF, 1938)	Henry King
Baby, Take a Bow (FFC, 1934)	Harry Lachman
The Beautiful Blonde from Bashful Bend (TCF, 1949)	Preston Sturges
The Best Things in Life Are Free (TCF, 1956)	Michael Curtiz
Big Boy (WB, 1930)	Alan Crosland
Bloodhounds of Broadway (TCF, 1952)	Harmon Jones
Bride of the Regiment (WB, 1930)	John Francis Dillon
Bright Eyes (FFC, 1934)	David Butler
Bright Lights (WB, 1930)	Michael Curtiz
Broadway Thru a Keyhole (TC, 1933)	Lowell Sherman
Call Me Mister (TCF, 1951)	Lloyd Bacon
Captain January (TCF, 1936)	David Butler
Carnival in Costa Rica (TCF, 1947)	Gregory Ratoff
Carousel (TCF, 1956)	Henry King
Centennial Summer (TCF, 1946)	Otto Preminger
The Cock-Eyed World (FFC, 1929)	Raoul Walsh
Coney Island (TCF, 1943)	Walter Lang
Crooner (WB, 1932)	Lloyd Bacon
Delicious (FFC, 1931)	David Butler
Diamond Horseshoe (TCF, 1945)	George Seaton
Dimples (TCF, 1936)	William A. Seiter
Doctor Dolittle (TCF, 1967)	Richard Fleischer
Doll Face (TCF, 1945)	Lewis Seiler
The Dolly Sisters (TCF, 1945)	Irving Cummings
Down Among the Sheltering Palms (TCF, 1953)	Edmund Goulding
Down Argentine Way (TCF, 1940)	Irving Cummings
Folies Bergère (TC, 1935)	Roy Del Ruth
Footlight Serenade (TCF, 1942)	Gregory Ratoff
42nd Street (WB, 1933)	Lloyd Bacon

Fox Movietone Follies of 1929 (FFC, 1929)	David Butler
Gentlemen Prefer Blondes (TCF, 1953)	Howard Hawks
George White's Scandals (FFC, 1934)	George White, Harry Lachman, Thornton Freeland
George White's 1935 Scandals (FFC, 1935)	George White
Golden Girl (TCF, 1951)	Lloyd Bacon
Golden Dawn (WB, 1930)	Ray Enright
Gold Diggers of Broadway (WB, 1929)	Roy Del Ruth
Greenwich Village (TCF, 1944)	Walter Lang
Hello, Frisco, Hello (TCF, 1943)	H. Bruce Humberstone
Her Majesty Love (WB, 1931)	William Dieterle
Hollywood Cavalcade (TCF, 1939)	Irving Cummings
Iceland (TCF, 1942)	H. Bruce Humberstone
Hello, Dolly! (TCF, 1969)	Gene Kelly
How To Be Very, Very Popular (TCF, 1955)	Nunnally Johnson
The I Don't Care Girl (TCF, 1953)	Lloyd Bacon
If I'm Lucky (TCF, 1946)	Lewis Seiler
I'll Get By (TCF, 1950)	Richard Sale
In Old Chicago (TCF, 1938)	Henry King
I Wonder Who's Kissing Her Now (TCF, 1947)	Lloyd Bacon
The Jazz Singer (WB, 1927)	Alan Crosland
Just Around the Corner (TCF, 1938)	Irving Cummings
King of Jazz (U, 1930)	John Murray Anderson
The King and I (TCF, 1956)	Walter Lang
Kiss Me Again (WB, 1931)	William A. Seiter
Let's Make Love (TCF, 1960)	George Cukor
The Life of the Party (WB, 1930)	Roy Del Ruth
Lillian Russell (TCF, 1940)	Irving Cummings
The Little Colonel (TCF, 1935)	David Butler
The Littlest Rebel (TCF, 1935)	David Butler
Mammy (WB, 1930)	Michael Curtiz
Married in Hollywood (FFC, 1929)	Marcel Silver
Meet Me After the Show (TCF, 1951)	Richard Sale
Monte Carlo (Par, 1930)	Ernst Lubitsch

Moon Over Miami (TCF, 1941)	Walter Lang
Mother Wore Tights (TCF, 1947)	Walter Lang
Moulin Rouge (TC, 1934)	Sidney Lanfield
Music in the Air (FFC, 1934)	Joe May
My Blue Heaven (TCF, 1950)	Henry Koster
My Gal Sal (TCF, 1942)	Irving Cummings
My Man (WB, 1928)	Archie Mayo
Now I'll Tell (FFC, 1934)	Edwin Burke
Oh, You Beautiful Doll (TCF, 1949)	John Stahl
On the Avenue (TCF, 1937)	Roy Del Ruth
Pin Up Girl (TCF, 1944)	H. Bruce Humberstone
Poor Little Rich Girl (TCF, 1936)	Irving Cummings
Rebecca of Sunnybrook Farm (TCF, 1938)	Allan Dwan
Rose of Washington Square (TCF, 1939)	Gregory Ratoff
Sally (WB, 1929)	John Francis Dillon
Say It with Songs (WB, 1929)	Lloyd Bacon
She Learned About Sailors (FFC, 1934)	George Marshall
The Shocking Miss Pilgrim (TCF, 1947)	George Seaton
Sing, Baby, Sing (TCF, 1936)	Sidney Lanfield
Song of the Islands (TCF, 1942)	Walter Lang
Song O' My Heart (FFC, 1930)	Frank Borzage
The Sound of Music (TCF, 1965)	Robert Wise
South Pacific (TCF, 1958)	Joshua Logan
Spring Is Here (WB, 1929)	John Francis Dillon
Springtime in the Rockies (TCF, 1942)	Irving Cummings
Stand Up and Cheer! (FFC, 1934)	Hamilton MacFadden
Star! (TCF, 1968)	Robert Wise
State Fair (TCF, 1945)	Walter Lang
State Fair (TCF, 1962)	Jose Ferrer
Stowaway (TCF, 1936)	William A. Seiter
Sunny (WB, 1930)	William A. Seiter
Sun Valley Serenade (TCF, 1941)	H. Bruce Humberstone
Susannah of the Mounties (TCF, 1939)	William A. Seiter
Swanee River (TCF, 1940)	Sidney Lanfield

Sweet Kitty Bellairs (WB, 1930)	Alfred E. Green
Sweet Rosie O'Grady (TCF, 1943)	Irving Cummings
Thanks a Million (TC, 1935)	Roy Del Ruth
That Lady in Ermine (TCF, 1948)	Ernst Lubitsch, Otto Preminger
That Night in Rio (TCF, 1941)	Irving Cummings
There's No Business Like Show Business (TCF, 1954)	Walter Lang
Three Little Girls in Blue (TCF, 1946)	H. .Bruce Humberstone
Tin Pan Alley (TCF, 1940)	Walter Lang
Viennese Nights (WB, 1931)	Alan Crosland
Wabash Avenue (TCF, 1950)	Henry Koster
Wake Up and Dream (TCF, 1946)	Lloyd Bacon
Week-End in Havana (TCF, 1941)	Walter Lang
Wee Little Winkie (TCF, 1937)	John Ford
When My Baby Smiles at Me (TCF, 1948)	Walter Lang
Where Do We Go from Here? (1945)	Gregory Ratoff
Wintertime (TCF, 1943)	John Brahm
Young People (TCF, 1940)	Allan Dwan

INDEX

ABOUT THE AUTHOR

Credit: Autumn Years

Bernard F. Dick is professor of communication and English at Fairleigh Dickinson University and is author of many books, including *That Was Entertainment: The Golden Age of the MGM Musical*; *The Screen Is Red: Hollywood, Communism, and the Cold War*; *The President's Ladies: Jane Wyman and Nancy Davis*; *Hollywood Madonna: Loretta Young*; *Forever Mame: The Life of Rosalind Russell*; and *Claudette Colbert: She Walked in Beauty*, all published by the University Press of Mississippi.